Professional Management Spectrum, Inc.
P.O. Box 30330   Pensacola, FL 32503
PH: (850) 432-7697   FAX: (850) 432-3908   ORDERS: 1-800-346-6114

FOR NAVY, MARINE CORPS, COAST GUARD

NAVY EVAL & FITREP WRITING GUIDE

For Navy (new Eval/Fitrep system) and Coast Guard use. This is the **most popular writing guide** in the military today, with more than **100,000 satisfied users.** This guide covers the "nuts & bolts" of FITREPs and Evals.

It is ideally suited for the person who:
- Is new to writing EVALs/FITREPs
- Wants to **Maximize use** of allowable space
- Does not enjoy continually writing appraisals "from scratch"
- Does not know how to word or document performance/potential
- Wants to submit good, effective write-ups to impress the "boss"

The Guide contains:

* **Instruction, direction, & guidance** (with samples) on submitting smooth appraisals in a style that will positively influence selection boards.

* **200+ pages of example bullet statements** tailored toward the New Navy Eval/Fitrep system.

* **500 of the most popular,** descriptive adjectives used in appraisals.

* **LDO/CWO** info with 20+ Command Endorsement samples

* **CPO, SCPO, MCPO Selection Board** information (with worksheet)

Much more....

NAVY EVAL & FITREP WRITING GUIDE (2nd Edition) .... **$24.95 Each**

NAVY & MARINE CORPS PERFORMANCE WRITING GUIDE (2nd Edition)

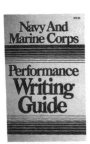

(For use by Navy, USMC, & USCG) This book picks up where the *Navy Eval & Fitrep Writing Guide* and the *Fitness Report Writing Guide for Marines* leaves off on Evals and Fitreps, and covers **new writing and performance areas,** such as Awards & Medal write-up, plus Letters of Appreciation/Commendation.

The Guide Contains:

* **Personal Awards** (Achievement/Commendation Medals, etc.)

* **Sailor/Marine of the Month, Quarter, Year** - Samples, Info .

* **Superior & Substandard** sections in every area of performance

* **2,000 Word Dictionary** - A listing of the most used adjectives, nouns, and verbs in the English language on PERSONAL PERFORMANCE, and PERSONALITY traits.

* **2,000 Word Thesaurus** - Grouped in unique, ready, and easy to use sections by SUPERIOR - to - SUBSTANDARD PERFORMANCE, and PERSONALITY TRAIT sections.

* **2,500 BULLET PHRASES** - Ready to use. FAVORABLE and UNFAVORABLE sections.

NAVY & MARINE CORPS PERFORMANCE WRITING GUIDE (2nd Edition) .... **$24.95 Each**

FITNESS REPORT WRITING GUIDE FOR MARINES

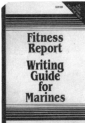

This book has helped **thousands of Marines** draft Fitreps.

* It covers what information should be included in narrative remarks, with instruction & direction on how to submit polished Fitreps in the format & style that will influence promotion selection boards.

Includes:

* More than 600 ready-to-use **BULLET PHRASES,**

* Plus, nearly 500 of the most **popular descriptive adjectives.**

* A special section on **Brag Sheets,** and much more.

FITNESS REPORT WRITING GUIDE FOR MARINES .... **$ 24.95 Each**

WE DID ALL THE HARD-WORK RESEARCH. YOU GET ALL THE CREDIT.

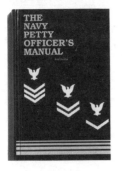

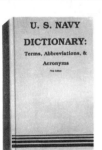

Professional Management Spectrum, Inc.

P.O. Box 30330 Pensacola, FL 32503
(850) 432-7697 FAX: (850) 432-3908

"Serving Professionals With Pride"

ORDER FORM

Prices Subject to Change
Military Purchase Orders Accepted

FOR FASTER DELIVERY
Monday-Friday 9:00 - 5:00 Eastern Time
CALL 1-800-346-6114
For orders using VISA, MasterCard, AMEX only

ORDERED BY: (Please Print or Type)

Rank	First	Middle Initial	Last	Service

Address:

Phone #:

SHIP TO: Use ONLY if different from "Ordered By" (Please Print or Type)

Rank	First	Middle Initial	Last	Service

Address:

Item Description (Please be Specific with Title of Book/Clip Art Set)	Quantity	Price Each	Total Price

FOR PACKAGING, SHIPPING, HANDLING & INSURANCE, PLEASE ADD THE FOLLOWING:

	REG.	AIR
1 ITEM	$ 3.00	$ 5.00
2 ITEMS	$ 6.00	$10.00
3 ITEMS	$ 9.00	$14.00
4 ITEMS	$11.00	$16.00
5 ITEMS	$13.00	$18.00
6 ITEMS	$15.00	$20.00

NOTE: We do NOT Ship to non-U.S. ZIP CODES.

Amount for Merchandise	
Shipping SEE CHART	
SUB TOTAL	
6% Sales tax (Florida Only)	
GRAND TOTAL	

METHOD OF PAYMENT: ☐ Check ☐ Money Order ☐ VISA ☐ MasterCard ☐ AMEX

Expiration Date:

Card No.

Signature:

Professional Management Spectrum, Inc.
P.O. Box 30330   Pensacola, FL 32503
PH: (850) 432-7697   FAX: (850) 432-3908   ORDERS: 1-800-346-6114

FOR ALL SERVICES & CIVILIANS

THE DEFINITIVE PERFORMANCE WRITING GUIDE

FOR USE BY NAVY, ARMY, AIR FORCE, COAST GUARD, & CIVILIAN PERSONNEL. This guide is packed full of BULLET PHRASE STATEMENTS and WORD BANKS. It provides simple, straight-forward, and easy-to-use information to utilize when writing on anyone's PERFORMANCE, BEHAVIOR, or CHARACTER. This unique, powerful writing guide lets you become your own successful "wordsmith." This guide does not cover how to draft performance appraisals. The other service writing guides cover that subject.

This book has:
* 5,500 + Bullet Phrases,   * 2,300 + Word Bank   * 2,000 Word Thesaurus
These are broken down **into 5 performance areas (Superior to Unsatisfactory)**

and, FAVORABLE & UNFAVORABLE areas for:
6 - PERSONALITY & WORK RELATIONSHIPS   7 - LEADERSHIP, SUPERVISION, & MANAGEMENT
8 - SELF-EXPRESSION SKILLS
PLUS: Action words; Important DOs & DON'Ts; Objective & Subjective Analysis; Helpful Hints; Key Words; A "Bell Curve"Breakdown, and much more.
THE DEFINITIVE PERFORMANCE WRITING GUIDE .... **$25.95 Ea.**

SUCCESSFUL LEADERSHIP TODAY

Today's book for today's leaders.
This hardcover book **contains info on:** * How to work with others and lead others.
* How to develop & strengthen your **personal leadership skills**.
Also contains:
Quotes from Napoleon to Halsey and MacArthur (and others) on leadership qualities & traits that hold true today. Hundreds of tips, ideas, & suggestions to improve yourself and your leadership/management skills. Presented in a straight-forward, easy to read format.   **And, information on:**
* Motivation * Delegating * Goals * Incentives * Authority * Initiative * Counseling
* Self-confidence * Earning trust * Confidence & respect * Role model * Emotional need
* Loyalty * Responsibility * Quality * Opportunities * Image * Socializing * Leadership style
* Brainstorming * Dedication * Favoritism * Policy voice * Career goals
* Job placement   * Commitment * Professional growth,   and Much more.
SUCCESSFUL LEADERSHIP TODAY   (Hardcover) .... **$25.95 Ea.**

ARMY & AIR FORCE

WRITING GUIDE FOR ARMY EFFICIENCY REPORTS   WRITING GUIDE FOR AIR FORCE EFFICIENCY REPORTS

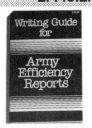

Do away with the countless hours of frustration you spend on "reinventing the wheel" every time you draft an efficiency report, or other personal performance document. **Thousands of Army & Air Force personnel** have already benefited from these books. These books can help anyone, **AT ANY LEVEL,** write **TOP NOTCH** efficiency reports, award recommendations, and other performance documents. Equally useful and **beneficial to supervisors, middle and top managers** from E-5 through O-6.

HIGHLIGHTS OF ARMY & AIR FORCE GUIDES:
* **2,500 BULLET PHRASES** - Favorable & Unfavorable Sections
* **2,000 WORD DICTIONARY** - Alphabetical listing of the MOST EFFECTIVE adjectives, nouns, & verbs on personal performance and personality traits in the English language (with definitions).
* **2,000 WORD THESAURUS** - Words groups in unique, easy-to-use sections by SUPERIOR-to-SUBSTANDARD PERFORMANCE and PERSONALITY TRAIT sections.
SPECIAL SECTIONS ON: ** Preparation Check-List * Drafting Narratives * Opening Format * Closing Format
* Favorable Efficiency Reports * Individual Recognition Write-Ups, More.
WRITING GUIDE FOR ARMY EFFICIENCY REPORTS (2nd Edition) .... **$ 24.95 Ea.**
WRITING GUIDE FOR AIR FORCE EFFICIENCY REPORTS (2nd Edition) .... **$ 24.95 Ea.**

PURCHASE ORDERS/IMPAC ACCEPTED. Prices Subject to Change.

Professional Management Spectrum, Inc.
P.O. Box 30330   Pensacola, FL 32503
PH: (850) 432-7697   FAX: (850) 432-3908   ORDERS: 1-800-346-6114

COMPUTER CLIP ART GRAPHICS
For IBM Compatibles (3 1/2" Disks)

Black & White Clip Art @ 300 dots-per-inch resolution. Fine detail! The clip art pictures can be used for memos, letters, signs, posters, illustrated covers of manuals, standard operating procedures, etc. Pictures in .PCX FORMAT. All graphics packages come complete with a Pictorial Reference Guide, listing all graphics included, disk by disk. This guide provides the user with a ready reference in finding pictures. **BEFORE ORDERING YOUR CLIP ART**, be sure your computer has a "GRAPHICS," (like Harvard Graphics), "PAINT" (Paintbrush), or a WORD PROCESSOR (Microsoft WORD, WordPerfect, Enable, etc.) that can import .PCX graphic pictures. Always follow Program instructions concerning "pictures" or "graphics" when using these clip art packages. All Computer Clip Art Sets are $19.95 Ea.

FOR ALL SERVICES

AIRCRAFT CLIP ART

Pictures Include:
* 60 United States Military Aircraft, many with top, side, and front views, including: A10, A3, A37, A4, A6, A7, AV8, B1, C123, C130, C135, C141, C5, C7, C9, E2, E3, E4, E6, EA6, F104, F105, F106, F14, F15, F16, F4, F5, FA18, AH1, H2, H3, H46, H47, OH6, UH1, AH64, CH54, H60, O2, OH58, OV1, OV10, T2, T34, T38, T39, T41, T43, T45, U2, B2, B52, FB111, F117, P3, S3, SR71. More than 160 total pictures

-----
AIRCRAFT CLIP ART .... $ 19.95

MILITARY GRAPHICS COLLECTION

Our collection of "generic" pictures, including Military People (comical & in the workplace), commercial/military ships, submarines, commercial/military aircraft, sailboats, rifles, pistols, tanks, office machinery, utensils, & furniture.
Perfect pictures for newsletters, command newspapers, home or office use. Over 250 images!

MILITARY GRAPHICS COLLECTION .... $ 19.95

NAVY

NAVY SHIP GRAPHICS

Pictures Include:
* Over 90 Line-Drawn Illustrations and Silhouettes of United States Navy ships, including: AO, AD, AS, ATS, AE, AFS, ASR, BB, CG, CGN, CV, CVN, DD, DDG, FF, FFG, LCC, LHA, LHD, LKA, LPD, LPH, LSD, LST, PG, PHM, and SUBMARINES.

NAVY SHIP GRAPHICS .... $ 19.95

NAVY OFFICER CLIP ART

100 + Pictures Including:
* Sleeve & Collar Devices (Ensign thru Fleet Admiral)
* Special qualification insignia (SWO, SUB, AVIATOR, NFO, etc.)
* Specialty Devices (Supply, Nurse, Medical, Law, Chaplain, etc.)
* Warrant Officer/LDO Insignia (Boatswain, Opstech, Elect. Tech, Ships Clerk, etc.), plus special logos, and more

-----
NAVY OFFICER CLIP ART .... $ 19.95

NAVY ENLISTED CLIP ART

100 + Pictures Including:
* CPO Insignia, plus Command Master Chief, Command Senior Chief, Command Chief, and "Navy Chief-Navy Pride" logo, etc.
* All Navy Rating Insignia
* Sleeve & Collar Devices (E-1 thru E-9)
* Qualification Badges (ESWS, EAWS, EOD, SUB, DIVER, A/C, etc)
* Special Duty Pins/Logos (Small Craft, Career Counselor, Company Commander, etc.), plus many extras.

NAVY ENLISTED CLIP ART .... $ 19.95

AIR FORCE, ARMY, COAST GUARD, & MARINE CORPS

AIR FORCE CLIP ART

Pictures Include:
* Rank Insignia from Airman thru 4-Star General
* Qualification Insignia and Designations, including Pilo Aircrew, Navigator, Surgeon, Nurse, Security, Missil Parachutist, Astronaut, Instructor, and many more.
* Command Badges & Seals, including Air Comb Command, Air University, JCS, Recruiting Service, etc.

AIR FORCE CLIP ART .... $ 19.95

ARMY CLIP ART GRAPHICS

Pictures Include:
* Rank Insignia from Private thru 4-Star General
* Designator Insignia (such as Infantry, Armor, Enginee Ordnance, Aviation, Cavalry, Medical, Dental, Intelligence Special Forces, Transportation, Police, etc.)
* Line Art Illustrations and Silhouettes of Tanks, Fightin Vehicles, Army Aircraft, plus Army caps, badges, etc.

ARMY CLIP ART GRAPHICS .... $ 19.95

COAST GUARD ENLISTED CLIP ART

Pictures Include: * Coast Guard Pay Grade Insignia (E-1 thru E-9) & Rating Insignia(RM, BM, ET, etc.)
* Special Qualification Insignia (Coxswain, Cutterman, Diver OIC, etc.)
* Badges (Recruiting, Presidential Svc, SECDEF Svc, etc.)
* Coast Guard Aircraft, Boats, Cutters, More

USCG ENLISTED CLIP ART .... $ 19.95

COAST GUARD OFFICER CLIP ART

Pictures Include: * All Rank Insignia for Ensign through Admiral, including collar devices & shoulder boards.
* Warrant Officer Insignia, such as Communications, Aviation Engineering, Electronics, Boatswain, etc.
* Special Qualification Insignia, such as Aviator, Diver, Flight Officer, Command Ashore/Afloat, OIC, SWO, etc.
* Coast Guard Aircraft, Boats, Cutters, More.

USCG OFFICER CLIP ART .... $ 19.95

MARINE CORPS CLIP ART

Pictures Include: * All Insignia for Pay Grades E-1 thru E-9 and Warrant Officer thru General
* Iwo Jima Memorial Picture, NFO Wings, Marine Aviator, Circle USMC Logo, Eagle Globe & Anchor, Navy Dept Badges, JCS, etc.
* American Flag, Various Line Art Drawings and Silhouettes of Tanks and Vehicles
* Several Pre-made Memo Forms (Colonel, Major, etc.)

MARINE CORPS CLIP ART .... $ 19.95

Professional Management Spectrum, Inc.

P.O. Box 30330   Pensacola, FL 32503
(850) 432-7697   FAX: (850) 432-3908
"Serving Professionals With Pride"

ORDER FORM

Prices Subject to Change
Military Purchase Orders Accepted

FOR FASTER DELIVERY
Monday-Friday 9:00 - 5:00 Eastern Time
CALL 1-800-346-6114
For orders using VISA, MasterCard, AMEX only

ORDERED BY: (Please Print or Type)

Rank	First	Middle Initial	Last	Service

Address:

Phone #:

SHIP TO: Use ONLY if different from "Ordered By" (Please Print or Type)

Rank	First	Middle Initial	Last	Service

Address:

Item Description (Please be Specific with Title of Book/Clip Art Set)	Quantity	Price Each	Total Price

Amount for Merchandise
Shipping **SEE CHART**
SUB TOTAL
6% Sales tax (Florida Only)
GRAND TOTAL

FOR PACKAGING, SHIPPING, HANDLING & INSURANCE,
PLEASE ADD THE FOLLOWING:

	REG.	AIR
1 ITEM	$ 3.00	$ 5.00
2 ITEMS	$ 6.00	$10.00
3 ITEMS	$ 9.00	$14.00
4 ITEMS	$11.00	$16.00
5 ITEMS	$13.00	$18.00
6 ITEMS	$15.00	$20.00

NOTE: We do NOT Ship to non-U.S. ZIP CODES.

METHOD OF PAYMENT: ☐ Check ☐ Money Order ☐ VISA ☐ MasterCard ☐ AMEX

Expiration Date:

Card No.

Signature:

THE NAVAL OFFICER'S MANUAL
2nd Edition

Published by:
Professional Management Spectrum, Inc.
P. O. Box 30330
Pensacola, FL 32503

ISBN: 1-879123-01-0

Printed in the United States of America

NOTE 1: The "boxed" quotes used in this book are from the hardcover book *SUCCESSFUL LEADERSHIP TODAY*. Ordering information on this and other professional books can be found in the front/back of this book.

THE NAVAL OFFICER'S MANUAL
TABLE OF CONTENTS

CHAPTER 1

COMMISSIONED OFFICERS

OATH OF OFFICE

Having been appointed an officer in the Armed Forces of the United States I do hereby accept such appointment and do solemnly swear (or affirm) that I will support and defend the Constitution of the United States against all enemies, foreign and domestic; that I will bear true faith and allegiance to the same; that I take this obligation freely, without any mental reservation or purpose of evasion; that I will well and faithfully discharge the duties of the office on which I am about to enter; so help me God.

CODE OF A NAVAL OFFICER

It is, by no means, enough that an officer of the Navy should be a capable mariner. He must be that, of course, but also a great deal more. He should be, as well, a gentleman of liberal education, refined manner, punctilious courtesy, and the nicest sense of personal honor. He would not only be able to express himself clearly and with force in his own language both with tongue and pen, but he should be versed in French and Spanish.

He should be the soul of tact, patience, justice, firmness, and charity. No meritorious act of a subordinate should escape his attention or be left to pass without its reward, if even the reward be only one word of approval. Conversely, he should not be blind to a single fault in any subordinate, though at the same time he should be quick and unfailing to distinguish error from malice, thoughtlessness from incompetence, and well-meant shortcoming from heedless or stupid blunder. As he should be universal and impartial in his rewards and approval of merit, so should he be judicial and unbending in his punishment or reproof of misconduct.

John Paul Jones

COMMISSIONED OFFICERS

All commissioned officers hold a commission granted by the President and signed by the Secretary of the Navy. Officers take precedence according to their grade, and within the grade according to the date of appointment to that grade.

OFFICER GRADE

The word "rank" is often used interchangeably with "grade" when referring to an officer. This is INCORRECT. Officers hold a grade (lieutenant, commander, etc.); they outrank a junior; or they rank from the date of appointment to their grade (date of rank). An officer gets "promoted" to the next higher grade while an enlisted person gets "advanced" to the next higher grade.

OFFICER CATEGORIES

Officers receive a commission as either a line or staff officer, depending on educational and physical qualifications, personal interests, and prior experience.

LINE OFFICERS. Within the line designation, you are either an unrestricted line (URL) officer or a restricted line (RL) officer. Defined simply, the URL officers are those considered eligible for command at sea within one of the five areas of warfare expertise:
1. SURFACE
2. AVIATION
3. SUBMARINE
4. SPECIAL OPERATIONS
5. SPECIAL WARFARE

URL officers who are not qualified in any warfare specialty are classified as general URL officers. General URL officers are eligible for command of shore activities, with emphasis on shore management specialties.

2

The restricted line (RL) officer category includes those officers qualified to serve in highly specialized jobs, such as engineering duty or aeronautical engineering and maintenance duty. RL officers may command auxiliary vessels and designated shore activities.

STAFF CORPS. Like RL officers, staff corps officers are not eligible for command at sea but may assume command of activities within their own corps.

There are nine Navy staff corps groups. These are listed below in order of precedence:
1. MEDICAL (consists entirely of physicians and surgeons)
2. SUPPLY
3. CHAPLAIN
4. CIVIL ENGINEER
5. JUDGE ADVOCATE GENERAL
6. DENTAL
7. MEDICAL SERVICE (pharmacists, medics, administrative officers, medical technologists, etc.)
8. NURSE
9. NAVY BAND (musicians)

Commissioned officers of the staff corps have all the rights and privileges of their grade.

Staff corps officers should not be confused with staff officers. Staff officers may be either line or staff corps officers assigned to the staffs of high-ranking officers.

LINE AND STAFF CORPS DISTINCTIONS

Line officers wear grade-indicating devices on both collars of their uniform. Staff corps officers wear their grade insignia on the right collar and the corps device on the left collar.

Flag line officers personal flag consists of a blue background with white stars. A staff corps flag officer's personal flag is a white background with blue stars.

ASSIGNMENTS AND CAREER PATHS

Specific types of duty assignments for each officer will vary, dependent on the officer's specialty, educational training, and interests. Those officers who plan a career in the unrestricted line will find additional information in the Unrestricted Line Officer Career Planning Guidebook, OPNAV P-13-1-86.

Figure 1 on the following page is a typical professional development pattern for a SURFACE WARFARE OFFICER. It illustrates the general progression of assignments and promotions that a surface warfare officer can expect, along with the years' continuous service, and promotion times as an average. No two officers will follow identical career patterns; however, on the average, the successful surface warfare officer will meet most of the career milestones in about the same sequence shown in Figure 1. For instance, if you select a career as a surface warfare officer, you may stay at sea the first 4 years because of operational requirements and/or personal choice. During this time you will strive to complete personnel qualification standards (PQS) and qualify as division officer, officer of the deck (OOD), department head, and surface warfare officer. Then you may rotate ashore for staff duty or to attend the Naval Postgraduate School. Although you did not follow the development plan exactly, you will have obtained the experience and qualifications necessary to make you competitive with your year-group peers.

Figures 2 through 8 are examples of professional development patterns in other career specialty fields. The career path for female officers in RL and staff corps categories parallels that of male officers except as constrained by law.

SUBSPECIALTIES

The Navy places considerable emphasis on an officer developing a subspecialty in addition to a primary area of naval warfare. A subspecialty is a secondary area of expertise coded to show levels of education.

If you desire a certain code status, you can enroll in further study under a Navy-sponsored program or an off-duty program.

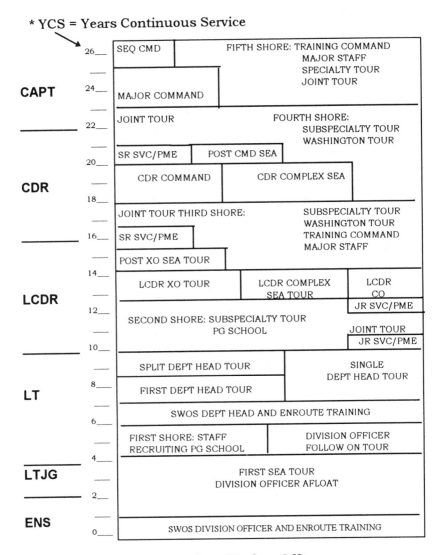

* YCS = Years Continuous Service

YCS			
26	SEQ CMD	FIFTH SHORE: TRAINING COMMAND / MAJOR STAFF / SPECIALTY TOUR / JOINT TOUR	
24 (CAPT)	MAJOR COMMAND		
22	JOINT TOUR	FOURTH SHORE: SUBSPECIALTY TOUR / WASHINGTON TOUR	
20	SR SVC/PME	POST CMD SEA	
(CDR)	CDR COMMAND	CDR COMPLEX SEA	
18			
	JOINT TOUR THIRD SHORE:	SUBSPECIALTY TOUR / WASHINGTON TOUR	
16	SR SVC/PME	TRAINING COMMAND / MAJOR STAFF	
14	POST XO SEA TOUR		
(LCDR)	LCDR XO TOUR	LCDR COMPLEX SEA TOUR	LCDR CO
12			JR SVC/PME
	SECOND SHORE: SUBSPECIALTY TOUR / PG SCHOOL		JOINT TOUR
10			JR SVC/PME
	SPLIT DEPT HEAD TOUR		SINGLE DEPT HEAD TOUR
8 (LT)	FIRST DEPT HEAD TOUR		
6	SWOS DEPT HEAD AND ENROUTE TRAINING		
	FIRST SHORE: STAFF RECRUITING PG SCHOOL	DIVISION OFFICER FOLLOW ON TOUR	
4 (LTJG)	FIRST SEA TOUR / DIVISION OFFICER AFLOAT		
2			
0 (ENS)	SWOS DIVISION OFFICER AND ENROUTE TRAINING		

1. Surface Warfare Officer

NAVPERS 15839F, Volume 1, broadly defines subspecialty areas available to all UNRESTRICTED, RESTRICTED, and STAFF CORPS officers.

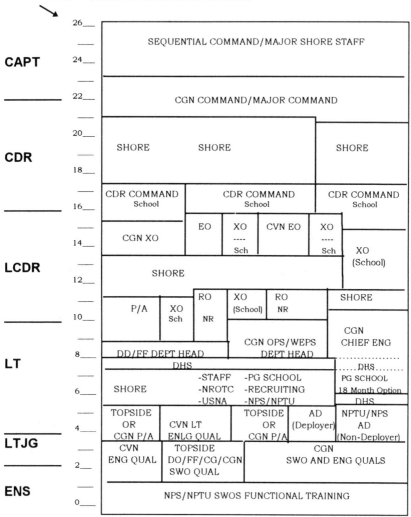

2. Surface Warfare Officer (Nuclear).

CAPT

CDR

LCDR

LT

LTJG

ENS

26__

24__

22__

20__

18__

16__

14__

12__

10__

8__

6__

4__

2__

0__

			SECOND MAJOR COMMAND
MAJOR COMMAND			
POST COMMAND SHORE		DC SHORE	
	POST COMMAND ASHORE	MAJOR COMMAND	
SENIOR SVC COLLEGE			
COMMAND			
PCO			
XO	POST XO ASHORE	XO	
POST DEPT HEAD SHORE	XO	POST DEPT HEAD SHORE	
NAV	NAV	WEPS TSO	IMA RADCOM	SLO
ENG	ENG	WEPS TSO	ENG	WEPS/TSO NAV	ENG NAV WEPS/TSO
SOAC			
POST JO SHORE TOUR/PG SCHOOL			
FIRST SEA TOUR			
INITIAL TRAINING			

3. Nuclear Submarine Officer.

7

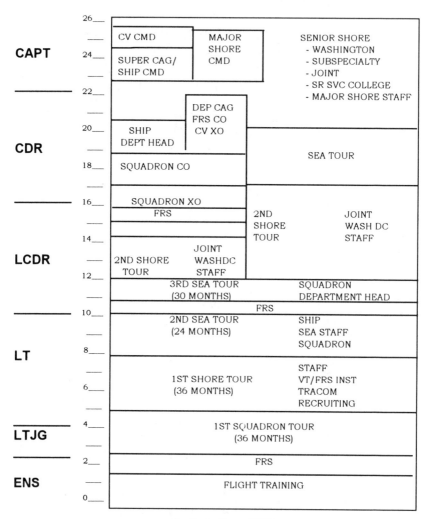

4. Aviation Officer.

Rank	Years	Career Path	
CAPT	26 — — 24 — — 22 —	FOURTH SHORE TOUR	- MAJOR COMMAND - MAJOR SHORE STAFF - SHORE COMMAND - SUBSPECIALTY UTILIZATION
CDR	20 — — 18 — — 16 —	THIRD SHORE TOUR SENIOR OPERATIONAL TOUR	-SHORE STAFF, JOINT STAFF -SR SVC COLLEGE -SUBSPECIALTY UTILIZATION -COMMAND -OPERATIONAL STAFF
LCDR	14 — — 12 — — 10 —	OPERATIONAL TOUR -XO SEAL TEAM/XO NSWU/ XO SPECBOAT UNIT/XO SDV TEAM SECOND SHORE TOUR -JR SVC COLLEGE -PG SCHOOL	-CO (LCDR) SPECBOAT UNIT - JOINT STAFF - NSW STAFF -MAG/MISSIONS -JOINT STAFF -SHORE STAFF
LT	— 8 — — 6 — — 4 —	OPERATIONAL TOUR -DEPT HEAD/OPS/SEAL TEAM, SDV TEAM, SPECBOATRON/UNIT FIRST SHORE TOUR -PG SCHOOL -SHORE & OVERSEAS SHORE DUTY STAFF	-XO (LT) SPECIAL BOAT UNITS -NSW STAFF -PEP -NAVAL SPECIAL WARFARE CENTER
LTJG	— 2 —	INITIAL OPERATIONAL TOURS -SEAL TEAM PLATOON CDR/ASST	-SDV TEAM PLATOON CDR/ASST -SPECIAL BOAT UNIT CRAFT OIC
ENS	— 0 —	BUDS TRAINING	

5. Naval Special Warfare Officer

9

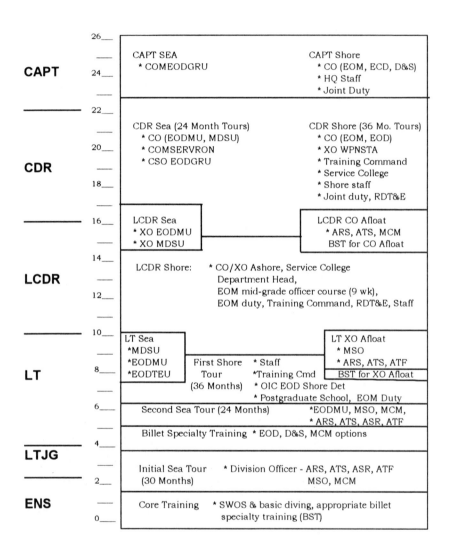

6. Special Operations Officer

Rank	Years	Primary Career Requirement	Major Service/Joint Staff & Related
CAPT	26 24 22	* MAJOR CMD TOUR - RECRUITING AREA - TRAINING CMS - MSC AREA CMD - NARDAC - OCEANSYSCOM - EPMAC - NCTAMS - NMEC - NETPMSA - NAVSTA	** MAJOR SERVICE/JOINT STAFF (NOTES 2 & 3) SENIOR PME (NOTE 1) SUBSPECIALTY TOUR
CDR	20 18 16	* COMMANDER CMD TOUR -NAVSUPPACT - PSA -NAVFAC/FLTSURVC - NCTC - NRD - NCS/NCU - MSCO EXECUTIVE OFFICER -NAVSTA/NAVSUPPACT - NROTC -SPASURVSYS/FLTSURVC - NARDAC -TRANING CMD -EPMAC -NCTAMS/NCTS -DPSCPAC - SIMA - NPRDC	** MAJOR SERVICE/JOINT STAFF (NOTES 2 & 3) SENIOR PME (NOTE 1) SUBSPECIALTY TOUR
LCDR	14 12	* EXECUTIVE OFFICER TOUR -MEPS - TPU/BRIG -PSA/PSD - SIMA -NRD -MSCO/COMFSRON -NAVFAC/NOPF - NTTC -NCTC/NCS - FACSFAC	** MAJOR SERVICE/JOINT STAFF (SEE NOTES 2 & 3) -DISTRIBUTION - PLANS/POLICY -CAREER PROGRESSION - PROJECT SPT -PROGRAM/RESOURCE APPRAISAL JUNIOR PME (1) SUBSPECIALTY TOUR
LT	10 8 6	* DEPT HEAD TOUR - OIC/ASS'T OIC - OPS OFFICER - DIR FAMILY SERVICE CTR/CAAC - ADMIN OFFICER - PROGRAMS OFFICER (RECRUITING) - COMM OFFICER - DIR OF TRAINING - SECURITY OFFICER	* SUBSPECIALTY DEVELOPMENT/PROVEN DESIGNATION POSTGRADUATE SCHOOL
LTJG **ENS**	4 2 0	* DIVISION OFFICER TOUR - WATCH OFFICER - PORT/BASE SVCS OFFICER - LEGAL OFFICER - COMM/CMS CUSTODIAN -ADMIN/PERS OFFICER -ASS'T OIC - FIRST LT/FACILITIES MGR - ADP - COMPANY OFFICER	* SUBSPECIALTY DEVELOPMENT GENERAL EXPERIENCE TOUR -INSTRUCTOR -PROTOCOL - PAO -TRANSPORTATION - INTEL - HUMAN RESOURCES - LOGISTICS - ACTION OFFICER (SERVICE/JOINT STAFF)

LEGEND:
* PRIMARY CAREER REQUIREMENT
** SEE 0-4 LEVAL FOR ILLUSTRATIVE TYPE OF ASSIGNMENTS
NOTE:
(1) OFFICER WILL NORMALLY ATTEND ONLY ONE PROFESSIONAL MILITARY
EDUCATION (PME) INSTITUTION
(2) COMPLETION OF ONE JOINT TOUR IS REQUIRED FOR PROMOTION TO FLAG RANK
(3) SERVICE STAFF (TYPICAL)   JOINT STAFFS (TYPICAL)

SERVICE STAFF (TYPICAL)	JOINT STAFFS (TYPICAL)
- OPNAV	- THE JOINT STAFF
- CHNAVPERS	- OSD
- TYCOM	- ALLIED
- FLEET	- DEFENSE AGENCIES
- TRAINING CMD	- UNIFIED COMMANDS

7. General Unrestricted Line Officer Career Path

11

	30__	CONUS/Foreign Shore	**CAREER DEVELOPMENT MANAGE-MENT/LEADERSHIP** * Command * Material Professional * Increasing Specialization or Depth Depending on the Need of the Service
CAPT	26__		
	——		
	24__		
	——	CONUS	
	22__		
	——		
CDR	20__		
	——	Sea/Foreign Shore	
	18__		
	——		**MANAGEMENT DEVELOPMENT** * Development of Indepth Proficiency Operational Experience Proficiency Growth Subspecialty Assignment - three tours in function Management Skill Development - two related functions to develop depth and breadth Service College
	16__	CONUS	
LCDR	——		
	14__		
	——	Sea/Foreign Shore	
	12__		
	——		
	10__		
		CONUS	
	8__	PG/CONUS	
LT	——		**TECHNICAL DEVELOPMENT** *Development of Prerequisite Experience * Subspecialty Development * Post Graduate School * Supply Afloat * Basic Qualification
	6__	Sea/Foreign Shore	
	——		
	4__	CONUS	
LTJG	——		
	2__	Sea	
	——		
ENS	0__	NSCS	

8. General Supply Corps Officer

SPECIALTY AND SUBSPECIALTY CONCEPT

The area of specialization (specialty) required in a particular job (billet) is identified by a unique designator code. Certain billets requiring additional qualifications beyond those indicated by a designator code are further identified by subspecialty codes. Subspecialty codes define the field of application and additional education, experience, and training qualifications needed to satisfy special requirements that meet specific criteria of the subspecialty validation process.

Subspecialties are applicable to the URL, RL, and STAFF CORPS and are professional development fields secondary to specialties.

SUBSPECIALTY CODE DESCRIPTION

A subspecialty code is made up of FIVE characters consisting of four numerals and an alphabetic suffix. The following provides a detailed description of subspecialty codes.

DESCRIPTION OF SUBSPECIALTY CODES

UNRESTRICTED LINE REQUIREMENTS

(FIRST SUBSET) 1st & 2nd Characters. (a) The Functional Field subspecialty codes, 20XX through 90XX, may be applied to URL officers and billets in the grades of LCDR-CAPT to indicate background experience in one of the functional fields. These codes are assigned to officers as a result of subspecialty selection boards
(b) URL subspecialty billet requirements below the grade of LCDR will be expressed by "OO" entered in the first subset, i.e. OOXX.

(SECOND SUBSET) 3rd & 4th Characters. (c) Codes XX10 through XX9X are used to express the broad or discrete Education/Skill fields as they are acquired by officers of required in billets.

(SUFFIX) 5th Characters. (d) The alphabetic suffix states the level of the educational/skill pertaining to the field stated in the second subset.

(e) The Proven Subspecialists codes
"C" (Doctorate),
"M" (Post Masters),
"Q" (Masters),
"F" (Functional Education), and
"R" (Significant Experience)
may be used to identify URL officers and requirements in the LCDR-CAPT grades. A proven subspecialty code must always be accompanied by one of the specific Functional field codes in the first subset.

RESTRICTED LINE/STAFF CORPS REQUIREMENTS

(FIRST SUBSET) 1st & 2nd Characters. (a) The first subset will be coded 00XX except for those subspecialty fields considered unique to the staff Corps, as listed below.

(SECOND SUBSET) 3rd & 4th Characters. (b) Codes 0010 through 009X are used to express the broad or discrete Educational/Skill Fields.

(SUFFIX) 5th Character. (c) The alphabetic suffix states the level of education/skill pertaining to unique Staff Corps subspecialty. The "Proven Subspecialist" codes to not apply.

UNIQUE STAFF CORPS REQUIREMENTS

(a) The first subset of these subspecialty codes denotes a unique Staff Corps field as follows:

11XX - CEC	12XX - JAG
13XX - SUPPLY	14XX - CHAPLAIN
15XX & 16XX - MEDICAL	17XX - DENTAL
18XX - MEDICAL SERVICE	19XX - NURSE

(b) Describes the educational/skill field within each of the unique Staff Corps subspecialties; must always be expressed in conjunction with the unique Staff Corps field in the first subset
(c) The alphabetic suffix states the level of education/skill pertaining to the unique Staff Corps subspecialty. The "Proven Subspecialist" codes do not apply.

SUBSPECIALTY CODE EXAMPLES

CODE	DESCRIPTION
0036P	Master's level in Manpower/Personnel Management.
9095Q	Proven Subspecialist; Master's level education in Computer Systems Management; experience in the Manpower/ Personnel field.
7068G	Functional education in Strategic Weapons (FBM) with experience in Strategic Plans.
1306P	Supply Corps requirement for Master's level in Procurement Management.
1970V	Nurse Corps requirement for certified Hyperbaric Nurse.

OBTAINING A SUBSPECIALTY. Officers interested in developing a subspecialty based upon postgraduate (PG) education should indicate a preference for such graduate work (including curriculum) on their officer preference card before they complete their first tour. This will permit a significant number of PG-selected officers to pursue graduate studies during second or subsequent tours of duty. The Navy needs officers with graduate degrees in technical areas. Therefore, the majority of quotas are for study in technical curricula.

Officers who miss going to postgraduate school during their first shore tour have additional opportunities for selection and attendance during their second and subsequent shore tours.

Of primary importance to new unrestricted line officers is the attainment of the basic skills and qualifications associated with their warfare specialty. Unrestricted line officers should strive to gain the necessary warfare qualifications leading to command.

Your sustained superior performance in your present assignment is the most important factor in determining your future assignments and promotion opportunities. Therefore, whatever your job and whether or not you consider it important, always strive to do your best.

DUTY PREFERENCES. The needs of the Navy come first in deciding your duty assignments. However, the Navy does consider your personal preferences and requires you to submit an Officer Preference and Personal Information Card (NAVPERS 1301/1) to inform your detailer of your duty preferences. Changes in postgraduate preference, marital of dependency status, members of household, current residence, or next duty preference are reasons for submitting a new card. You DO NOT submit a card reading "No Change."

Make realistic choices of duty and duty stations on your preference card. The Commander, Naval Military Personnel Command (NMPC), issues the Biennial Officer Billet Summary, NAVPERS 15994H, on an annual basis. This summary provides officers with a ready reference of billets relative to geographic location, required designator and rank, subspecialty, and primary duties. All ships and stations receive this publication. Consult the Biennial Officer Billet Summary before you fill out your preference card.

Your detailer works on your transfer several months before you actually receive your orders. Using your preference card, and again, according to the Navy's needs, your detailer attempts to locate an assignment commensurate with your preference and one that will "round out" your experience for promotion.

Your detailer's recommendation goes to the Placement Desk with your name and qualification. If the Placement Desk accepts you, they notify the Order Writing Section. If the Placement Desk does not accept you, your detailer will start the process again.

FLIGHT AND SUBMARINE TRAINING. Article 6610360 of the Naval Military Personnel Manual (MILPERSMAN) outlines the necessary qualifications and requirements for officers interested in FLIGHT TRAINING.

Article 6610320 of the MILPERSMAN sets forth the necessary qualifications and requirements for officers interested in SUBMARINE TRAINING.

TRANSFER TO THE REGULAR NAVY. Naval Reserve officers and Regular Navy temporary officers may transfer to the Regular Navy. The primary objective of this program is to meet deficiencies in the numbers of Regular Navy officers in the various staff corps and line communities. Regular permanent appointments are made to the active-duty list of the Navy in both the line and staff corps as appropriate.

The Secretary of the Navy convenes a selection board twice a year, normally in April and October, to consider the records of those officers applying for transfer to the Regular Navy. As with other competitive selections in your career, performance is critical to selection. Refer to MILPERSMAN, Article 102012, for details on application, processing, and appointment procedures.

If you request transfer to the Regular Navy in conjunction with a request for a lateral transfer between restricted line, unrestricted line, and staff, follow the procedures in MILPERSMAN, Article 1020120. Refer to MILPERSMAN, Article 1020150, to request lateral transfer without augmentation.

Reserve officers are eligible for permanent appointment in the Regular Navy after they have completed 3 years on active duty (while serving under a 4-year obligation). Those who serve under a 2-year agreement are eligible to transfer to the Regular Navy after 1 year of active commissioned service.

OFFICER SERVICE RECORDS

PERMANENT NATURE OF AN OFFICER'S RECORD. Any matter rightfully placed in the official record of an officer MAY NOT BE REMOVED EXCEPT BY SPECIAL AUTHORIZATION OF THE SECRETARY OF THE NAVY. THE RECORD IS PERMANENT. A Fitness Report once submitted for the record becomes the property of the Navy Department and is NOT SUBJECT TO CHANGE. A controversial report may be amended by correspondence forwarded via official channels, such correspondence to be attached to and made a part of the report in question.

Pursuant to Navy Regulations, adverse matter shall NOT be placed in an officer's record without his/her knowledge. In all cases it shall be referred to the officer reported on for such official statement as he/she may choose to make in reply. If the officer reported on desires to make NO STATEMENT, he/she shall so state officially in writing.

1. OFFICER MICROFICHE RECORD (microfiche file)
Serves as an official history of each officer's naval career. Maintained at NMPC.
a. MICROFICHE NO. 1 (Fitness reports and awards)
  (1) Latest official photograph
  (2) Fitness reports
  (3) Medals and awards
b. MICROFICHE NO. 2 (Professional history)
  (1) Civilian and military education and training
  (2) Appointments and promotions
  (3) Qualifications
  (4) Reserve status
  (5) Miscellaneous professional history
c. MICROFICHE NO 3 (Personal data)
  (1) Medical history
  (2) Security clearances
  (3) Record of Emergency Data
  (4) Citizenship & Biography
  (5) Record changes
d. MICROFICHE NO 4 (Copies of orders)
e. MICROFICHE NO 5 (Privileged information) Adverse or derogatory information when/if needed
f. MICROFICHE NO 6 (Enlisted record) Used only if the individual has more than two years of enlisted active duty.

RECORD ACCESS. The individual, detailer, placement officer, selection board members, and anyone the officer designates in writing. The individual's commanding officer is prohibited by law from seeing another officer's record.

COMMENTS. Anytime you are going before a selection board or are up for orders, review your microfiche for currency and accuracy (microfiche 1, 2, and 5).

To request a copy of the microfiche record from NMPC, use form NAVPERS 1070/879.

2. OFFICER SERVICE RECORD

Maintained at the local command by deploying commands. Shore commands usually keep the Officer Service Record at the local Personnel Support Detachment (PSD). The commanding officer has access to this service record.

The purpose of this service record copy is to provide a ready file of documents from which information required for proper assignment, promotion, and administration of an officer may be obtained. This record does not contain any adverse information or Fitness Reports.

a. RIGHT SIDE

Reserved for documents affecting the utilization and assignment of the officer concerned.

Documents will be filed in reverse order to make sure item (1) is on top when the record is opened for reading.
(1) Copy of NAVPERS 1210/5 Officer Qualification Questionnaire
(2) NAVPERS 318, original of Training School Record (Applicable to officers commissioned prior to March 1965)
(3) Copies of NAVPERS 1210/2, Annual Qualifications Questionnaire - Inactive Duty Reserve Officers
(4) Copy of NAVPERS 1301/1, Officer Preference and personal Information Card
(5) Copy of NAVPERS 1301/51, Officer Data Card
(6) Copy of DD 398, Statement of Personal History, or superseding Personnel Security Questionnaire (BI/SBI), as appropriate
(7) Permanent letters of designation or revocation of special qualifications, such as Submarine Qualification designations, SWO, Command at Sea, etc.
(8) Any official correspondence affecting the utilization and assignment of an officer

b. LEFT SIDE

Documents will be filed in reverse order to make sure item (1) is on top when the record is opened for reading.
(1) NAVPERS 5510/1, Personnel Reliability Program, if applicable
(2) NAVPERS 5510'3, Personnel Reliability Program (PRP) Screening and Evaluation Record, if appropriate
(3) OPNAV 5521/429, Certificate of Personnel Security Clearance

(4) Copy of NAVCRUIT 1000/20, Officer Appointment Acceptance and Oath of Office

(5) Copy of NAVPERS I000/22, Acceptance and Oath of Office for present grade

(6) Copy of NAVPERS 1421/7, Delivery of Temporary/Permanent Appointment

(7) Copy of NAVPERS 1070'26, Statement of Service, as appropriate

(8) Signed copy of NAVPERS 1070'602, Dependency Application/Record of Emergency Data. Copy of Servicemen's Group Life Insurance (SGLI)

(9) Copies of official correspondence originated at present command and endorsements or copies of replies

(10) Copies of Correspondence Course Completion Letters

(11) Recording of Code of Conduct Training

(12) NAVPERS 5512/1, Application for Armed Forces ID Card, or superseding DD 1172, Application for Uniformed Services ID Card/DEERS Enrollment

(13) DD 803, Certificate of Termination

(14) Latest photograph

(15) NAVPERS 1070/74, Officer's Report of Home of Record and place from which ordered to a tour of active duty

(16) Copy of DD 214, Certificate of Release or Discharge from Active Duty

(17) Official correspondence relative to assignment cancellation, or termination in the Naval Reserve Program

(18) Orders or copies of all endorsements relative to assignment, cancellation, or termination in the Naval Reserve Program

(19) Correspondence indicating satisfactory completion of driver improvement/training, as applicable

(20) Documents and correspondence of courses and schools completed, medals, awards, commendations, equator crossings, round-the-world cruises, etc.

(21) Letters of temporary designation that apply while at present command such as Command Security Manager, Top Secret Control Officer, Naval Courier, etc.

"Hidden talent counts for nothing." NERO
From the book: ***Successful Leadership Today***

CHAPTER 2

SELECTION BOARDS

OFFICER PROMOTION OVERVIEW

U.S. STATUTE. The overall maximum number of officers that may serve in the Navy is established by U.S. Statute. The maximum number of officers in paygrade of 0-4 and above that may serve in the Navy is also established by U.S. Statute.

SECNAV. The Secretary of the Navy (SECNAV) establishes the actual number of officers to be selected for promotion in each competitive category. This is determined by U.S. Statute (mentioned above) and the projected needs of the Navy.

SELECTION BOARD. The selection board selects the "best qualified" officers to fill the available slots and recommends the individual officers to be promoted.

PRESIDENT. The President approves recommendations of the selection board.

U.S. SENATE. The Senate confirms appointments to the next paygrade.

OFFICER. Individual officers accept or decline the appointment.

OFFICER PROMOTION PROCESS

SELECTION BOARD. Members are nominated by NMPC and selected by the Secretary of the Navy. The board is required to be balanced with a proportional representation from each line or staff community. Each designator up for promotion must be represented.

ELIGIBILITY. Time in paygrade is the only requirement to be considered for promotion by selection board process.

1.   BELOW ZONE - Minimum time in grade requirement. Records are reviewed and normally only the absolute "front runners" are promoted from the below zone list. If not selected, this does not count as being "passed over."

2. IN ZONE - Primary candidates eligible for promotion. Most officers should expect to be promoted when they are in the "in zone" list of candidates. Those not selected when "in zone" are considered to have been "passed over" for promotion for the first time.

3.   ABOVE ZONE - Last chance for those officers that have been passed over.   Officers not selected from "above zone" have been "passed over" twice in the same paygrade.

SELECTION BOARDS

TYPES.   There are two types of selection boards, statutory boards and administrative boards.   Statutory boards include promotion (including special and spot promotion boards), and the various continuation boards.   All others are administrative boards.

THE DIFFERENCES
1. Statutory boards are governed by law, primarily Title 10 of the U.S. Code.   Administrative boards are governed by instruction or policy.

2. Statutory boards are convened by SECNAV; admin boards are convened by CNP or DCNP.

3.   Statutory board results are approved by the President, SECDEF or SECNAV. Admin boards are approved by CNP or DCNP.

4.   Membership on statutory boards is set by statute and SECNAVINST 1401.3 (which is very specific as to designator mix and paygrade). Membership requirements for admin boards are determined by the board sponsor.

> *"Want a valuable asset? Tell someone they are."*
> From the book: ***Successful Leadership Today***

PRECEPTS. Each year, SECNAV approves language used in the current year's statutory selection board precepts. A precept is the document, signed by the convening authority and directed to the president of the board, giving general and specific guidance to the board regarding the criteria upon which their selections should be based.

The only information allowed before a statutory board is an officer's official service record microfiche, officer summary record (OSR), any correspondence the officer submits to the board, and the board precept. Admin boards work the same except for those board requiring an application package (LDO/CWO Inservice Procurement, Federal Executive Fellowship, Test Pilot, etc.) which is also reviewed by board members. No other information is allowed to be discussed or presented before a board.

The statutory "best qualified" criterion is based on performance. Additional guidance in the precept addresses equality in the selection of minority officers and consideration of non-warfare career paths of General Unrestricted Line Officers. Language is also directed at non-traditional career paths of officers with subspecialties, to ensure the future needs of the Navy are met by officers with particular skills. Also singled out in the precept for consideration by the board are an officer's performance of duty in a joint billet and the unique career paths and needs of the Navy with respect to the Materiel Professional (MP) community.

Admin board precepts are standardized and mirror the language used in statutory boards. Precepts convening admin boards may be modified by an additional section in which the board sponsor provides specific guidance to the board, tailored for that particular board's function. This may include quotas or numbers to select, including alternates; additional program eligibility criteria; amplification of unique career paths; or, other information deemed necessary by the board sponsor.

Admin boards are pivotal to most officers at one or more points in their career. Prepare for an admin board as diligently as you would for a promotion board. Review your microfiche, OSR and ODC for accuracy well in advance of the board. Your OSR is particularly critical because it is used to present your record to board members. The other board members do not review your microfiche. They see only the OSR. Also, ensure your photograph is current and in the correct uniform.

Admin boards are important and can affect your standing in a promotion board three or four years away. Virtually all officers in all designators have career milestones they must meet to maintain upward mobility within their communities. Many of these career milestone opportunities are determined through admin board action. You must succeed in the admin board selection process to remain truly competitive for your next statutory board.

SELECTION BOARD CONVENINGS

Promotion selection boards are convened by the Secretary of the Navy (SECNAV) as authorized by statute. At least 30 days before the first scheduled convening date for selection boards of the next fiscal year, SECNAV provides (via ALNAV) the board schedule and promotion zones. This ALNAV is released each October.

SELECTION BOARD PREPARATION. Preparation for a promotion selection board begins four months before its convening date. The initial list of eligible officers is compiled and modified as required. The eligibles list is continually synchronized with the official automated database to ensure consideration of all eligible officers. One week before the board convening date, the assistant recorders review the record of each eligible officer, transcribe missing microfiche data onto the Officer Summary Record (OSR), and ensure fitness report continuity for at least the last five years.

The promotion selection board reviews the record of each eligible officer whether in the promotion zone (IZ), above zone (AZ), or below zone (BZ). For the record he or she will brief, each board member transcribes information from the microfiche record to the OSR.

BOARD ACTION. When the selection process begins the annotated OSR is projected onto large screens in the board meeting room, and the record is briefed by the board member who reviewed the officer's microfiche record. The board, using the precept as guidance, recommends (within the numbers authorized) those officers it considers "best qualified" for promotion.

RELEASING THE RESULTS. Once the selection board provides a select list to the Secretary of the Navy, and it is subsequently approved by the Secretary of Defense. A select ALNAV message will be released usually four to five weeks after the selection board adjourns. For those officers selected for LCDR and above, Senate confirmation is required before promotion or frocking.

CHECK YOUR RECORD. Although the recorders check for current and complete fitness reports, you owe it to yourself to make sure the board has your complete and accurate record. Six months before the board for which you are eligible convenes, you should order your microfiche record from PERS-313 and your OSR from PERS-323. If you discover errors or omissions, contact PERS-313 to correct your record as soon as possible. Fitness report correction information goes to PERS-323.

CORRESPONDING WITH THE BOARD. Copies of documents you receive after you have reviewed your record (such as fitness reports, personal awards, etc.) should be forwarded in a letter to the president of your selection board. Any corrections you have made to your record should also be addressed. A command endorsement to your letter to the president of the board is not necessary. Only those officers who are eligible before a selection board may correspond with its president. Any endorsement or letter written on your behalf must go via you or it will be returned to the originator. To ensure safe arrival of your correspondence, use overnight delivery service and obtain a signed receipt. All correspondence must be received by the board convening date. All late correspondence will be returned.

SPECIAL BOARD PROCEDURES. Frequently when an officer fails to select for promotion, he or she feels an injustice has occurred and immediately requests a special selection board. However, failure of selection for promotion is not in itself grounds for requesting a special promotion selection board. The following describes what constitutes grounds for a board, the administrative routine to expect when requesting a board, and what can make or break the effectiveness of a request.

Statute and SECNAVINST 1401.1 require consideration by a special promotion selection board for only one reason:

The SECNAV determines that an eligible officer was not considered by a regularly scheduled promotion selection board because of administrative error.

SECNAV may grant a special promotion selection board for an officer who was considered but not selected by a regular board when SECNAV determines that the action of the board was contrary to law, involved material error of fact, or material administrative error; or determines that the board did not have certain material information before it for consideration.

Officers are required to exercise reasonable diligence to discover and correct any error or omission in the official record prior to the convening date of the regularly scheduled board. If they have not, they should not expect approval of special selection board requests.

Administrative processing of a special board request begins at BUPERS in the Officer Promotions, Appointments, and Enlisted Advancements Division. The special board coordinator researches the case using pertinent records retained by BUPERS, in addition to the materials and information provided by the aggrieved officer when submitting the board request. A recommendation is then formulated and submitted to PERS-06 (BUPERS legal counsel) for legal scrutiny. This recommendation becomes the basis for the Chief of Naval Personnel's (CNPs) recommendation to the SECNAV.

CNP then reviews the entire case, makes a recommendation and forwards the completed package with the officer's request and any pertinent material facts to SECNAV via the Office of the Judge Advocate General (OJAG).

OJAG researches the legality of the case and forwards it to SECNAV for final determination. Officer promotion selection boards are regulated by federal statute. These circumstances mandate meticulous attention to legal detail in all matters pertaining to officer promotions.

Normal processing time is four months from date of receipt of the members request in PERS-26 to the release of SECNAV's decision.   If the request is approved, the next major administrative step is the board itself.

Special promotion selection boards are convened when necessary based on demand. Due to cost, scheduling and other needs-of-the Navy considerations, it is practical to convene a special promotion selection board only when there are several approved requests.   Boards are scheduled quarterly unless demand necessitates more.

An officer whose request is denied is immediately notified by personal letter from PERS-26.   An officer whose request is approved is notified via message at least 30 days before the convening date of the special board.

The process for setting up and administering a special promotion selection board is the same as for a regular board. Special board recommendations go through the same approval chain as do those of regular boards. However, special board results usually take longer to be released than normal promotion selection boards.

YOUR RESPONSIBILITY. The responsibility for ensuring the accuracy of your microfiche lies with you.   You should periodically review and update your microfiche record to ensure completeness and accuracy.   Once the board has met, it's too late to correct your record for that board.

Missing photographs, personal awards, or designation letters are not normally considered material to a board's deliberations. Missing regular FITREPs (greater than 90 days) may be grounds for a special board if the officer has made every effort possible to update the record.

To maximize your chances for promotion at regular boards, first make sure you have done all you reasonably can to correct errors in your record.   If not selected, review SECNAVINST 1401.1 and any regulation that pertains to the reason for your request before initiating action to BUPERS. Ask questions of your detailer, legal officer, and others held accountable for expertise on the specific issue involved in your potential request. Detailers are required to provide you with failure of selection counseling.

CHAPTER 3

OFFICER UNIFORMS

There are four (4) basic categories of officer uniforms.

1. WORKING UNIFORMS
a. General Characteristics:
- (1) No ribbons
- (2) Not a liberty uniform
- (3) Never a "Uniform of the Day"
- (4) Name tags are optional

b. OCCASIONS: There are no specific occasions for the wearing of a working uniform. If the situation, location or type of work to be done meets the requirements then a working uniform will be worn.

c. TYPES:
(1) WORKING KHAKI
Also known as "Wash Khaki." May wear Khaki combination or garrison cover. A command ball cap may also be authorized. Black shoes. Brown shoes are optional for aviation related fields.
(2) WINTER WORKING BLUE
All black (Navy blue), identical to the Winter Blue uniform except no ribbons or no tie.
(3) AVIATION WORKING GREEN
Worn with black shoes, green combination or green garrison cover. Brown shoes optional.

2. SERVICE UNIFORMS
a. GENERAL CHARACTERISTICS:
- (1) Ribbons will be worn
- (2) Used as a liberty uniform
- (3) Used as the "Uniform of the Day"
- (4) Name tags are optional

b. OCCASIONS:
(1) Worn at all official functions where Formal Dress, Dinner Dress or Full Dress uniforms are not prescribed and the civilian equivalent is coat and tie.
(2) Worn when in a travel status.

c. TYPES:
    (1) SERVICE DRESS BLUE

The basic uniform of the Navy. Authorized for year round wear at all official functions. White combination cover, white long sleeve or optional short sleeve for women and men (except for ceremonial occasions or inspections). Long sleeve shirts may have epaulets and soft shoulder boards will be worn. Wear black shoes.

    (2) SERVICE DRESS WHITE ("Choker Whites")

White combination cover, white shoes/socks and hard shoulder boards for male and female.

    (3) SUMMER WHITE

Optional summer dress uniform. Hard shoulder boards for male and female uniforms.

    (4) WINTER BLUE

Same as the Winter Working Blue but with the addition of ribbons and a tie.

    (5) SUMMER KHAKI

Basic Naval Service Dress uniform. Brown shoes optional for aviators, Khaki combination or garrison cover authorized.

3. CEREMONIAL/FULL DRESS UNIFORMS

a. GENERAL CHARACTERISTICS:
    (1) Large medals, above left breast pocket
    (2) White gloves
    (3) Swords (prescribable for 0-4 and above)
    (4) No name tags
    (5) Ribbons, not having medals, above right breast pocket

b. OCCASIONS:
    (1) When assuming or relinquishing command; or participating in the ceremony.
    (2) Official visits with honors as prescribed in Navy Regulations.
    (3) Visits of ceremony to Foreign Men-Of-War and foreign officials.
    (4) Graduation, commissioning, weddings or funerals.

c. TYPES:
    (1) FULL DRESS BLUE (winter)

White combination cover, white long sleeve or optional short sleeve for women and men (except for ceremonial occasions or inspections). Long sleeve shirts may have epaulets and soft shoulder boards will be worn. Wear black shoes.

      (2) FULL DRESS WHITE (summer)
White combination cover, white shoes/socks and hard shoulder boards for males.

4. DINNER DRESS UNIFORMS
a. GENERAL CHARACTERISTICS:
      (1) Miniature medals
      (2) Miniature breast insignia
      (3) White gloves
      (4) No name tags
b. OCCASIONS: As prescribed.
c. TYPES:
      (1) DINNER DRESS BLUE JACKET (winter)
Prescribable for 0-4 and above, high waisted black pants, short jacket with sleeve insignia, gold cummerbund, pleated white shirt with gold studs and cufflinks, and with combination cover.
      (2) DINNER DRESS WHITE JACKET (summer)
Prescribable for 0-4 and above, high waisted black pants, short jacket with hard shoulder boards, gold cummerbund, pleated white shirt with gold studs and cufflinks, and with combination cover.
      (3) DINNER DRESS BLUE (winter)
White combination cover, white long sleeve or optional short sleeve for women and men (except for ceremonial occasions or inspections). Long sleeve shirts may have epaulets and soft shoulder boards will be worn. Wear black shoes. Bow tie, pleated shirt (gold studs and cufflinks optional). No cummerbund.
      (4) DINNER DRESS WHITE (summer)
White combination cover, white shoes/socks and hard shoulder boards for males. No cummerbund.
      (5) FORMAL DRESS (white tie)
Worn normally when civilians wear evening clothes (white tie). This uniform may be prescribed for Captains, Flag Officers, and other officers assigned to duty where required by protocol. See Navy Uniform Regulations for description.

5. MISCELLANEOUS UNIFORMS
a. TROPICAL DINNER DRESS
This uniform is intended for wear in climates where the use of other dinner dress uniforms would be uncomfortable.

(1) MALE. Blue dress trousers (same as Summer Dress Blues), gold wraparound cummerbund, white summer short sleeve shirt with hard shoulder boards, black dress shoes.

(2) FEMALES. Blue unbelted skirt (same as Summer Dress Blue), gold wraparound cummerbund, white short sleeve shirt with hard shoulder boards, black dress shoes.

b. SERVICE DRESS BLUE (YANKEE)

This uniform is a combination of the Service Dress Blue and Service Dress White uniforms. From the waist up it is the Summer Dress Blue. From the waist down it is the Summer Dress White. Will be worn when prescribed.

c. TROPICAL KHAKI

This is a working uniform that could be worn in tropical climates where other working uniforms would be uncomfortable. Same as working khaki except khaki short trousers and knee-length black socks.

d. TROPICAL WHITE

This is a service uniform which may be worn in tropical climates where other dress uniforms would be uncomfortable. Same as summer white uniform except white short trousers and knee-length white socks.

A GOOD leader inspires others with his or her own confidence; A GREAT leader inspires them with confidence in themselves."
From the book: ***Successful Leadership Today***

CHAPTER 4

UNIFORM INSIGNIA

COMMAND AT SEA. This insignia is worn by persons below flag rank who have, or had, command of commissioned ships or aviation squadrons at sea. Officers currently in command wear the insignia on the right breast. Those not presently in command, but who have held command, wear it on the left breast below any ribbons, medals or other insignia.

COMMAND ASHORE/PROJECT MANAGER. Worn by officers below flag rank who have, or had, command ashore or served as project manager. Those currently occupying those positions wear the insignia on the right breast. Those not presently in command, or a project manager, but who have been in that position, wear it on the left breast below any ribbons, medals or other insignia.

SMALL CRAFT. The small craft insignia is worn by personnel currently serving, or having previously served, as officer in charge of small craft. This insignia is worn in the same manner as the Command at Sea and Command Ashore/Project Manager insignia.

"Nothing is more difficult, and therefore more precious, than to be able to decide." NAPOLEON
From the book: **Successful Leadership Today**

The insignia described below are worn on the left breast above any medals, ribbons, or insignia.

SURFACE WARFARE (SWO & ESWS). This insignia is worn by personnel who have qualified in all phases of surface warfare.

Surface Warfare Officer

Enlisted Surface Warfare Specialist

SUBMARINE(SS). This insignia is worn by personnel who have qualified to serve in submarines. In addition to the basic insignia, other submarine insignia include those for submarine medical, engineering, and supply officers, and for all who participated successfully in combat patrols. The Officer's "dolphins" are gold, and the enlisted "dolphins" are silver.

NAVAL AVIATOR. This insignia is worn by personnel qualified to serve as pilots of Navy & Marine Corps aircraft.

NAVAL FLIGHT OFFICER (NFO). The insignia is worn by unrestricted line officers qualified to operate the sophisticated airborne weapons systems in our modern Navy aircraft.

SPECIAL WARFARE. This insignia is worn by personnel qualified in underwater and beach reconnaissance, demolition, and special warfare tactics. They are usually associated with underwater demolition teams (UDT) or Sea, Air, Land (SEAL) team detachments.

EXPLOSIVE ORDNANCE DISPOSAL (EOD). Worn by personnel who are qualified in the identification and safe disposal of many different types of ordnance produced by the United States, our allies, and our enemies.

SSBN DETERRENT PATROL. Worn by personnel who successfully complete a patrol on a fleet ballistic missile submarine. Gold stars are mounted on the scroll to indicate each successful patrol subsequent to that which the original insignia was awarded.

DIVER. The diver insignia is worn by personnel qualified in various classes of diving.

> *"No one is offended by writing that is easy to understand."*
> From the book: *Successful Leadership Today*

**Command
Master Chief**

**Command
Senior Chief**

**Command
Chief**

**Career
Counselor**

**Recruit
Company
Commander**

**Enlisted Aviation
Warfare Specialist**

Naval Parachutist

Aircrewman

**Supply Surface Warfare
Officer**

**CB Combat Warfare
Pin**

INSIGNIA OF U.S. ARMED FORCES OFFICERS

	WARRANT				COMMISSIONED										
PAY GRADE	W-1	W-2	W-3	W-4	0-1	0-2	0-3	0-4	0-5	0-6	0-7	0-7 – 0-8		0-9 – 0-10	
NAVY	WARRANT OFFICER W1 (GOLD–BLUE)	CHIEF WARRANT OFFICER W2 (GOLD–SCARLET)	CHIEF WARRANT OFFICER W3 (SILVER–BLUE)	CHIEF WARRANT OFFICER W4 (SILVER–BLUE)	ENSIGN (GOLD)	LIEUTENANT JUNIOR GRADE (SILVER)	LIEUTENANT (SILVER)	LIEUTENANT COMMANDER (GOLD)	COMMANDER (SILVER)	CAPTAIN (SILVER)	COMMODORE (SILVER)	REAR ADMIRAL (SILVER) / VICE ADMIRAL (SILVER)		ADMIRAL (SILVER)	FLEET ADMIRAL (SILVER)
MARINES	WARRANT OFFICER W1 (GOLD–SCARLET)	CHIEF WARRANT OFFICER W2 (GOLD–SCARLET)	CHIEF WARRANT OFFICER W3 (SILVER–SCARLET)	CHIEF WARRANT OFFICER W4 (SILVER–SCARLET)	SECOND LIEUTENANT (GOLD)	FIRST LIEUTENANT (SILVER)	CAPTAIN (SILVER)	MAJOR (GOLD)	LIEUTENANT COLONEL (SILVER)	COLONEL (SILVER)	BRIGADIER GENERAL (SILVER)	MAJOR GENERAL (SILVER) / LIEUTENANT GENERAL (SILVER)		GENERAL (SILVER)	
ARMY	WARRANT OFFICER W1 (SILVER–BLACK)	CHIEF WARRANT OFFICER W2 (SILVER–BLACK)	CHIEF WARRANT OFFICER W3 (SILVER–BLACK)	CHIEF WARRANT OFFICER W4 (SILVER–BLACK)	SECOND LIEUTENANT (GOLD)	FIRST LIEUTENANT (SILVER)	CAPTAIN (SILVER)	MAJOR (GOLD)	LIEUTENANT COLONEL (SILVER)	COLONEL (SILVER)	BRIGADIER GENERAL (SILVER)	MAJOR GENERAL (SILVER) / LIEUTENANT GENERAL (SILVER)		GENERAL (SILVER)	GENERAL OF THE ARMY (SILVER)
AIR FORCE	WARRANT OFFICER W1 (GOLD–SKY BLUE)	CHIEF WARRANT OFFICER W2 (GOLD–SKY BLUE)	CHIEF WARRANT OFFICER W3 (SILVER–SKY BLUE)	CHIEF WARRANT OFFICER W4 (SILVER–SKY BLUE)	SECOND LIEUTENANT (GOLD)	FIRST LIEUTENANT (SILVER)	CAPTAIN (SILVER)	MAJOR (GOLD)	LIEUTENANT COLONEL (SILVER)	COLONEL (SILVER)	BRIGADIER GENERAL (SILVER)	MAJOR GENERAL (SILVER) / LIEUTENANT GENERAL (SILVER)		GENERAL (SILVER)	GENERAL OF THE AIR FORCE (SILVER)

36

INSIGNIA OF ENLISTED PERSONNEL

ENLISTED

PAY GRADE	E-1	E-2	E-3	E-4	E-5	E-6	E-7	E-8	E-9	E-10 *
NAVY								SENIOR PETTY OFFICERS COLLAR DEVICES		
	SEAMAN RECRUIT	SEAMAN APPRENTICE	SEAMAN	PETTY OFFICER THIRD CLASS	PETTY OFFICER SECOND CLASS	PETTY OFFICER FIRST CLASS	CHIEF PETTY OFFICER	SENIOR CHIEF PETTY OFFICER	MASTER CHIEF PETTY OFFICER	MASTER CHIEF PETTY OFFICER OF THE NAVY
MARINES	PRIVATE	PRIVATE FIRST CLASS	LANCE CORPORAL	CORPORAL	SERGEANT	STAFF SERGEANT	GUNNERY SERGEANT	FIRST SERGEANT / MASTER SERGEANT	SERGEANT MAJOR / MASTER GUNNERY SERGEANT	SERGEANT MAJOR OF THE MARINE CORPS
ARMY	PRIVATE	PRIVATE	PRIVATE FIRST CLASS	CORPORAL / SPECIALIST 4	SERGEANT / SPECIALIST 5	STAFF SERGEANT / SPECIALIST 6	SERGEANT FIRST CLASS	FIRST SERGEANT / MASTER SERGEANT	COMMAND SERGEANT MAJOR / SERGEANT MAJOR	SERGEANT MAJOR OF THE ARMY
AIR FORCE	AIRMAN BASIC	AIRMAN	AIRMAN FIRST CLASS	SERGEANT / SENIOR AIRMAN	STAFF SERGEANT	TECHNICAL SERGEANT	MASTER SERGEANT	SENIOR MASTER SERGEANT	CHIEF MASTER SERGEANT	CHIEF MASTER SERGEANT OF THE AIR FORCE

ALL STARS SILVER

STARS LIGHT BLUE

* AUTHORIZED ONLY WHILE SERVING AS THE SENIOR ENLISTED MEMBER OF ANY BRANCH OF MILITARY SERVICE.

STAFF CORPS INSIGNIA

Medical Corps

Chaplain Corps (Christian)

Chaplain Corps (Jewish)

Supply Corps

Dental Corps

Medical Service Corps

Nurse Corps

Navy Band Leader

Judge Advocate General's Corps

Law Community

Civil Engineer Corps

WARRANT OFFICERS INSIGNIA

Aerographer

Air Traffic Control Tech.

Av. Electronics Tech.

Av. Maintenance Tech.

Aviation Boatswain

Aviation Operations Tech.

Aviation Ordnance Tech.

Bandmaster

Boatswain

Civil Engineering Corps

Communications Tech.

Cryptologic Technician

**Data
Processing
Tech.**

**Electronics
Technician**

**Engineering/Nuc.
Power Tech.**

EOD Technician

**Intelligence
Tech.**

**Operations
Technician**

**Ordnance/Spec.
Warfare Tech.**

Photographer

**Med/Dental
Svc/Phys. Asst.**

**Repair
Technician**

**Security
Technician**

Ship's Clerk

**Supply Clerk/
Food Svc**

CHAPTER 5

THE NAVAL OFFICER'S SWORD

GENERAL RULES

1. The Navy officer's scabbard is worn straight except when rotated 180 to draw or return sword.

2. Officers draw and return sword, without command, when the commander of their unit draws his/hers. Unless members of the commander's staff, they execute all other movements of the sword manual on the commander's command to the unit. The commander of a unit and his staff execute all other movements of the sword manual on the commander's separate command to his staff, given after his command to the unit. The sword will be drawn whenever with armed troops, except when at ease, rest, route step, at ease march, inspecting troops, or when the commander of a unit is being inspected.

3. Carry sword is assumed when:
    a. Giving commands.
    b. Changing position in formation at quick time.
    c. Addressing or being addressed by a senior.
    d. The preparatory command for, and while marching at quick time, has been given.
    e. Any manual of arms movement has been ordered except parade rest, at east, rest, present arms, order arms, or eyes right (left). When in formation with personnel to your front at normal distance or less (organization staffs excluded), remain at carry sword except during rest or at ease.

4. Present sword is assumed when:
    a. Saluting with the sword.
    b. The unit is presented to the colors or to any person, or when the National Anthem, To The Color, Retreat, or Hail to the Chief is played.
    c. Executing eyes right (left) while marching past a reviewing officer or stand. If in the interior of a formation, remain at carry sword.

5. While marching with sword at the carry, the arms should swing 6 inches to the front and 3 inches to the rear. Do not hold the scabbard or sling.

6. While marching at double time, hold the sword diagonally across the chest with the sharp edge to the front. Hold the scabbard with the left hand just below the lower brass ring mounting.

7. When calling roll, reading documents, or publishing orders to a formation, slip the fingers of the left hand between the sword grip and guard. Allow the sword to hang, with the grip to the front across the knuckles. Keep the left elbow against the side and hold the document with both hands.

8. When not in formation, keep the sword in its scabbard. Salute by executing the hand salute.

DRAW SWORD

When drawing the sword, the given command is (1) Draw, (2) SWORD

On Draw, grip the scabbard below the upper ring mounting with the left hand. Turn the scabbard clockwise 180 and tilt it forward to form an angle of 45 with the deck. Take the sword grip in the right hand and pull it about 6 inches from the scabbard, as in Figure 1. The right forearm should now be parallel to the deck, the left hand holding the scabbard against the side. See Figure 1.

Fig. 1. Position for "Draw"

Fig. 2. Drawing Sword on Command Word "Sword"

On SWORD:

1. Draw the sword smartly, raising the right arm to its full extent, directly to the front at an angle of about 45, the sword in a straight line with the arm, edge down; drop the left hand by the side (Figure 2).

2. Pause for one count.

3. Bring the back of the blade against the shoulder seam of the coat, the blade vertical, back of the grip to the rear, the arm nearly extended, the thumb and

Fig 3. Position of Carry Sword

forefinger embracing the lower part of the grip, the thumb against the trouser seam, the fingers joined behind the end of the hilt (Figure 3). This is the position of carry sword.

PRESENT SWORD

The command for presenting the sword may be (1) Present, (2) SWORD; (1) Present, (2) ARMS; or (1) Eyes, (2) RIGHT (or LEFT).

Fig 4. Position for "Present"

Fig. 5. Position for the word "Sword"

Present, SWORD (ARMS)

The command Present, SWORD (ARMS) is given only when halted at order or carry sword.

On Present, raise your right hand to the level of and 6 inches in front of the neck. Keep your thumb on the left side of the grip, wrist straight, and elbows against the body, as in Figure 4. The blade should tilt forward at 30

On the word SWORD (ARMS) whip the point down smartly to a position 3 inches above the deck and slightly right of your right foot (Figure 5). Straighten your arm so the guard is against your trouser seam. The blade is inclined down and to the front with the sharp edge to the left. The thumb remains on the left side of the grip.

Eyes, RIGHT (LEFT)
The command Eyes, RIGHT (LEFT) is given only when halted at order sword or when marching at carry sword.

On the preparatory word Eyes and the word of execution RIGHT (LEFT), execute precisely the same motions as on the words Present and SWORD (ARMS) described in the preceding section. As the sword is brought down, however, turn your head and eyes 45 to the right or left, except that those in the extreme right or left file continue to look straight ahead.

The command to carry sword from eyes right (left) is Ready, FRONT. On the word Ready, turn the sharp edge of the sword down. On the FRONT, raise the sword to carry, at the same time turning your head and eyes to the front.

PARADE REST

The command Parade, REST normally is given only from order sword. When given at another position, come to order sword on the preparatory word Parade. Otherwise, no action is taken on Parade.

On REST, move the left foot smartly 12 inches to the left. Simultaneously lower the point of the sword, and place your left hand behind you, just below the belt, as in Figure 5. The fingers of the left hand are straight and joined, your palm flat and facing rear.

AT EASE; REST
The commands AT EASE and REST may be given from any position of the sword.

On AT EASE, come to order sword if not already in that position. Then move your left foot 12 inches to the left and lower the point of the sword to the deck. Rest your weight equally on both feet with your legs straight. At the same time place your left hand behind you. Keep your fingers straight and joined, your palm flat and facing rear. You may relax and, except for your right foot, move about. DO NOT talk.

The command REST is executed in the same manner as at ease, the only difference being that you may talk.

ORDER SWORD

The position of order sword is shown in Figure 6. In this position your right arm hangs naturally with your thumb along the trouser seam.

Being at present arms, the command to order sword is Order, SWORD (ARMS), executed in one count. On SWORD (ARMS) turn the sharp edge of the sword down.

Being at eyes right or left, the command is Ready, FRONT, also executed in one count. On FRONT, turn the sword edge down while turning head and eyes smartly to the front.

Fig 6. Position for "Order Sword"

Fig. 7. Returning sword to the scabbard

To order sword from parade rest, the command is (command, etc.), ATTENTION, executed in one count. On ATTENTION, bring your left heel smartly against your right and your left hand back to your side.

46

To order sword from at ease or rest, the command is (command, etc.), ATTENTION. On Command, come to parade rest. On ATTENTION, bring your left heel smartly against your right and your left hand back to your side.

RETURN SWORD

Being at carry or order sword, the command to return the sword to the scabbard is Return SWORD.

On Return, execute the first motion of present sword (Figure 4). At the same time grip the scabbard with your left hand just above the upper ring mounting, tilt it forward, and turn it clockwise 180; the scabbard should form a 45 angle to the deck.

Looking down at the opening of the scabbard lower the sword point to a position just above the opening with your left thumb and forefinger, as in Figure 7. Raise your head back to attention. Your right forearm should not be across your body, parallel to the deck. Your left hand holds the scabbard against your side.

On SWORD, push smartly down on and release the grip of the sword so that is slides all the way into the scabbard. In the same motion bring your right hand back to your right side. Turn the scabbard clockwise 180, then release the scabbard (Figure 8).

Fig. 8. Position at completion of "Return Sword"

47

CHAPTER 6

TRADITIONS, HONORS, AND CEREMONIES

INTRODUCTIONS. Aboard ship, the regularly assigned commanding officer is addressed as "Captain" regardless of grade. The regularly assigned executive officer may be addressed as "commander" without appending his/her name.

In general, it is preferable to call officers of the rank of commander or above by their title and name; that is, "Commander..." rather than by the impersonal "sir"/"ma'am." Other officers are addressed in the same manner. In prolonged conversation, where repetition would seem forced or awkward, the shorter "sir"/"ma'am" naturally is used more often.

Naval officers are introduced to civilians by title, and the method of introduction should give the cue as to how they should be addressed from then on. If you were introducing an officer below the grade of commander, you might say, "This is Lieutenant Jones. Mr. Jones is an old shipmate of mine." This serves a double purpose; it gives the officer's to whom you are introducing an officer knowledge of the naval man's grade in the event that person does not know it, and it also gives the correct method of address, "Mr. Jones."

Because many people are not familiar with Navy grade insignia and corps devices, it is usually a good idea to make any introduction however brief, reasonably informative. A woman lieutenant may be introduced with the words, "This is Lieutenant Jones. Miss (or Ms. Mrs.) Jones is in the Nurse Corps."

"Respect yourself and others will respect you." CONFUCIUS
From the book: *Successful Leadership Today*

Who was the Navy's first black admiral?
SAMUEL L. GRAVLEY, JR. (1971)

ADDRESSING NAVY OFFICERS TO NAVY PERSONNEL

Person Addressed or Introduced	**Introduce As**	**Address As**
Admiral	Admiral Jones	Admiral Jones
Vice Admiral	Vice Admiral Jones	Admiral Jones
Rear Admiral	Rear Admiral Jones	Admiral Jones
Captain	Captain Jones	Captain Jones
Commander	Commander Jones	Commander Jones
Lieutenant Commander	Lieutenant Commander Jones	Commander Jones
Lieutenant	Lieutenant Jones	Lieutenant Jones
Lieutenant Junior Grade	Lieutenant JG Jones	Lieutenant Jones
Ensign	Ensign Jones	Ensign Jones
Chief Warrant Officer	Chief Warrant Officer Jones	Chief Warrant Officer Jones
Midshipman	Midshipman Jones	Midshipman Jones

ADDRESSING NAVY OFFICERS TO CIVILIANS

Person Addressed or Introduced	**Introduce As**	**Address As**
Admiral	Admiral Jones	Admiral Jones
Vice Admiral	Vice Admiral Jones	Admiral Jones
Rear Admiral	Rear Admiral Jones	Admiral Jones
Captain	Captain Jones	Captain Jones
Commander	Commander Jones	Commander Jones
*Lieutenant Commander	Lieutenant Commander Jones	(Mr., Mrs., Ms., Miss) Jones
*Lieutenant	Lieutenant Jones	(Mr., Mrs., Ms., Miss) Jones
Lieutenant Junior Grade	Lieutenant JG Jones	(Mr.,Mrs.,Ms.,Miss) Jones
Ensign	Ensign Jones	(Mr., Mrs., Ms.,Miss) Jones
Chief Warrant Officer	Chief Warrant Officer Jones	(Mr.,Mrs.,Ms.,Miss) Jones
Midshipman	Midshipman Jones	(Mr., Mrs., Ms.,Miss) Jones

*When not in uniform a captain or lieutenant would be introduced as "of the Navy" to distinguish the grade from other services.

MEDICAL AND DENTAL CORPS OFFICERS

Officers of the Medical and Dental Corps in the grade of Commander and above are introduced, and addressed, as above unless they prefer to be addressed as "Doctor."

Officers in the grade of Lieutenant Commander and below are addressed as "Doctor."

When Medical and Dental Corps officers are introduced, "of the Dental/Medical Corps" should follow their grade ("Lieutenant Jones of the Navy Medical Corps").

CHAPLAIN CORPS

Officers of the Chaplain Corps in the grade of Commander and above are introduced, and addressed, as above unless they prefer to be addressed as "Chaplain."

Officers in the grade of Lieutenant Commander and below are addressed as "Chaplain."

In what year was the U.S. Navy Reserve established?
1915

"Another word for satisfaction is responsibility."
From the book: **Successful Leadership Today**

"Who uttered the now-famous words, "Don't give up the ship?"
JAMES LAWRENCE

50

ADDRESSING NAVY ENLISTED PERSONNEL
TO NAVY PERSONNEL

**Person Addressed
or Introduced**   **Introduce As**   **Address As**

Person Addressed or Introduced	Introduce As	Address As
Master Chief Petty Officer	Master Chief Jones	Master Chief Jones
Senior Chief Petty Officer	Senior Chief Jones	Senior Chief Jones
Chief Petty Officer	Chief Jones	Chief Jones
Petty Officer First Class	Petty Officer Jones	Petty Officer Jones
Petty Officer Second Class	Petty Officer Jones	Petty Officer Jones
Petty Officer Third Class	Petty Officer Jones	Petty Officer Jones
Seaman, Fireman, Airman, etc	Seaman Jones	*Jones
Seaman, Fireman, Airman, etc. Apprentice	Seaman Apprentice Jones	*Jones
Seaman, Fireman, Airman, etc. Recruit	Seaman Recruit Jones	*Jones

* Some Navy people prefer to address all E-1, E-2, and E-3s as "Seaman/Airman Jones." In this case the "modifier" of Apprentice and Recruit are dropped.

> *"A good leader has a likable personality.
> People like being around a good leader."*
> From the book: ***Successful Leadership Today***

> Women became an official and a permanent part of
> the U.S. Navy the year Congress authorized the
> establishment of the Women's Reserve. In what year
> did this occur?   1942

ADDRESSING NAVY ENLISTED PERSONNEL
TO CIVILIANS

Person Addressed or Introduced	Introduce As	Address As
Master Chief Petty Officer	Master Chief Jones	(Mr.,Mrs.,Ms.,Miss) Jones
Senior Chief Petty Officer	Senior Chief Jones	(Mr. Mrs.,Ms., Miss) Jones
Chief Petty Officer	Chief Jones	(Mr., Mrs., Ms., Miss) Jones
Petty Officer First Class	Petty Officer Jones	(Mr., Mrs.,Ms., Miss) Jones
Petty Officer Second Class	Petty Officer Jones	(Mr., Mrs.,Ms., Miss) Jones
Petty Officer Third Class	Petty Officer Jones	(Mr., Mrs.,Ms., Miss) Jones
Seaman, Fireman, Airman, etc.	Seaman Jones	(Mr., Mrs.,Ms., Miss) Jones
Seaman, Fireman, Airman, Apprentice, etc.	Seaman Apprentice Jones	(Mr., Mrs., Ms., Miss) Jones
Seaman, Fireman, Airman, etc. Recruit	Seaman Recruit Jones	(Mr., Mrs., Ms., Miss) Jones

SENIORS AND JUNIORS. There is only one proper response to an oral order--"Aye, aye, sir/ma'am." This reply means more than "yes." It indicates that "I understand and will obey." Such responses to an order as, "O.K. sir," or "All right, sir," are taboo. "Very well" is proper when spoken by a senior in acknowledgment of a report made by a junior, but a junior never says, "Very well" to a senior.

The word "sir/ma'am" should be employed as a prefix to an official report, statement, or question addressed to a senior. It should also be used when addressing an official on duty representing a senior. For example, the officer of the deck, regardless of grade, represents the commanding officer, and should be addressed as "sir"' "ma'am."

Juniors addressing a senior should introduce themselves unless certain the senior knows them by sight.

There are certain differences in phrasing which should be noted. Senior officers send their "compliments" to juniors. For example, "Admiral Jones presents his compliments to Captain Smith." Juniors send their "respects." When making a call upon a commanding officer, one is correct in saying, "Captain, I came to pay my respects," or to say to the orderly before entering the captain's office, "Tell the captain that Ensign Jones would like to pay his/her respects."

In written correspondence, a senior officer may "call" attention to something, but a junior may only "invite" it. For many years, it was Navy custom that a junior writing a memorandum to a senior subscribed it "Very respectfully,"; a senior writing to a junior used "Respectfully," Some officers and enlisteds still follow this custom when writing memorandums, However, the Navy Correspondence Manual, SECNAVINST 5216.5(), states that "A complimentary close is not desired or required."

QUARTERDECK ETIQUETTE. It is well to remember when on the quarterdeck that this has always been the honored, ceremonial part of the ship and that it still retains its sanctity.

You cannot just walk on and off a ship as you would enter and leave your home; you must follow certain procedures.

BOARDING A SHIP IN UNIFORM. When boarding ANY ship in uniform, and the national ensign is flying, you halt at the gangway, face aft, and salute the ensign. You then turn to the officer of the deck (OOD) and salute. If you are returning to your own ship, you say, "I report my return aboard, sir/ma'am." The OOD returns both salutes and says, "Very well, " or a similar expression.

When you salute the ODD upon boarding a ship other than your own, you say, "I request permission to come aboard, sir/ma'am." You should then add the purpose of your visit.

When you leave your ship, the order of saluting is reversed. You salute the OOD first and say, "I have permission to leave the ship, sir/ma'am." If you are leaving a ship that you have visited, you salute the OOD and say, "With your permission, I shall leave the ship, sir/ma'am." After receiving permission, you then face and salute the ensign (if it is flying) and depart.

BOARDING A SHIP IN CIVILIAN ATTIRE. When boarding a ship in civilian attire, and the national ensign is flying, you will halt at the gangway, at attention, and face aft. Remaining at attention, you then turn to the officer of the deck (OOD). If you are returning to your own ship, you say, "I report my return aboard, sir/ma'am." The OOD salutes and says, "Very well," or similar expression. When you board a ship other than your own, you say: "I request permission to come aboard, sir/ma'am." You should then add the purpose of your visit. The OOD will then say, "Permission granted" or "Permission not granted."

When leaving a ship in civilian attire, the procedure is reversed. You stand at attention in front of the OOD first and say, "I have permission to leave the ship, sir/ma'am." After receiving permission, you then stand at attention facing the ensign (if it is flying) and depart.

BOARDING SHIPS WITH PETTY OFFICERS STANDING OOD WATCH. On many ships, particularly those of destroyer size and smaller, there may be a first class or chief petty officer instead of an officer on the quarterdeck. Although you do not usually salute enlisted personnel, you must salute an enlisted person who is the OOD because you are saluting the position and authority represented--not the individual.

QUARTERDECK CONDUCT. The etiquette of the quarterdeck should be strictly enforced by the watch officer. The quarterdeck should be kept immaculate and its ceremonial character maintained. For officers and enlisted persons alike, adherence to these rules is required:
  -Avoid appearing out of uniform.
  -Never smoke.
  -Refrain from putting hands in pockets.
  -Refrain from horseplay.

54

-Don't engage in recreational athletics on the quarterdeck unless it is sanctioned by the captain, and then only after work hours.

OOD RESPONSIBILITY/AUTHORITY. The officer of the deck (OOD) is the officer on watch in charge of the ship (normally on duty for four hours) and represents the captain. The OOD is responsible for the safety of the ship, subject however, to any orders received from the commanding officer. All officers or other persons on board ship, whatever their rank, who are subject to the orders of the commanding officer, except the executive officer, are subordinate to the officer of the deck. However, when circumstances warrant, the commanding officer may delegate to another officer, for a specified watch (for example, Command Duty Officer)), authority to direct the OOD in time of danger or during an emergency. Such an officer, while on watch, bears the same relation to the officer of the deck, both in authority and responsibility, as that prescribed for the executive officer, but shall be subordinate to the executive officer.

WARDROOM ETIQUETTE. The officers' mess is organized on a business-like basis. There is a mess fund to which all officers must contribute their share on joining the mess. Officers receive a subsistence allowance from the Navy and it is a courteous gesture for them to ask the mess treasurer, within the first 24 hours aboard, for their mess bill and mess entrance fee and pay them at once. The monthly mess assessments defray the cost of food and other items purchased by the mess.

The fund is administered by the mess treasurer, who is elected by the members. In messes where the treasurer does not also act as caterer, the commanding officer appoints a mess caterer. The treasurer then is responsible for accounting for all receipts and expenditures, while the duties of the caterer involve the purchase of food, preparation of menus, and supervision of service. At the close of each month, the mess treasurer gives the mess members a statement of the mess accounts.

> *"Either attempt it not, or succeed."* OVID
> From the book: *Successful Leadership Today*

The wardroom is the commissioned officers' mess and lounge room. Some basic rules of etiquette are as follows:

-Don't enter or lounge in the wardroom out of uniform.
-Except for breakfast, don't sit down to meals before the presiding officer is seated.
-If necessary to leave before the completion of the meal, ask to be excused.
-Introduce guests to wardroom officers, especially on small ships.
-Never be late for meals. If you are unavoidably late, make your apologies to the presiding officer.
-Don't loiter in the wardroom during working hours.
-Avoid wearing a cap in the wardroom; especially when your shipmates are eating.
-Avoid being boisterous or noisy.
-Don't talk shop continuously.
-Do pay mess bills promptly
-In general, the young officer pursues the correct course by being the best listener in the mess.
-Religion, sex, and politics are not discussed in the wardroom. In the wardroom, good manners, with a consideration for other members and their guests, constitute the first principle to which all others are secondary.

The executive officer normally is president of the mess. On a small ship such as a DD, however, a separate mess is not provided for the commanding officer. In this case the CO, who eats his meals in the wardroom, is president of the mess.

Officers are assigned permanent seats at the table, alternately, in the order of grade, to the right and left of the presiding officer, except that the seat opposite that of the presiding officer is occupied by the mess caterer. (Second ranking officer sits on the right of the presiding officer, third on the left, and so on.)

"A leader is a dealer in hope." NAPOLEON
From the book: **Successful Leadership Today**

In what year was the rank of Rear Admiral created in the U.S. Navy? 1862

COURTESY AND SUPERIORS

1. Statements by seniors, such as the ones listed below, may not be issued as a direct order, but they should be taken as though a direct order was issued:
    a. I desire...
    b. I Wish...
    c. Could you...
    d. Would you...

2. At command social gatherings, juniors should remain in attendance until the commanding officer has departed. If the social gathering is at the residence of the commanding officer, don't stay more than 45 minutes or an hour after completing your meal, unless specifically asked.

3. DO NOT speak to a superior in the "third person." That is do not say, "Would the Captain/Commander care to...." Instead say, "Would you care to...."

4. It is not proper courtesy for a subordinate to pay a compliment directly to a superior. This could be construed as "polishing up" your superior to gain favor.

5. When speaking of the commanding officer, never say "The Old Man," or "Skipper."

6. Do not criticize or find fault with a superior in public.

7. Avoid the use of foul and vulgar language. It shows bad taste. It also shows an inability to express oneself in the English language.

8. When in the presence of a superior, either stand up or sit down, as appropriate. DO NOT slouch or lean on objects.

9. DO NOT discuss religion, politics, or sex with others in public.

10. Always give a smart, proper salute. Not many things in the Navy look worse than a sloppy salute. A good or bad salute reflects directly on the person giving the salute as well as the person receiving the salute. Look sharp, show your pride.

11. DO NOT offer excuses or explain some problem or situation if something goes wrong unless specifically asked.

SALUTING. The right hand is raised smartly until the tip of the forefinger touches the lower part of the headgear or forehead above and slightly to the right of the right eye.

Thumb and fingers are extended and joined. The palm is turned slightly inward until the person saluting can just see its surface from the corner of the right eye.

The upper arm is parallel to the ground. The elbow is slightly in front of the body. The forearm is inclined at a 45-degree angle. The hand and wrist are in a straight line.

The salute is completed by dropping the arm to its normal position in one sharp, clean motion.

One should be at attention when saluting, except when walking. The first position of the hand salute is executed when six paces from the person being saluted, or at the nearest point of approach, if more than six paces. Thirty paces is generally regarded as the maximum saluting distance. The salute position should be held until the person saluted has passed or the salute is returned.

Salutes are not appropriate when:
(1) Uncovered, except where failure to salute might cause embarrassment or misunderstanding;
(2) In formation, except on command;
(3) On work detail (person in charge of detail salutes);
(4) Engaged in athletics or assembled for recreation or entertainment;
(5) Carrying articles with both hands, or otherwise so occupied as to make saluting impracticable;
(6) In public places where obviously inappropriate (theaters, restaurants, etc.);
(7) In public conveyances;
(8) A member of the guard is engaged in performance of duty which prevents saluting;
(9) In action or under simulated combat conditions; and,
(10) At mess.

> *"You make the best impression by doing the "every day" things right."*
> From the book: **Successful Leadership Today**

BOAT ETIQUETTE

-Unless otherwise directed by the senior officer present, officers enter boats in inverse order of rank (juniors first) and leave them in order of rank (juniors last).

-It is proper to stand and salute when a senior enters or leaves a boat.

-When a senior officer is present, do not sit in the stern seats unless asked to do so.

- The seniors are ordered the most desirable seats.

-Always offer a seat to a senior.

-When leaving a ship, be in the boat a minute before the boat gong, or when the officer of the deck says the boat is ready; don't make a last-second dash down the gangway.

-If the boat is crowded, juniors embark in the next boat.

-Juniors in boats take care to give seniors room to move about.

"Success is a journey, not a destination." H.T. COLLARD
From the book: *Successful Leadership Today*

What Navyman and future President served as a Supply Officer in World War II?   RICHARD NIXON

"What motivates one person may not motivate the next person."
From the book: *Successful Leadership Today*

In what year was the U.S. Navy Nurse Corps established?   1908

Official	Gun Salute		Official	Gun Salute	
	Arrival	Departure		Arrival	Departure
President	21	21	Governor General or Governor of a commonwealth or possession of the United States or area under United States administration	....	17
Ex-President or President-elect	21	21			
Secretary of State when acting as special foreign representative of the President	19	19	Other Under Secretaries of Cabinet, the Solicitor General, the Deputy Attorney General, and the Deputy Postmaster General	....	17
Vice President	....	19			
Speaker of the House of Representatives	....	19			
Governor of a state of the United States	....	19			
Chief Justice of the United States	....	19	Members of Congress	....	17
Ambassador, High Commissioner, or special diplomatic representative whose credentials give him authority equal to or greater than that of an Ambassador	....	19	Envoy Extraordinary and Minister Plenipotentiary	....	15
			Minister Resident	....	13
			Charge d'Affaires	....	11
Associate Justices of Supreme Court	....	19	Career Minister, or Counselor of Embassy or Legation	....	....
US representative to the UN	....	19	Consul General; or Consul or Vice Consul when in charge of a Consulate General	....	11
Secretary of Defense	19	19			
Deputy Secretary of Defense	19	19	First Secretary of Embassy or Legation	....	....
Cabinet officer other than Secretary of Defense	....	19			
Secretaries of the Army, Navy, and Air Force	19	19	Consul; or Vice Consul when in charge of a Consulate	....	7
Director of Defense Research and Engineering	19	19	Mayor of an incorporated city	....	....
President pro tempore of the Senate	....	19	Second or Third Secretary of Embassy or Legation	....	....
Assistant Secretaries of Defense	17	17			
General Counsel of the DOD	17	17	Vice Consul when only representative of United States, and not in charge of a Consulate General or Consulate	....	5
Under Secretaries of the Army, Navy, and Air Force	17	17			
Assistant Secretaries of the Army, Navy, and Air Force	17	17	Consular Agent when only representative of the United States	....	....

Gun Salutes - U.S. Civil Officials During Official Visits

Officer	Gun Salute	
	Arrival	Departure
Chairman, Joint Chiefs of Staff.	19	19
Chief of Staff, U.S. Army	19	19
Chief of Naval Operations	19	19
Chief of Staff, U.S. Air Force	19	19
Commandant of the Marine Corps.	19	19
General of the Army. . .	19	19
Fleet Admiral	19	19
General of the Air Force	19	19
Generals	17	17
Admirals.	17	17
Naval or other military Governor, commissioned as such by the President, within the area of his jurisdiction	. . . .	17
Vice Admiral or Lieutenant General . . .	. . . .	15
Rear Admiral or Major General	. . . .	13
Commodore or Bridgadier General. . .	. . . .	11
Other commissioned officers	. . . .	. . . .

Gun Salutes - U.S. Military Officers During Official Visits

SHIPS ENTERING OR LEAVING PORT. The crew is paraded at quarters during daylight on entering or leaving port on occasions of ceremony except when weather or other circumstances make it impracticable or undesirable to do so.

Ordinarily, occasions of ceremony are construed as:
- visits that are not operational;
- at homeport when departing for or returning from a lengthy deployment;
- visits to foreign ports not visited recently; and,
- other special occasions so determined by a superior.
In lieu of parading the entire crew at quarters, an honor guard may be paraded in a conspicuous place on weather decks.

DIPPING THE NATIONAL ENSIGN.
1. When any vessel, under the United States registry or the registry of a nation formally recognized by the Government of the United States, salutes a ship of the Navy by dipping her ensign, it is answered dip for dip. If not already being displayed, the national ensign is hoisted for the purpose of answering the dip. An ensign being displayed at half-mast is hoisted to the truck or peak before a dip is answered.

2. No ship of the U. S. Navy dips the national ensign unless in return for such compliment.

3. Of the colors carried by a naval force on shore, only the battalion or regimental colors are dipped in rendering or acknowledging a salute.

4. Submarines, or such other ships of the line in which it would be considered hazardous for personnel to do so, are not required to dip the ensign.

> *"To really motivate people offer
> rewards not punishment."*
> From the book: **Successful Leadership Today**

ENSIGN AT HALF-MAST

1.   In half-masting the national ensign it is, if not previously hoisted, first hoisted to the truck or peak and then lowered to half-mast. Before lowering from half-mast, the ensign is hoisted to the truck or peak and then lowered.

2.   When the national ensign is half-masted, the union jack, if displayed from the jackstaff, is likewise half-masted.

3.   When directed by the President, the national ensign is flown at half-staff at military facilities and naval vessels and stations abroad whether or not the national ensign of another nation is flown full-staff alongside that of the United States.

DRESSING AND FULL-DRESSING SHIP

1.   On occasions of dressing ship, the largest national ensign with which the ship is furnished is displayed from the flagstaff, and except as prescribed for a ship displaying a personal flag or command pennant, a national ensign is displayed from each masthead. The national ensigns displayed at the masthead are of uniform size, except when, due to a substantial difference in heights of masthead, a difference in the size of national ensigns is appropriate.

2.   On occasions of full-dressing ship, in addition to the dressing of the mastheads, a rainbow of signal flags, arranged in the order prescribed in Navy Department publications, is displayed, reaching from the foot of the jackstaff to the mastheads and thence to the foot of the flagstaff. Peculiarly masted or mastless ships make a display as little modified from the rainbow effect as is practicable.

3.   When dressing or full-dressing ship in honor of a foreign nation, the national ensign of that nation replaces the United States national ensign at the main, or at the masthead in the case of a single-masted ship; provided that when a ship is full-dressed or dressed in honor of more than one nation, the ensign of each nation is displayed at the main, or at the masthead in a single-masted ship.

> In what year did the first women graduate
> from the U.S. Naval Academy?   1980

63

4. Should half-masting of the national ensign be required on occasions of dressing or full- dressing ship, only the national ensign at the flagstaff is half-masted.

5. When full-dressing is prescribed, the senior officer present may direct that dressing be substituted if, in that officer's opinion, the state of the weather makes such action advisable. The senior officer present may also, under such circumstances, direct that the ensigns be hauled down from the mastheads after being hoisted.

6. Ships not underway are dressed or full-dressed from 0800 until sunset. Ships underway are not dressed or full-dressed.

"Many receive advice, few profit by it."
PUBLILIUS SYRUS
From the book: **Successful Leadership Today**

The U.S. Navy's first iron-hulled ship, the steamer MICHIGAN, was launched in what year?   1843

The rank of Lieutenant (Junior Grade) was introduced in the Navy in what year?   1883

"Knowledge comes from action, not inaction."
From the book: **Successful Leadership Today**

CEREMONIES FOR NATIONAL HOLIDAYS

1.   On WASHINGTON'S BIRTHDAY, the third Monday in February, and on INDEPENDENCE DAY, the 4th of July, every ship of the Navy in commission, not underway, displays full-dress ship. At noon each saluting ship and each naval station equipped with a saluting battery fires a national salute of 21 guns.

2. On MEMORIAL DAY, the last Monday in May, each saluting ship, and each naval station having a saluting battery, fires at noon a salute of 21 minute-guns. All ships and naval stations display the national ensign at half-mast from 0800 until the completion of the salute or until 1220 if no salute is fired or to be fired.

3.   When the 4th of July occurs on Sunday, all special ceremonies are postponed until the following day.

> "We confide in our strength without boasting of it; we respect that of others, without fearing it." THOMAS JEFFERSON
> From the book: *Successful Leadership Today*

> What officer was Chief of Naval Operation longer than any other person?
> ARLEIGH A. BURKE

> "Never promise more than you can perform." PUBLILIUS SYRUS
> From the book: *Successful Leadership Today*

CHAPTER 7

AWARDS

An AWARD is an all-inclusive term covering any decoration, medal, badge, ribbon, or an attachment thereof bestowed on an individual.

A UNIT AWARD is an award made to an operating unit and worn only by members of that unit who participated in the cited action.

A SERVICE AWARD is an award made to those who have participated in designated wars, campaigns, expeditions, etc., or who have fulfilled, in a creditable manner, specified service requirements.

A DECORATION is an award bestowed upon an individual for a specific act of gallantry or meritorious service.

A MEDAL is an award presented to an individual for performance of certain duties, acts, or services. It consists of a suspension ribbon made in distinctive colors and from which hangs a medallion.

A MINIATURE MEDAL is a replica of a large medal, made to a scale one-half that of the original.

A BADGE is an award to an individual for some special proficiency apart from the duties of the individual's grade or rate. It consists of a medallion hung from a bar or from bars.

A RIBBON or ribbon bar consists of a portion of the suspension ribbon of a medal and is worn instead of the medal. The dimensions of all ribbons are 1 3/8 inches by 3/8 inches.

An ATTACHMENT is any appurtenance, such as a star, clasp, or device, worn on the suspension ribbon of a medal or on the ribbon, or ribbon bar.

PRECEDENCE LIST OF MEDALS/AWARDS

(From Navy/Marine Corps Awards Manual, SECNAV INST 1650.1)

ORDER OF PRECEDENCE

I Military Decorations
II Unit Awards
III Nonmilitary U. S. Decorations
IV Campaign and Service Medals
V Non Military Service Awards
VI Foreign Military Decorations
VII Marksmanship Awards

I - MILITARY DECORATIONS

1 - Medal of Honor
2 - Navy Cross
3 - Defense Distinguished Service Medal
4 - Distinguished Service Medal
5 - Silver Star
6 - Defense Superior Service Medal
7 - Legion of Merit
8 - Distinguished Flying Cross
9 - Navy and Marine Corps Medal
10 - Bronze Star Medal
11 - Purple Heart
12 - Defense Meritorious Service Medal
13 - Meritorious Service Medal
14 - Air Medal
15 - Joint Service Commendation Medal
16 - Navy Commendation Medal
17 - Joint Service Achievement Medal
18 - Navy Achievement Medal
19 - Combat Action Ribbon

II - UNIT AWARDS

1 - Presidential Unit Citation
2 - Joint Meritorious Unit Award
3 - Navy Unit Commendation
4 - Meritorious Unit Commendation
5 - Navy "E" Ribbon

III - NONMILITARY U. S. DECORATIONS

Nonmilitary decorations are worn in the order earned. These include, but are not limited to, the following:

- Presidential Medal of Freedom
- National Security Medal
- National Sciences Medal
- Gold Life Saving Medal
- Silver Life Saving Medal
- Medal for Merit
- National Intelligence Distinguished Service Medal
- National Intelligence Medal of Achievement
- National Distinguished Civilian Service Award
- Navy Award for Distinguished Achievement in Science
- President's Distinguished Federal Civilian Service Medal
- Department of Defense Distinguished Civilian Service Medal
- Navy Distinguished Public Service Award
- NASA Distinguished Service Medal
- NASA Flight Medal
- NASA Medal for Exceptional Bravery
- NASA Medal for Exceptional Service
- Merchant Marine Distinguished Service Medal
- Merchant Marine Meritorious Service Medal
- Merchant Marine Mariners Medal
- Selective Service Distinguished Service Award
- Selective Service Exceptional Service Award
- Selective Service Meritorious Service Award
- Congressional Space Medal of Honor

IV - CAMPAIGN AND SERVICE AWARDS

1 - Prisoner of War Medal
2 - Good Conduct Medals (Navy & USMC)
3 - Naval Reserve Meritorious Service Medal
4 - Selected Marine Corps Reserve Medal
5 - Navy Fleet Marine Force Ribbon
6 - Expeditionary Medals (Navy & USMC)
7 - China Service Medal
8 - American Defense Service Medal
9 - American Campaign Medal
10 - European-African-Middle Eastern Campaign Medal
11 - Asiatic-Pacific Campaign Medal
12 - World War II Victory Medal
13 - Navy Occupation Service Medal
14 - Medal for Humane Action

15 - National Defense Service Medal
16 - Korean Service Medal
17 - Antarctica Service Medal
18 - Armed Forces Expeditionary Medal
19 - Vietnam Service Medal
20 - Southwest Asia Service Medal
21 - Humanitarian Service Medal
22 - Sea Service Deployment Ribbon
23 - Navy Arctic Service Ribbon
24 - Naval Reserve Sea Service Ribbon
25 - Navy and Marine Corps Overseas Service Ribbon
26 - Navy Recruiting Service Ribbon
27 - Armed Forces Reserve Medal
28 - Naval Reserve Medal
29 - Marine Corps Reserve Ribbon

V - NON-MILITARY SERVICE AWARDS
Non-military service awards are worn after all campaign and service awards.

1 - Merchant Marine Gallant Ship Unit Citation
2 - Merchant Marine Defense Bar
3 - Merchant Marine Combat Bar
4 - Merchant Marine War Zone Bar (Atlantic, Mediterranean-Middle East, & Pacific)
5 - Merchant Marine WWII Victory Medal
6 - Merchant Marine Korean Service Bar
7 - Merchant Marine Vietnam Service Bar

VI - FOREIGN MILITARY DECORATIONS

1- Foreign Unit Awards (No Medals)
-Philippine Presidential Unit Citation
- Korean Presidential Unit Citation
- Vietnam Presidential Unit Citation
- Republic of Vietnam Meritorious Unit Citation (Gallantry Cross Medal   Color w/Palm)
- Republic of Vietnam Meritorious Unit Citation (Civil Actions Medal First   Class Color w/Palm)

2 - Non-U.S. Military Service Awards
- Philippine Defense Ribbon
- Philippine Liberation Ribbon

- Philippine Independence Ribbon
- United Nations Service Medal
- United Nations Medal
- Multinational Force and Observers Medal
- Inter-American Defense Board Medal

3 - Foreign Service Medals
- Republic of Vietnam Campaign Medal
- Kuwait Liberation Medal

VII - NAVY MARKSMANSHIP AWARDS
- U.S. Distinguished International Shooter Badge
- Distinguished Marksman Badge
- Distinguished Pistol Shot Badge
- National Trophy Match Rifleman Excellence in Competition Badge (Gold)
- National Trophy Match Pistol Shot Excellence in Competition Badge (Gold)
- Interservice Rifleman Excellence in Competition Badge (Gold)
- Interservice Pistol Shot Excellence in Competition Badge (Gold)
- Navy Rifleman Excellence in Competition Badge (Gold)
- Navy Pistol Shot Excellence in Competition Badge (Gold)
- Fleet Rifleman Excellence in Competition Badge (Gold)
- Fleet Pistol Shot Excellence in Competition Badge (Gold)
** (National, Interservice, Navy & Fleet Badges in silver and bronze continue in the above order with silver taking precedence over bronze)

- Expert Rifleman Medal
- Navy Rifle Marksmanship Ribbon
- Expert Pistol Shot Medal
- Navy Pistol Marksmanship Ribbon
- President's Hundred Award (Rifle or Pistol) (enlisted personnel only)

---

*"Establish a professional working relationship
with others for life."*
From the book: **Successful Leadership Today**

LARGE MEDALS

The arrangement of awards is by seniority from top down and from inboard to outboard. All medals may be worn, but a minimum of five must be worn by those possessing five or more. The Medal of Honor, worn when either large or miniature medals are prescribed, is worn from a suspension ribbon placed around the neck.

Full-size medals are worn on full-dress uniforms. The holding bar of the lowest row of medals is located approximately 1/4 inch above the left breast pocket and clear of the lapel. The medal bottoms dress in a horizontal line.

When more than one row is worn, no row must contain a lesser number than the row above it. As far as possible, except for the top row, all rows contain the same number of medals. Overlapping is equal and the right, or inboard, medal shows in full. Upper rows are mounted so as to cover the suspension ribbons of the medals below.

MINIATURE MEDALS

Miniature medals are worn with formal dress and dinner dress uniforms. On male tail coats and mess jackets, the holding bar of the lowest row of medals is positioned on the left lapel, 3 inches below the notch and centered on the lapel. If the bar exceeds a length of 2 3/4 inches, the bar extends over the outboard edge of the lapel. When worn on a male officer's blue or white service coat, the lowest bar is centered immediately above the left breast pocket. On a woman officer's uniform, the lowest bar is centered on the left pocket flap of the blue and white service coat. On other uniforms, it is attached in the same relative position.

The number of miniature medals worn on one holding bar may not exceed 11. When more than 11 are worn, they are arranged in two rows. Miniature medals may be equally overlapped up to 50 percent, the right (inboard) medal showing in full.

SERVICE RIBBONS

Service ribbons are worn in the order of their precedence, from top down and from inboard outward. The ribbons are worn with all service dress uniforms. There are no intervals between ribbons or rows of ribbons. They may be sewed to the uniform or arranged on holding bars to be pinned to the uniform. They may not be impregnated with preservatives that change their appearance or be worn with transparent covers. On male uniforms, the lower edge of the bottom row of ribbons is centered approximately 1/4 inch above the left breast pocket. On women's blue and white uniforms, one or two rows are centered on the left pocket flap; additional rows are worn immediately above the flap.

Three ribbons or less are worn in a single horizontal row. When more than three are authorized, they are worn in rows of three each. If not in multiples of three, the uppermost row contains the lesser number, the center of the row to be over the center of the row beneath. A minimum of three ribbons must be worn by those possessing three or more; all may be worn if desired.

ATTACHMENTS

A variety of stars, devices, and clasps are authorized for wear on medal suspension ribbons and corresponding service ribbons.

STARS

A GOLD star is worn instead of a second or subsequent award of a military decoration.

BRONZE stars indicate:
(1) Service in a cited unit at the time of an action for which the unit was awarded a unit citation;
(2) Second and subsequent awards of a campaign or service medal;
(3) The number of battle engagements during a given campaign for which a medal is authorized; and,
(4) First individual award of the Air Medal.

A SILVER star is authorized for wear instead of five gold or bronze stars.

A single star is centered on the ribbon. If more than one star is worn, they are placed in a horizontal line close to and symmetrically about the center of the ribbon. The silver star is located as near the center of the ribbon as symmetry permits. A star, worn in addition to a silver star or letter device, is worn on the wearer's right. A second star is worn on the wearer's left, etc. When medals overlap, all stars may be worn to the wearer's left. Stars are placed on the ribbon with two rays pointing down.

LETTER DEVICES

Metal letter devices, when authorized, are worn centered on the appropriate ribbon.

Individuals awarded the Legion of Merit, Bronze Star Medal, Joint Service Commendation Medal, Navy Achievement Medal, or the Commendation Medal for acts or services involving direct participation in combat operations may be authorized to wear a bronze letter "V."

Personnel who qualify may wear the bronze "S" signifying sharpshooter or bronze "E" signifying expert on their Pistol or Rifle Marksmanship ribbons, as appropriate. A silver "E" is worn upon qualifying for the third "E."

CLASPS

Clasps, when authorized ,are worn only on suspension ribbons of large medals although stars or other devices worn instead of clasps may be displayed on the suspension ribbons of miniature medals and on ribbon bars.

CHAPTER 8

LEADERSHIP PRINCIPLES AND CONCEPTS

1. PROFESSIONALISM. There is no place in your organization for amateurs or for amateur workmanship. The professional approach is the only acceptable one. Each person should be able to master the structure and content of his/her job, and to delve into the fine grain of the plans, programs, and problems in his/her area of cognizance. Guestimates at the answers to operational or administrative problems is permissible only on a stop-gap basis when time permits nothing better, and must be labeled as such.

2. LEADERSHIP BY EXAMPLE. Display, demand, and accept only top-quality professional approach. Leaders reap what they sew.

3. GOLDEN RULE. The Golden Rule is the best guide to all personal and professional relationships--up and down the chain of command.

4. TRUTHFUL. Good leadership fundamentals demand being truthful. A particular advantage of telling the truth is that you then don't have trouble trying to remember what you said.

5. MUTUAL TRUST. You should assume that all persons with whom you conduct business are honest and are doing their best to further the mission or their organization, in the absence of evidence to the contrary. It is essential for integrity of action that your relationships be founded on mutual trust and confidence.

6. INITIATIVE. Another stamp of the professional is the habit of taking the initiative, to move in the correct direction without prompting. Almost by definition a leader is someone who doesn't have to await specific directions from superiors. A leader leads.

7. CONSIDERATION. Any action, however large and significant, or however trivial, should be preceded by careful consideration of the potential impact of the action on any other people involved.

8. UNENFORCED RULES. You should have no unenforceable rules. You should also have no rules which, although enforceable, are not enforced. Rules and regulations which are not observed in letter and spirit are corrosive and undermine the effectiveness of all rules and regulations. You should either enforce the effective rules, regulations, and instructions, or take action to have them changed so that they can and will be observed and enforced.

9. NO ONE IS INDISPENSABLE. Being the "person to see" in an organization has good and bad points. An organization that cannot operate when someone is missing, especially "the boss'" is not properly structured or led. Leaders, at all levels, must ensure that key subordinates know what is to be done, how it is to be done, and what factors impacted on the decision process. Operational procedures and administrative routine should not slow down simply because the "person to see" is unavailable. A good leader should work himself out of a job, not into one.

10. ASSIGNING RESPONSIBILITY. Assign responsibility to an individual, not a group. Assigning responsibility to groups diffuses clear lines of authority, control, and specific responsibility. If two seamen are detailed to do a job, place the senior person in charge and hold him/her personally accountable to you for the execution of the job.

11. SUBORDINATE REPORTING. The old saying that "a person cannot have two masters" is especially true in the Navy. One subordinate should report to only one senior for any particular task.

12. TASKS AND RESPONSIBILITY. Every individual is entitled to be assigned explicit, written tasks and areas of responsibility, and be given the authority, training, and tools necessary to accomplish the tasks. Explaining the need and importance of a job should become common leadership practice. When anything less is made available, job accomplishment will not meet expectations and leadership is at fault.

13. LOWEST COMPETENT LEVEL. Decisions and actions should be taken at the lowest competent level in your organization. To push decisions or actions to a higher level than is justified has many ill effects. Specifically, the lower level individuals are deprived of opportunities to exercise their judgment. Also, they may lose interest as well as confidence. Additionally, the upper levels can become bogged down with details to the point where focus cannot be placed on the broader aspects of responsibility. One way to define the "lowest competent level" is to ask whether the matter at hand is entirely within the purview of a single individual. If that individual's responsibilities encompass all aspects of the matter at hand, then it should probably be acted upon by that individual. On the other hand, matters which establish or alter organizational policy should always be made at the highest levels.

14. FOLLOW-UP. One of the keys to administrative and operational success is constant follow-up. Follow-up is essential because of the tendency to shy away from irritating or difficult problems. Lack of follow-up can clog the operational and administrative process and force the periodic re-learning of lessons previously learned.

15. ANSWERS TO PROBLEMS. When you bring a problem to the attention of your boss, it is part of your duty to present, if time permits, possible solutions. In any organization the boss always has enough problems. What is needed is well thought out solutions to problems. There are any number of problems and only a limited number of correct solutions. If a problem area has been examined closely enough to know that there is a problem, the person conducting the evaluation must have some idea for proper resolution.

16. ABIDE BY DECISIONS. When a superior brings up a matter for subordinate discussion, that is the time for open deliberation. Once a decision is made, all concerned should be able to live with that decision and to do their part. A good test of loyalty is the extent to which a subordinate can implement a decision from a superior that he/she personally disagreed with during discussion.

17. CONSTRUCTIVE SUGGESTIONS. The indiscriminate griping on the part of an individual is a sure sign of immaturity. It is also an indication that that individual has never been successful in a position of responsibility. If you have a complaint or a constructive suggestion, it is irresponsible to sound- off in the general public. Put your complaint or suggestion in front of the person who can do something about it. You are expected to identify shortcomings in your organization and to do something about these shortcomings.

18. WORKING FOR THE BOSS. When your superior asks you to do something, never respond with, "We can't do that," or "It can't be done." Rather, say, "I'll research that and get back to you." In this way you don't have to make a snap judgment that could be at least partially wrong. Investigate the matter and proceed accordingly.

19. KEEP THE BOSS INFORMED. No one likes bad news surprises. If you break bad news, or even potential bad news, to your boss it is not a surprise. If someone else breaks bad news to the boss about something in your area of responsibility, that is a surprise. Keep the boss informed.

20. CHANGE. Some ways of doing things are better than others. At a given time procedures for doing something were devised because of a need or requirement. At that time the procedure decided upon was seen as the best choice. New people bring in new ideas. Do not "change for change sake," but be alert to possible improvement ideas from others.

"Destiny is not a matter of chance,
it is a matter of choice...it is a thing
to be achieved." WILLIAM JENNINGS BRYAN
From the book: *Successful Leadership Today*

What officer is commonly referred to as
the "father of the steam navy.
COMMODORE MATTHEW PERRY

LEADERSHIP PRINCIPLES

<u>The "winner" vs. the "loser"</u>

A WINNER says, "Let's find out." A LOSER says, "Nobody knows."

When a WINNER makes a mistake, he says, "I was wrong." When a LOSER makes a mistake, he says, "It wasn't my fault."

A WINNER isn't nearly as afraid of losing as A LOSER is secretly afraid of winning

A WINNER works harder than a loser and has more time; A LOSER is always "too busy" to do what is necessary.

A WINNER goes through a problem; A LOSER goes around it, and never gets past it.

A WINNER makes commitments; A LOSER makes promises.
A WINNER says, "I'm good, but not as good as I ought to be"; A LOSER says, "I'm not as bad as a lot of other people."

A WINNER listens A LOSER just waits until it's his turn to talk.

A WINNER respects those who are superior to him and tries to learn something from them; A LOSER resents those who are superior to him, and tries to find chinks in their armor.

A WINNER explains; A LOSER explains away.

A WINNER feels responsible for more than his job; A LOSER says, "I only work here."

A WINNER says, "There ought to be a better way to do it"; A LOSER says, "That's the way it's always been done."

A WINNER paces himself; A LOSER has only two speeds-- hysterical and lethargic.

Who was the U.S. Navy's first Rear Admiral, Vice Admiral, and full Admiral?
DAVID FARRAGUT

LEADERSHIP PRINCIPLES

The "leader" vs. the "driver"

THE DRIVER	THE LEADER
Says "I"	Says "we"
Depends on own authority	Depends on good morale & esprit de corps
Inspires fear	Inspires enthusiasm
Throws own weight around	Throws own weight behind a mission
Fixes the blame for breakdown	Fixes the breakdown
Rubs a mistake in	Rubs a mistake out
Knows how it's done	Shows how it's done
Makes work drudgery	Makes work interesting

CLIMBING THE LADDER OF SUCCESS

It takes more than luck to get ahead. Look closely at the below tips.

1) **BE A GOOD LISTENER.**   By getting all the facts and information the first time you save time and avoid mistakes. Listen attentively.

2) **BE OBSERVANT**. Train yourself to identify areas of waste and inefficiency.

3) **BE PROFESSIONAL**. Care about your job.   Never be indifferent about the way you do your work.

4) **BE PLEASANT**. Make it a habit to be pleasant, cordial and courteous. Cheerfulness is contagious.

5) **BE DEPENDABLE**. Show others they can depend on you, any time, all of the time.

6) **BE A BRAIN-STORMER**. Think of new ideas, new ways of doing things. Write down your solutions and study them.

7) **BE A TIME MANAGER**. If you don't manage your time, others will do it for you. Plan your time.

8) **BE LOYAL**. Practice loyalty to the Navy, your command and your organization on a daily basis. If you want others to be loyal, you should settle for no less from yourself.

9) **BE EFFICIENT**. Don't waste your time or effort. Determine the best way to do your job and then do it without wasted effort.

10) **BE AWARE OF YOUR ABILITIES**. Know what you can do and what you cannot do. Practice improving in areas that need improving.

11) **BE ALERT** to learn new practices and procedures. Read and evaluate any new information you can find.

12) **BE HELPFUL**. Helping others builds team work and goodwill.

13) **BE ENTHUSIASTIC**. Be proud of what you do and energetic about your work.

14) **BE COOPERATIVE**. Work with others for the common good of a team effort.

15) **BE CONFIDENT**. Have confidence in yourself and your abilities. You can't be a good leader of people without self confidence. Others can easily spot a lack of confidence.

"People who fly into a rage always make a bad landing." WILL ROGERS
From the book: ***Successful Leadership Today***

In what year was the Navy's first battleship commissioned? 1895

CHAPTER 9

LEADERSHIP MANAGEMENT PRINCIPLES

TEAM WORK. To achieve maximum effectiveness your organization must function as a fine tuned team. You need team unity and team effort.

Keep the lines of communications open up and down the chain of command. Ensure each individual knows exactly what his or her job encompasses--how that individual fits into the team. The better each member of your team understands the organization's mission and priorities the better each member can contribute to the collective team effort.

Explain and define the expected performance of each individual. Explain why an individual's performance is important to the team effort.

Most importantly, perhaps, delegate authority and responsibility. Most people have a higher sense of duty and obligation when they are in charge of some aspect of the operation.

Finally, explain the importance of feedback. Everyone should be able to provide feedback in a timely manner. Navy organizations are dynamic in nature. New, outside factors are always being entered into the operating and management equation. You and the people who work for you must stay alert for the need to update existing policies and procedures.

DEVELOP SUBORDINATES. An important aspect of leadership is to develop subordinates. The people working for you must be placed in a position where they have the opportunity to grow professionally and personally. This should be followed up with your personal involvement.
-Offer encouragement
-Hold subordinates accountable for actions and performance
-Monitor results
-Provide feedback

-Know the difference between an honest mistake and a mistake caused by carelessness--and respond accordingly. Remember, praise in public and condemn in private.

MATCH PEOPLE AND JOBS

You need to know your people, to know what motivates them. Once this is accomplished, your people should be matched with the correct jobs.

HARD CHARGERS. Difficult and demanding jobs should be given to your few "hard chargers." This is best for you because you can be sure that these people will give their best in an important job or billet. This is also best for the hard chargers because they want a challenge. This elite group prides itself on overcoming obstacles and getting the job done. Anything less challenging dampens their spirit and morale. Reward accordingly.

AVERAGE WORKERS. The routing tasks should be assigned to the average workers. This group should not be put in to jobs over their head. The average worker will openly complain if faced with hard or difficult tasks. This could have a negative impact on morale and job accomplishment. The morale of this group is satisfied with simply getting the job completed. However, keep an open mind on this group. If someone shows potential for more difficult assignments, don't let it slip without notice.

BELOW AVERAGE WORKERS. As a general rule people in this group should be given the more menial, repetitive tasks. Close supervision is recommended. Almost any below average performer can improve to at least an average worker with the correct motivation. The ultimate motivation must come from within each individual. Proper outside leadership and supervision can help prompt this internal motivation.

This group will require extra time and effort on your part. Give this time and effort willingly. The more below average workers you have in your organization the more inefficient your organization will operate and the more this group will adversely affect morale. Continue to demand and expect good performance. Re-think possible motivation and encouragement aspects of each individual. Don't give up on individuals in this group until all efforts have been expended.

OPERATING PHILOSOPHY. It is generally considered good management philosophy to periodically announce your goals, objectives, and concerns. The following examples are intended to serve as a guide in formulating your own operating philosophy.

EXAMPLE #1

1. Know and take care of your people. Division officers and chiefs must be attuned to their sailors' personal problems and committed to resolving them or knowing where to seek assistance with thorough follow-up.
2. Retention....
3. Training....
4. Preventive Maintenance....
5. Administration....
6. Finally, each of you need to set goals to achieve whatever specific objectives you have set for yourselves within your individual organizations. Your own leadership style will dictate how to make your objectives known to your organization. When you evaluate your subordinates it should be, in the main, an analysis of how well they have worked toward and achieved the command, department, and division objectives.

EXAMPLE #2

1. We must be prepared at all times to ensure that...
2. Our management philosophy should be guided by these principles:

> -Run (organization) the right way and let it be known that when we do something, we do it the right way the first time, all of the time.
> -Inspire job satisfaction and self pride in everyone working for us.
> -Keep the pressure on pride and professionalism.

"Win the heart and the body will follow."
From the book: ***Successful Leadership Today***

EXAMPLE #3

1. Adherence to rules, regulations, and authority.
2. Use the chain of command.
3. Take care of and know your people.
4. Leadership by example.
5. A day's work for a day's pay.
6. Superior's Tasking Priorities:

-A superior's 1st TASK is to keep subordinates busy in accomplishing established goals and objectives.

-A superior's 2nd TASK is to monitor and evaluate subordinate performance (providing training and guidance as necessary).

-A superior's 3rd TASK is to pursue personal duties and responsibilities. (If a superior is busy and the subordinates are sitting around idle, the superior is NOT doing the job correctly).

EXAMPLE #4

While conducting our daily operations, it is important that all personnel know the goals we are striving to achieve so our efforts may lead, ultimately, to the attainment of specific objectives.

1. Progress toward....
2. Establish....
3. Attain....
4. Continue to....
5. Improve....
6. Recognize outstanding, individual performance.
7. Emphasize....
8. Expedite efficient....
9. Eliminate....
10. Identify....
11. Upgrade....
12. Increase....

(NOTE: the above goals and concerns are put forth in positive, action words.)

Who appoints the Navy's Vice Chief of Naval Operations (VCNO)?   President

"Reason and judgment are the qualities of a leader." TACITUS
From the book: ***Successful Leadership Today***

CHAPTER 10

TAKING CHARGE

The following steps and procedures are recommended in preparation for taking over a Navy division, department, or other organization.

As quickly as possible, learn the identity of your personnel and call them by rate and name. Learn as much as you can about their personal histories and professional capabilities by using the division officer's notebook and each individual's service record as sources of information.

Establish communication with your personnel through formal and informal talks. Observe their appearance, military bearing, and cooperation among themselves and with members of other organizations.

Review the master training plan for all formal school requirements. Note the projected rotation date (PRD) of personnel and when a relief is to report. Review the Enlisted Distribution Verification Report (EDVR) for required Navy enlisted classification codes (NECs) for the organization to ensure the right mix of personnel are on board.

Perhaps the most important function that you can perform when preparing to take charge of a division, department, or other Navy organization is to immediately establish a good professional rapport with your chief petty officers. The chief petty officers in your organization are your most important personnel asset. They know their jobs and the jobs and capabilities of the people under them. Work through your chiefs. Maintain the chain of command. Your chiefs realize that you probably do not know all of the technical details of the organization. Tell them right off that there are areas you are not familiar with, but that you want them to teach you about them. Don't come off as a "know it all," especially in front of the chief petty officer community.

Talk informally with your superiors and members of other organizations to get a feeling of the general impression of your organization. As a military organization, how does it compare with others? Professionally, does your organization work smoothly with other organizations, or is your organization poorly coordinated and in conflict with other organizations? You need to know these and other important questions if you intend to get started on the right foot. The right questions, if asked in the right places, can give you an excellent picture of your organization's performance.

To maintain continuity, get your predecessor's opinion of each person, including areas of dependability, demeanor, personal problems, and any special leadership techniques (approaches) that work especially well with certain individuals.

During the relieving period, become familiar with established policies. Your administrative inspection will reveal many policies. To further clarify them, become familiar with Standard Organization and Regulations of the U.S. Navy (OPNAVINST 3120.32), ship's or station's instructions, other pertinent instructions, and letters that delegate authority.

You and your predecessor should inform organization personnel of your relieving plans and keep them informed in other matters so that they have no doubt about who is in charge. You can avoid many problems by early clarification of policies and changes in policies regarding matters such as the watch, quarter and station bill; sea bag and personnel inspections; leave; liberty; and, mess cooking. Remember, however, a good rule of management is to avoid making any drastic changes until you have been on board for a while.

Inspect the material condition of the organization for cleanliness, damage control, safety, and habitability. Inventory and inspect all equipage before assuming custody. Survey missing equipment. Do not accept responsibility for past bad housekeeping. A good aid in making a material inspection is the check-off list for the Board of Inspection and Survey (INSURV). Be sure to note the discrepancies on the last inspection to see of they have been corrected. Also, check file copies of all pending deferred action documents to get a firm idea of the organization's material readiness status. Make sure the planned maintenance system (PMS) is up to date and effective.

Conduct an administrative inspection. Note any discrepancies from the last administrative inspection. The predeployment check-off list can give you an excellent idea of what to do before you deploy. These administrative inspections will raise many questions, such as the following: Is the tickler file up-to-date? Does it contain due dates and references for all reports required? Are proper security procedures in effect and being followed?

Upon completion of all necessary inspections and transfers, you might need to report in writing to the commanding officer, or other person, stating your readiness to assume responsibility for the organization. This report should include a statement of the condition of the organization, its personnel, records, facilities, and state of readiness. Note any deficiencies that exist and recommend procedures for correcting them. Show the inventory status of all equipage and classified material assigned to your organization and that you have accepted custody. In the report, list anything that is seriously wrong and any discrepancies that cannot be corrected in short order. Ensure your boss is realistically aware of the conditions that exist in the organization at the time of your relieving. Avoid any personal attack on your predecessor unless that person's actions or attitude hampered the relieving process. Impersonal statements of conditions will suffice. Do not place yourself on the receiving end of grudging, minimal cooperation. A list of sample explanations of conditions and plans, including timing for correction, is not subject to misinterpretation.

> *"Leadership is solving problems."*
> From the book: ***Successful Leadership Today***

In what year was the Naval Reserve Officers Training Corps established?   1925

RELIEVING CHECK-LIST

_____ 1. Division Officer's Notebook
_____ 2. Billet Turnover Folder
_____ 3. Training Record
_____ 4. PQS Program
_____ 5. EDVR (Enlisted Distribution Verification Report)
_____ 6. NEC (Navy Enlisted Classification) Requirements
_____ 7. Sponsor Program
_____ 8. EMI (Extra Military Instruction) Policy
_____ 9. Morning Quarters (location, procedure, frequency)
_____ 10. Special Qualification (EAWS, ESWS, SS, etc.)
         Program
_____ 11. Advancement Performance
_____ 12. TEMMAD (Temporary Additional Duty) requirements/
         status
_____ 13. Drug & Alcohol Policy/Program
_____ 14. Physical Fitness Program
_____ 15. Admin Tickler File
_____ 16. Security Container Combination Changes
_____ 17. Listing of all materials to sign for (Page check and
         verify serial numbers as necessary)
_____ 18. Who Approves What Request Chits
_____ 19. Duties at Captain's Mast
_____ 20. Required Reading
_____ 21. Organization Manual
_____ 22. Instructions
_____ 23. SOPs
_____ 24. Outstanding/Pending Correspondence
_____ 25. Upcoming School Needs/Requirements
_____ 26. Past INSURV Results/Reports
_____ 27. CSMP (Current Ship's Maintenance Project)
_____ 28. Ship's Force Work List (Equipment Deficiency Log,
         JSN, 3M Suspense File)
_____ 29. Casualty Reports (CASREPS)
_____ 30. Casualty Corrections (CASCORS)
_____ 31. PMS (Preventive Maintenance System) Records
_____ 32. Budget/OPTAR (Operating Target) History/Status
_____ 33. Who Signs Requisitions?
_____ 34. Condition of Assigned Spaces
_____ 35. Condition of Assigned Equipment
_____ 36. Upcoming organization Events/Inspections/
         Deployments
_____ 37. Collateral Duties

GOOD FIRST IMPRESSION. It takes less than a minute to create a first impression. Initial impressions--good or bad--last a long time.

When meeting seniors and subordinates for the first time, look sharp. Your hair should be neatly groomed and you should be wearing your best "inspection-ready" uniform.

Learn each individual's name as soon as possible. When you are introduced to someone, repeat the name back to the person immediately (i.e. "How are you today, Chief Barnett"). The more often you use a name the sooner that name fits into your long term memory.

LEARN TO LISTEN PROPERLY. During the first few days at your new organization others will probably be doing most of the talking. You ask questions; they answer questions. If you want to learn and gain the respect of others, listen intently. As necessary, ask for clarification in unfamiliar areas. This shows that you are paying close attention and that you are interested in knowing what that person has to say. Proper listening includes:
1. Giving your complete attention
2. Thinking about what you hear
3. Compiling and digesting the information
4. Showing genuine interest
Above all, when speaking and listening, look the other person in the eye. Frequent eye contact during conversations is a lasting positive asset. Lack of regular eye contact can be taken as not being interested in the subject/speaker, being timid or shy, or, being unsure of yourself.

FIND REASON TO PRAISE OTHERS. Most people are either hard workers or good workers. And, human nature being what it is, almost everyone thinks that they are an asset to their organization. When meeting the new people who will be working for you, find some reason to praise something they have accomplished. This will get you going in a positive direction. The following examples might give you some ideas in this area.

"THAT LOOKS GREAT/SHARP. YOU MUST HAVE PUT IN A LOT OF HARD WORK TO ...."

"THAT'S A GREAT IDEA, I'VE NEVER SEEN ANYTHING LIKE THAT BEFORE."

"THE (SPACE/RECORDS, ETC.) LOOKS SHIPSHAPE. I CAN SEE THAT YOU PUT A LOT OF EFFORT INTO...."

BUILDING PERSONAL RELATIONSHIPS. You will meet many new people during your Navy career. When you transfer from a command that doesn't mean you have to leave friends and shipmates behind. Admiral Nimitz kept index cards on many shipmates he served with throughout his years of service. He would sent them notes, card, or letters from time to time (Christmas, birthdays, etc.). As he advanced through the ranks he became more and more known and respected throughout the Navy. This is an excellent practice for others to follow.

ARRANGING YOUR OFFICE. When you take over a new organization one of the first things to do is to organize your office to fit your personal and professional style. Arrange your office to inspire both yourself and others who enter your "home away from home." The people working for you will get a quick insight on how you operate based on the way your office is arranged. The following ideas are offered:

FRAME AND MOUNT A QUOTE
1. "DON'T GIVE UP THE SHIP." James Lawrence, U.S. Navy
2. "I HAVE NOT YET BEGUN TO FIGHT." John Paul Jones, U.S. Navy
3. "TAKE CARE OF YOUR MEN." Thomas Truxtun, U.S. Navy
4. "AN OFFICER IN CARRYING ON HIS DUTY SHOULD BE CIVIL AND POLITE TO EVERYONE, FOR CIVILITY DOES NOT INTERFERE WITH DISCIPLINE." Thomas Truxtun, U.S. Navy
5. SUCCESS IS:
      1 % INSPIRATION
      99% PERSPIRATION
6. LEADERSHIP IS SOMETHING YOU DO WITH PEOPLE; NOT TO THEM.
7. YOU WIN RESPECT BY DESERVING IT; NOT BY DEMANDING IT.

PICTURES
1. Family
2. Military (President, SECDEF, SECNAV, CNO, etc.)
3. Navy action picture (ship, submarine, aircraft, etc.)

OTHER - ACTION OR STATUS BOARD. Display major ongoing or upcoming projects, undertakings, events, etc.
"I.G. - NEXT WEEK"
"CPO FITREPS - BE ON TIME"

DISORGANIZED OFFICE. From time to time take a close look at your office with a critical eye. Individual items collected over time can collectively give your office a cluttered, disorganized appearance. Look at your office the way someone new at your organization might see it through their eyes. Items not used or needed should be removed. Required material should be stowed (in file cabinets if possible) and labeled.

Make sure that each piece of furniture and each filing container serves a needed purpose or function.

OFFICE FILING SYSTEM. Reference and historical information should be filed separately from on-going project material. You don't want to wade through mixed files looking for project papers. Institute a logical filing system that is simple and easy for you and others to locate needed files and papers quickly.

Each individual file should be labeled and filed with similar files. Each file cabinet drawer should be accurately labeled.

All personal items should be stowed in your desk.

MINIMIZE DESK CLUTTER. Most people would prefer to have an organized desk. That means getting rid of items that clutter the desk top.
APPROPRIATE DESK TOP ITEMS
1. In/Out/Pending Baskets
2. Telephone
3. Current project working on

OPTIONAL DESK ITEMS. These items should be placed under desk Plexiglas if possible.
1. Calendar (with upcoming events)
2. "Things To Do" list

Staples, paper clips, extra pens and other desk top clutter items will fit nicely into a desk drawer.

Stow information and reference material in desk drawers or in file cabinets, not on top of your desk or in your "pending" basket.

IN, OUT, AND PENDING BASKETS. Clear out your IN BASKET several times a day. Don't let paper work bog down in your in basket.

Try to handle each piece of paper that crosses your desk only once. Twice at most. Go over the paper and do something with it immediately. Either take action on it or pass action along to someone else and place it in your OUT BASKET. Don't keep paperwork in your in basket and look at it over and over again.

Keep the paperwork in your PENDING BASKET to a minimum. Reference and information material should be filed as soon as possible. Go through your pending basket at least every other day to ensure nothing gets "lost" on your desk.

"Don't expect inexperienced people
to make the right decisions."
From the book: ***Successful Leadership Today***

Only one naval officer has been both Chief of
Naval Operations and Chairman, Joint Chiefs
of Staff. Who was this officer?   THOMAS H. MOORER

"Being ANGRY is inefficient."
From the book: ***Successful Leadership Today***

To be a leader, you must know what motivates your subordinates. Superiors tend to take it for granted that they know the attitudes, likes, and dislikes of subordinates. Yet, superior and subordinate perceptions of job factors are seldom the same. Below are the results of a survey of what superiors and subordinates think is most important.

(1-highest, 10-lowest).

JOB FACTORS	PERCEPTIONS OF SUPERIORS	PERCEPTIONS OF SUBORDINATES
GOOD WAGES	1	5
JOB SECURITY	2	4
PROMOTION & UPWARD MOBILITY	3	7
GOOD WORKING CONDITIONS	4	9
INTERESTING WORK	5	6
SUPERVISOR LOYALTY TO WORKERS	6	8
TACTFUL DISCIPLINING	7	10
FULL APPRECIATION FOR WORK DONE	8	1
SYMPATHETIC UNDERSTANDING OF PERSONAL PROBLEMS	9	3
FEELING "IN" ON THINGS	10	2

"Offer people the opportunity to grow and most of them will flourish."
From the book: **Successful Leadership Today**

Who is the mythical God of the sea?
KING NEPTUNE

CHAPTER 11

BRAG FILE

You should keep a "Brag File'" The more information you have in a brag file the better. If you receive a "sounds good, say nothing" Fitrep, it is as much your fault as the person who wrote it--you let him/her get away with it. A good write-up must have some substance, some job accomplishment specifics. Your superiors don't have time to maintain a file of brag sheets on each person who works for them. You don't have time to maintain a file of brag sheets on each person who works for you. You keep your own, and tell your subordinates to keep one of their own. Then when it is time to provide an input to your Fitrep, break out everything you have, compile it and then decide what you want to use. If you don't come up with two or three items a week to place in the brag file, you aren't trying-- or you aren't doing your job.

The following items are offered to get you started. Add to it items particular or unique to your job or billet. These items could be appropriate to you individually, or to your work group.
1. Reenlistment (numbers/percentages)
2. Advancement (numbers/percentages)
3. PQS (military/professional)completed
4. Correspondence courses
5. Off-duty education
6. Inspection results: zone, material, security, command, safety, admin, personnel, berthing/ barracks. type training, 3M, retention team, etc.
7. Graded exercises
8. Financial budget (save $)
9. Organization manning allowance onboard
10. Average work-week hours
11. Accomplishments/Distinctions received
12. Organizational correspondence forwarded correct/timely
13. What your organization did to help meet command objectives and commitments.
14. Special/Additional assistance given others
15. New programs you had a hand in starting
16. Improvements to spaces/working conditions, etc.

17. Directives, SOPs, instructions originated/up-dated
18. Command and community involvement
19. Collateral duties (volunteer and be active in several)
20. Major evolutions participated in
21. Extra hours worked
22. Extra projects worked on (outside normal area of responsibility or outside normal working hours)

The above list could go on and on. The point is there is a list. Commit yourself to maintaining a "brag file" throughout all reporting periods. Tell your top performers to do the same, you will all look better.

"The only thing that makes a good idea work is a successful manager."
From the book: *Successful Leadership Today*

At one point in his career, Navy hero Commodore David Porter resigned his commission in the U. S. Navy to accept what position?
COMMANDER IN CHIEF, MEXICAN NAVY

"Great souls have wills; feeble ones have only wishes." PROVERB
From the book: *Successful Leadership Today*

CHAPTER 12

INCENTIVES AND AWARDS PROGRAM

To obtain maximum effort from each individual working for you, you must have an ongoing incentives award program. Your program should be structured to motivate people to put forth their very best effort on a continuing basis.

Selecting and providing the appropriate incentives is a cornerstone to any top notch organization. Many incentive programs encompass an awards system. **Awards should meet these three criteria:**
>   1) Must be timely
>   2) Must be appropriate
>   3) Must be meaningful

The type of award (or recognition) must vary directly with the accomplishment. Awards might take the following forms:
>   1) Verbal recognition at morning quarters
>   2) Verbal recognition at formal personnel inspections
>   3) Letter of Appreciation
>   4) Letter of Commendation
>   5) Sailor of the Month, Quarter, etc.
>   6) Appropriate Navy medal awards

Care should be taken to ensure that the incentive awards program is not overly generous. To give someone an award for merely doing a good job in a routine task can have bad side effects. First, it lessens the meaning of the award given to others who have honestly earned the award. Second, the entire incentives award program will crumble when you give special recognition to anyone and everyone who does a "good job" on an ordinary task. Doing a "good job" should be the norm in your organization--in any organization.

The best time to start an incentives and awards program is when you first report to a new organization. Nothing is more impressive to the people working for you than to see that you-- their new leader--are a professional who rewards superior performance.

CHAPTER 13

ORGANIZING YOUR ORGANIZATION

This section covers individual organizations. The principles noted are equally applicable to Navy divisions, departments, or other individual units.

The first principle of effective organization management is to fully understand the mission, objective, and role of the organization. While that may sound simple enough, don't be misled. Every time a new instruction or message is issued that effects an organization, to some extend the mission, objective, or role of that organization has been altered. Management practices and principles must be reviewed and updated on a regular basis. Once this is accomplished you are ready to get down to specifics.

1. Start with developing clear concepts of what the organization is going to do (GOALS).
2. Derive specific, measurable objectives from the definition of your goals.
3. Develop detailed strategy for achieving organizational objectives and purpose.
4. Assign responsibility and accountability for all organizational jobs and billets.
5. Set policy and administer the organization on a day-to-day basis.
6. Devise measures of performance (SET STANDARDS).
7. Use the performance measures to evaluate if strategy is working.
8. Undertake periodic comparisons of strategy and the actual performance (IDENTIFY NEED FOR CHANGE).
9. Demand contributions be spelled out and documented.

ORGANIZATION. Every organization should have a chain-of-command block diagram. Different organizations have different missions, so organization charts are seldom the same.

EXAMPLE DIVISION CHAIN OF COMMAND
BLOCK DIAGRAM

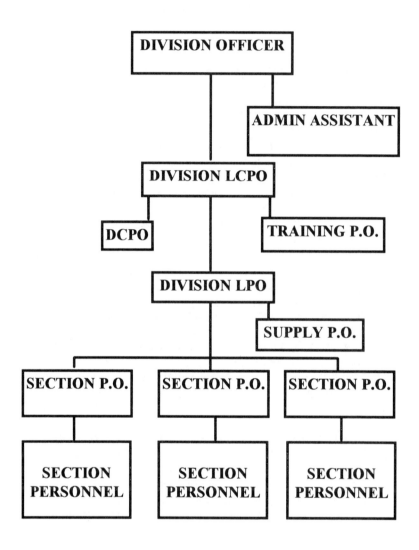

The organization chart should be built around the mission, tasks, and functions of the organization, and in direct relation to the quantity and quality of the people in that organization.

Any significant change--increase or decrease--in the number of people assigned to an organization will probably mean that there should be a change in the organization structure. Equally important, when one of the "key" individuals departs, a structure change may be needed.

The most important and crucial jobs should always be given to those few top performers you have available. If you have done this, when one of those top performers leaves and you don't have available an equal talent, then a structure change is needed. This may not mean some large scale adjustment that disrupts unity, but a "fine tuning" of the structure.

Most commands and departments are manned by enough people where this fine tuning might not be necessary. This may not be true for smaller organizations.

It is not uncommon for the organizational structure to change anytime a new boss arrives. Also, particular skills and talents vary among different officers and chiefs. Each time a new department/division officer or Leading Chief Petty Officer arrives, those two individuals should get together, go over their particular strong points and determine if an organization adjustment is necessary.

TOP 1% ACHIEVERS. When a new commanding officer reports aboard a command, he/she wants to run an efficient and effective organization. Additionally, that person had to be very competitive to assume command status in the first place. That new, competitive commanding officer is already planning ahead for his/her next promotion. Simply running an efficient and effective command is not all it takes to earn that next promotion. He/She must earn FITREPS superior to other commanding officers. When that new commanding officer reports aboard he/she probably has a list of command goals and objectives to be accomplished during his/her tenure. This same principle holds true if you are running a department, a division, or any other navy organization. If you want to be a TOP 1% ACHIEVER, review the following information closely.

If you want to have a top notch organization, consider one more point before starting on an organization chart. Not listed in your organization's "mission" are things like:
- Individual Advancement   - PQS Qualifications
- Educational Development   * "E" Awards -
- EAWS, ESWS, etc. Qualifications
- Etc ...

If you ever sat on a promotion selection board, you would occasionally come across a write-up that included a passage something like the following.
-100% of personnel passed advancement exams
-80% of personnel earned EAWS (ESWS, SS, etc.) pins
-2 previous non-high school grads earned high school diploma
-25% of completed 1 or more college classes
-100% of PQS qualified in ....
-5 personnel received Letters of Appreciation from ... for ...
-Only division in command(department) to ...
- Led command in ...

The above sample list could go on and on. As a note, organizations with small numbers of people might want to use percentages (80%, 100%, etc.) For large organizations, numbers like 50 people could be more impressive than 25%.

Individuals with comments such as these are invariably at the top of selection lists. And, the above list is limited only by one's imagination and willingness to go the extra mile. Fitrep write-ups such as the above example don't just magically appear in front of selection boards. They appear because the officer built into the organization the mechanism to produce these results.

After taking into account the mission, tasks, and functions handed down to you, and before you complete organization charts, job descriptions, etc., compile a list of personal goals you want your organization to accomplish. Only at this point in time are you ready to put together an organization structure with your key personnel filling the key positions.

Anytime you check into a new organization you should add your personal goals to the basic operating policy of that organization. In the above examples, the people working for you are better off, you are better off, and the command and the Navy are better off. If you do your job and organize properly, everyone wins.

> *"Attitude is Everything."*
> *"Image is reality."*
> From the book: **Successful Leadership Today**

ORGANIZATION PLANNING

PROCESS. Organization planning is the process of identifying and grouping duties to be performed, defining and delegating authority, assigning responsibility, and creating relationships enabling personnel to work effectively together in accomplishing objectives.

STRUCTURE. The organization structure is set up to promote cooperation and the effective exercise of executive leadership. Each person will give his/her best and will cooperate more effectively with others only when he/she understands his/her responsibilities and relationships to other members of the organization.

FUNCTIONS. Organization planning has been defined as, "determining which functions are necessary to a purpose and arranging them in groups that may be assigned to individuals."

HUMAN RELATIONS. Adequate consideration must be given to the human relations aspects in all organizing work. A sound organization allows personnel to work together effectively and harmoniously toward a common goal.

GENERAL PRINCIPLES
1. The mission and tasks of the command determine the functions to be performed.
2. The organization structure should be as simple as possible.
3. No billet should be set up unless it has a distinct job to perform.
4. The organization structure should be flexible enough to meet new and changing conditions.

THE FORMAL ORGANIZATION. Formal organization is a stable system of well defined jobs having definite measures of authority, responsibility and accountability. The formal organization enables personnel to work effectively together in achieving common objectives. Individuals must adjust to the formal structure which sets limits for personal work areas.

ORGANIZATION PLANNING. Organization planning is an important part of leadership enabling the accomplishment of short and long range objectives. It helps to define and arrange work and group people for effective mission accomplishment. For this purpose, manuals composed of organizational charts and functional guides are developed to describe and clarify the organizational structure.

Organization planning must be based on meeting the organization objectives and must consider the methods, facilities, procedures, and performance criteria of the organization. To be acceptable, solutions must be workable and not be affected by any conditions which would interfere with their adoption. These conditions must be understood and accepted by those who will be affected by them.

OBJECTIVES OF ORGANIZATION PLANNING

Three basic objectives of organization planning are:
1. To ensure that the organization structure is one that will carry out most effectively the mission and tasks of the organization.
2. To ensure that all essential functions are recognized and assigned as specific responsibilities to individuals.
3. To ensure that there is clear recognition and understanding of individual's duties, responsibilities, authority, and organizational relationships.

LACK OF ORGANIZATIONAL PLANNING. Typical results from a failure to provide organizational planning are:
1. Some functions are duplicated.
2. Importance of functions is out of proportion.
3. Some functions may be overlooked or neglected.
4. Individuals will stress their own areas of importance, which might or might not be the correct areas.

"Take minor setbacks for what they are."
From the book: *Successful Leadership Today*

ASSIGNMENT OF FUNCTIONS

1. Every significant function must be provided for to insure accomplishment of missions and tasks.

2. Every function should be assigned to a specific billet. Under normal circumstances, no single function should be assigned to more than one billet.

3. Closely related or similar functions should normally be assigned to a single billet.

4. Responsibilities of two or more billets that are related should be clearly defined.

"Talkers are no good doers."
WILLIAM SHAKESPEARE
From the book: *Successful Leadership Today*

The first Navy night carrier landing
took place in what year?   1925

"The best morale exists when you never hear the word mentioned. When you hear a lot of talk about it, it's usually lousy." GEN. DWIGHT D. EISENHOWER
From the book: *Successful Leadership Today*

5. There should be no overlapping, duplication, or conflict among organization billets.

The diagrams on the following pages provide guidance in constructing organizational charts and relationships.

Portrayal of Part-Time Splitting of Functions

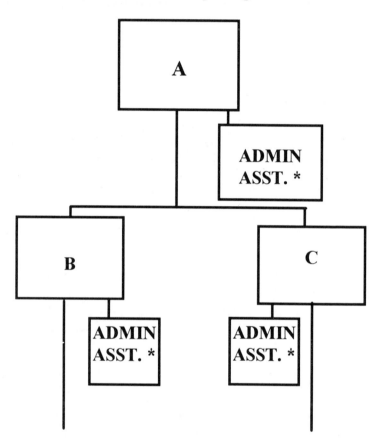

Legend: * Part-time splitting of function. Same person performs the duties of administrative assistant to A, B, and C.

STAGGERING BOXES

Numerous subdivisions on the same level of authority may be staggered as follows to make the chart more compact, particularly where space is limited.

TRY THIS

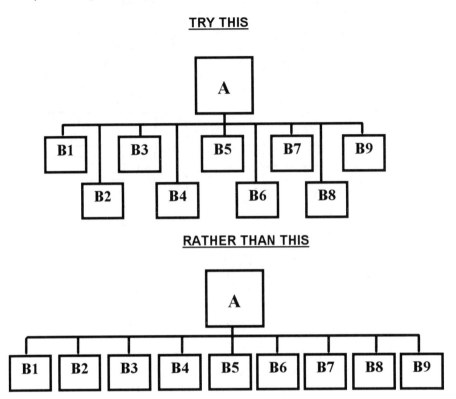

RATHER THAN THIS

Presentation of Lines of Authority to a Number of Subordinate Units.

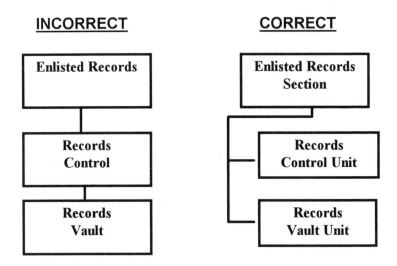

INCORRECT   CORRECT

| Enlisted Records | Enlisted Records Section |

| Records Control | Records Control Unit |

| Records Vault | Records Vault Unit |

EXPLANATION
1. Chart at left is wrong because head of Records Vault Unit does not report to head of Records Control Unit. Chart at right presents a more correct picture.
2. Organizational designation ("Section" and "Unit") should be shown.
3. Note preferred method of drawing line of authority.
4. Smaller "boxes" for units aids interpretation.

Achieving Simplicity in Organization Chart Layout
Example Nr. 1

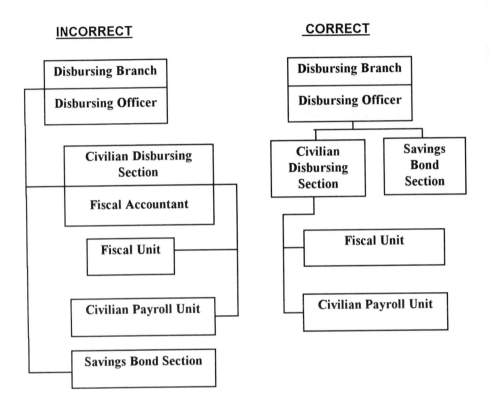

INCORRECT

CORRECT

| Disbursing Branch |
| Disbursing Officer |
| Civilian Disbursing Section |
| Fiscal Accountant |
| Fiscal Unit |
| Civilian Payroll Unit |
| Savings Bond Section |

| Disbursing Branch |
| Disbursing Officer |
| Civilian Disbursing Section | Savings Bond Section |
| Fiscal Unit |
| Civilian Payroll Unit |

EXPLANATION

1. Chart at left is unnecessarily complex for a basically simple organization.

2. Section boxes should be the same size, and, if possible, drawn on the same horizontal plane. If space is limited, subsidiary organization components should be drawn in a vertical line directly under a parent organization as shown for fiscal unit and civilian payroll unit.

Achieving Simplicity in Organization Chart Layout
Example Nr. 2

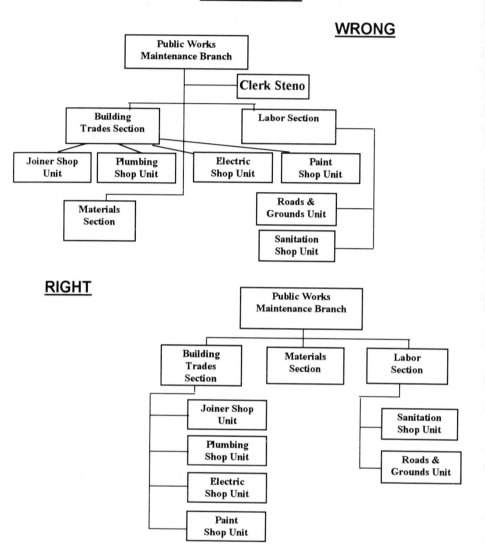

WRONG

RIGHT

EXPLANATION

EXPLANATION

1. Clerk-steno should not be shown as a separate component.
2. Sections, when space permits, should be drawn on the same horizontal plane.
3. Diagonal lines should not be used.
4. Avoid crossing lines of authority.
5. Note preferred method of drawing lines of authority for "Units," when drawn vertically under section.

Achieving Balance and Symmetry in Organization Chart Layout

INCORRECT

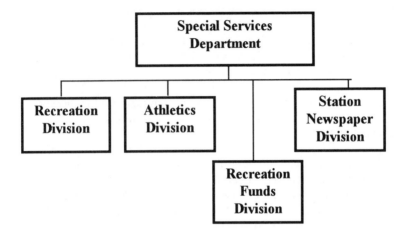

CORRECT

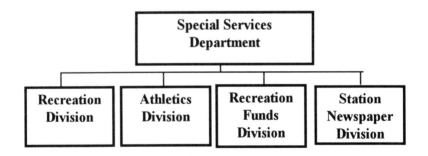

EXPLANATION

1. Balance and symmetry assist in presenting a clear picture of the organization. Chart on top is basically correct, but complicated by poor layout. Bottom example is preferred.

CHAPTER 14

ORGANIZATION AND REGULATIONS MANUAL

The single-most important document in any organization is an ORGANIZATIONAL DOCTRINE. This doctrine sets forth, in print, how an organization will be structured, who reports to whom, who is responsible for what, and what rules and regulations will be followed.

It would be difficult to imagine any navy organization functioning with any uniformity, cohesiveness, or consistency without an organizational doctrine.

OPNAVINST 3120.32 requires all departments and divisions to implement and maintain an organizational doctrine in the form of an Organization and Regulations Manual (O&R Manual). This manual may take the place of, be issued in addition to, or be used in conjunction with, numbered and dated instructions.

Prudent management practices dictate that a department and division have and enforce policies set forth in an O&R Manual. A new Head of Department or Division Officer's first priority should be to start, or update, a department/division O&R Manual. Periodic review is necessary to keep up with the dynamic nature of any Navy organization.

There are any number of ways an O&R Manual can be structured. A department manual should include:

(1) The duties, responsibilities, and authority of all key department billets; and,

(2) All operations, events, and procedures desired to be controlled, directed, or monitored at the department level.

All information required by a division officer that has not been covered in the Department O&R Manual should be included in the Division O&R Manual. Standard Operating Procedures (SOPs) are not included in an O&R Manual.

The below areas can be used as a guide for O&R Manual structure and content.

(1) Implementation/Promulgation Page
(2) Record of Changes Page
(3) Contents Page(s)
(4) Text

This chapter deals with constructing a department or division Organization and Regulations Manual (O&R Manual). The example used in this book is centered around a department O&R Manual. With only minor alterations, this information can be used to construct a division O&R Manual.

On the following pages, a department aboard a ship was used to cover as many areas of interest as possible. The "contents" section lists a variety of subjects to choose from in building your own O&R Manual. As a further aid, some samples of job descriptions and other information is included to assist you in starting your own O&R Manual.

This information is provided in the structure and format required of a department/division organization and regulations manual. Providing you with the information in this fashion, you can save many, many hours of painstaking labor in starting your own O&R Manual.

---

*"A leader should be visible and accessible.
You cannot lead setting behind a desk."*
From the book: **Successful Leadership Today**

What was the name of the world's first nuclear-powered submarine and in what year was it launched?
USS NAUTILUS, 1954

Who is considered the "father of the nuclear navy?"
ADMIRAL HYMAN RICKOVER

IMPLEMENTATION/PROMULGATION PAGE

xxx DEPARTMENT
NAME OF COMMAND
MAILING ADDRESS

xxxDEPTINST 5400.1
010:DLD;bdr
Date

xxx DEPARTMENT INSTRUCTION 5400.1
xxx Department Organization and Regulations Manual

Ref: (a) OPNAVINST 3120.32
(b) U.S. Navy Regulations, 1973
Encl: (1) Enlisted Evaluation Guide dtd ....
(Issued under separate cover)

1. Purpose. To promulgate the Organization and Regulations Manual of the xxx Department, (command).

2. Effective Date. This Organization and Regulations Manual is effective upon receipt.

3. Scope.
a. This manual is the basic organizational directive of the department. It is issued in support of command policy and in compliance with reference (a). The functional guides/billet descriptions contained herein constitute the formal delegation of responsibility and authority within the department chain of command as authorized by references (a) and (b). This manual shall in no way be construed as restricting the initiative or discouraging the resourcefulness of any individual in the department.

b. This manual outlines the total structural, functional, and personnel staffing organization of this department. It depicts the basic mission of the department, assigns specific functions and tasks to be performed in support of the mission, and describes inter-personal relationships of each billet's incumbent. Nothing contained herein shall be interpreted as contravening or superseding directives issued by higher authority.

4. Objectives.

a. To define, by means of organizational charts and functional guides/billet descriptions, a comprehensive and clearly presented department organizational structure.

b. To set forth explicitly the duties, responsibilities, limits of authority, and organizational relationships of specific billet assignments within the department.

c. To issue departmental regulations and policy guidance.

5. Action. All personnel attached to the xxx Department, (command), are responsible for being familiar with the contents of this manual and subsequent changes or additions. Compliance with this manual is mandatory.

_____
(Signed/Name)
(xxx Officer)

Distribution:
Executive Officer
xxx Division Officer
xxx Division Officer
xxx Division Officer
xxx Department Administrative Assistant
Files (5)

> _"No power is strong enough to be lasting if it labors under the weight of fear."_ CICERO
> From the book: **_Successful Leadership Today_**

RECORD OF CHANGE

Correction or Change #	Date of Change	Date Entered	By Whom Entered

---

"Failure to recognize someone's contributions to an organization is one of the most often voiced complaints by people."
From the book: **_Successful Management Today_**

Two future presidents enlisted in the Navy as Seaman in World War II and were later commissioned. What is the name of these two future presidents?
JOHN F. KENNEDY & GEORGE BUSH

xxx DEPARTMENT ORGANIZATION AND REGULATIONS MANUAL

CONTENTS

CHAPTER 1 - AUTHORITY AND RESPONSIBILITY

CHAPTER 2 - COMMAND ORGANIZATION

CHAPTER 3 - xxx DEPARTMENT MISSION AND ORGANIZATION

SECTION 3100 - DEPARTMENTAL BILLETS

116

CHAPTER 6 - COMMAND AND DEPARTMENT BILLS

> "TACT: The ability to describe others as they see themselves." ABRAHAM LINCOLN
> From the book: *Successful Leadership Today*

CHAPTER 13 - PERFORMANCE APPRAISAL

CHAPTER 14 - GOALS AND OBJECTIVES

14000   (information in this section determined by the individual heads of department and/or division officers ...Use goals, objectives, management concepts, principles, etc.)

"When you do something, you should be proud enough about it to sign your name to it."
From the book: **Successful Leadership Today**

The first woman to become an Admiral in the U.S. Navy was a member of which staff branch?
NURSE CORPS

"It is better to have one person working WITH you than to have three people working FOR you."
GEN. DWIGHT D. EISENHOWER
From the book: **Successful Leadership Today**

CHAPTER 1 AUTHORITY AND RESPONSIBILITY

1000 PRINCIPLES OF AUTHORITY AND RESPONSIBILITY

a. **UNITY OF COMMAND**. Unity of command requires that a person report directly to and receive orders from one superior. One person must have control over one segment of the organization, and he/she alone should issue all orders to, and should receive all reports from, that segment. All persons must know whom they direct and to whom they report. To ensure such unity within an organization, lines of authority should be definite, clear-cut, and understood by all.

b. **DELEGATION OF AUTHORITY AND ASSIGNMENT OF RESPONSIBILITY**. One primary measure of the ability of an officer or petty officer as an administrator is the ability to intelligently delegate authority. Authority should be delegated to the lowest level of competence within this or any organization.

Delegation of authority does not mean that the officer or petty officer relinquished his/her responsibility for the actions of the person to whom such authority is delegated.

Officers and petty officers at all levels are ultimately accountable for the performance of their individual organizational segments even if they have charged subordinates with the immediate responsibility for managing certain functions.

1010 OFFICER AND SENIOR PETTY OFFICER AUTHORITY

a. **AUTHORITY AND RESPONSIBILITY**. Authority is not absolute and it cannot be applied in an indiscriminate manner. Authority is tied directly to duties and responsibilities and it is only the fulfillment of assigned duties and responsibilities that authority within the Navy is granted to individuals. Exercise of authority, therefore, is inseparable from an acceptance of responsibility and is granted only to support the fulfillment of assigned duties and responsibilities.

(1) **GENERAL AUTHORITY**. General responsibilities and duties of all officers and petty officers within the Navy requires that they show in themselves a good example of subordination, courage, zeal, sobriety, neatness, and attention to duty.

They shall aid to the utmost of their ability and extent of their authority in maintaining good order and discipline as well as other matters concerned with the efficiency of command. Extent of authority to fulfill their general duties is set forth in Navy Regulations, which gives to all persons in the Naval Service the right to exercise authority over all persons who are subordinate to them. This authority charges all persons within the Naval Service to obey readily and strictly, and to execute promptly lawful orders of their superiors.

(2) **ORGANIZATIONAL AUTHORITY**. Organizational authority held by all officers and petty officers derives from their assigned billet within a particular organization. This command organizational structure is based upon guidance of reference (a) and is promulgated by organizational manuals such as the xxx Department Organization and Regulations Manual.

b. **LIMITATIONS OF AUTHORITY.** Authority includes the right to require actions of others. Actions of others are directed by oral or written orders which are subject to general limitations; they must be lawful since subordinates are only required to obey lawful orders (reference (b)), and they must not be characterized by tyrannical or capricious conduct, or by abusive language (reference (b)). Since authority is given only to fulfill duties and responsibilities, only so much organizational authority as may be considered necessary to fulfill responsibilities need be delegated and it should never be delegated beyond the lowest level of competence.

1020 **LAWFUL ORDERS**.

An order must be lawful and any order imposing punishment outside the framework of the Uniform Code of Military Justice (UCMJ) is illegal. Punishment may only be directed through judicial process or nonjudicially through Article 15 UCMJ. Authority to administer non-judicial punishment aboard (command) is reserved by UCMJ to the Commanding Officer. However, measures may be taken by officers and petty officers to correct minor infractions which do not merit punishment under Article 15, to correct deficiencies in a phase of military duty in which a subordinate may be deficient, or to direct completion of work assignments which may extend beyond normal working hours. This may be accomplished through Extra Military Instruction (EMI).

1030 LEADERSHIP

a. Officers and petty officers must encourage, inspire, teach, stimulate and motivate their subordinates to gain acceptance of the authority they hold by virtue of their assigned duties. Resorting to imposition of withholding of privileges and EMI should be taken ONLY when counseling and normal instruction and training fail to accomplish the necessary objective.

b. All officers and petty officers have the authority to do so and are expected to publicly commend their subordinates when appropriate and to take the initiative to recognize outstanding individuals by:

(1) Making recommendations for advancement, selection for specific programs, and reviewing personal performance evaluations.

(2) Initiating recommendations for personal awards and assignment to training schools.

(3) Assigning preferred duties.

(4) Initiating recommendations for special recognition such as sailor of the month, quarter, etc.

2000 COMMANDING OFFICER

a. **BASIC FUNCTION**.

As set forth in U.S. Navy Regulations, the commanding officer is charged with the absolute responsibility for the safety, well-being, and efficiency of his command.

b. **DUTIES, RESPONSIBILITIES, AND AUTHORITY**.

The duties and responsibilities of the commanding officer are established by U.S. Navy Regulations, general orders, customs, and tradition. The authority of the commanding officer is commensurate with his responsibility, subject to the limitations prescribed by law and U.S. Navy Regulations.

2010 EXECUTIVE OFFICER

a. **BASIC FUNCTION**.

The executive officer is the direct representative of the commanding officer. All orders issued by him as such representative will have the same force and effect as though issued by the commanding officer and shall be obeyed accordingly by all persons within the command.

b. **ORGANIZATIONAL RELATIONSHIPS**.
The executive officer is directly responsible to the commanding officer. All heads of departments and executive assistants report to the executive officer for all matters pertaining to the internal administration of the command.

2020 COMMAND DEPARTMENTS & COMPONENTS
a. **MAJOR DEPARTMENTS**
    (1) NAVIGATION
    (2) OPERATIONS
    (3) WEAPONS
    (4) DECK
    (5) ENGINEERING
    (6) AIR
    (7) AIMD
    (8) COMMUNICATIONS
    (9) SAFETY
b. **STAFF DEPARTMENTS**
    (1) SUPPLY
    (2) MEDICAL
    (3) DENTAL
c. **EXECUTIVE ASSISTANTS**
    (1) ADMINISTRATIVE OFFICER
    (2) SECURITY MANAGER
    (3) TRAINING OFFICER
    (4) SHIP'S SECRETARY
    (5) SENIOR WATCH OFFICER
    (6) PUBLIC AFFAIRS OFFICER
    (7) CHIEF MASTER-AT-ARMS
    (8) COMMAND CAREER COUNSELOR
    (9) SPECIAL SERVICES ASSISTANT
    (10) PERSONNEL OFFICER
    (11) 3-M COORDINATOR
    (12) EDUCATIONAL SERVICES OFFICER
    (13) LEGAL OFFICER
    (14) POSTAL OFFICER
    (15) CHAPLAIN ...etc...
d. **OTHER COMPONENTS**
    (1) COMMAND MASTER CHIEF
    (2) VARIOUS BOARDS, COMMITTEES & COUNCILS

2030 HEADS OF DEPARTMENT
a. GENERAL DUTIES.
The head of a department of a command is the officer detailed as such by competent authority. He/She is the representative of the commanding officer in all matters that pertain to the department. All other personnel in the department will be subordinate to head of department and all orders issued by him/her will accordingly be obeyed.

b. SPECIFIC RESPONSIBILITIES.
The head of a department, subject to the orders of the commanding officer, will:

(1) Organize and train his/her department to ensure readiness for battle.

(2) Prepare and maintain the bills and orders for the organization and operation of the department.

(3) Assign personnel to stations and duties within the department.

(4) Be responsible for the effectiveness of the department; to this end he/she will plan, direct, and supervise the work and training of personnel within the department via the established chain-of-command.

(5) Ensure that all prescribed or necessary security measures and safety precautions are strictly observed by all persons within the department and by others who may be concerned with matters under his/her control. He/She will ensure that all applicable safety precautions are kept properly posted in conspicuous and accessible places and that personnel concerned are frequently and thoroughly instructed and drilled in their observance.

(6) Make frequent inspections of the personnel and material of the department, including the spaces assigned thereto, and take necessary action to correct defects and deficiencies.

(7) Control the expenditure of funds allotted, and operate the department within the limit of such funds.

(8) Ensure economy in the use of public money and stores.

(9) Be responsible for the proper operation, care, preservation, and maintenance of the equipment and other material assigned to the department; and for the submission of such data in connection with the accounting thereof, including periodic inventories of assigned material, as may be prescribed by competent authority.

(10) Be responsible for the maintenance of records and the submission of reports required of the department.

(11) Be the custodian of the keys of all spaces and storerooms of the department, except such as are assigned by regulation to the custody of another officer.

(12) Be responsible for the cleanliness and upkeep of the spaces assigned to the department, except as prescribed by regulation or other competent authority.

(13) Anticipate the personnel and material needs of the department, and submit timely requests to fulfill requirements.

(14) Contribute to the coordination effort of the entire command by appropriate cooperation with other heads of department.

(15) Ensure that optimum conditions of readiness within the department are in accordance with NWIP 50-3.

(16) Perform other duties as may be assigned by competent authority.

In amplification of these responsibilities, a head of department will;

(1) Supervise the training and professional development of junior officers assigned to the department.

(2) Advise division officers on matters affecting the morale or discipline of personnel within the department, keeping the commanding officer informed of any matter which may adversely affect the department or the Naval Service.

(3) Maintain a maintenance and material manager system or a Current Ship's Maintenance Project (CSMP), as appropriate for the department.

(4) Approve exchanges of duty between similarly qualified officers or enlisted personnel of the department, subject to instructions promulgated by the executive officer and the senior watch officer.

(5) Maintain established standards of performance and conduct; evaluate performance by means of drills, exercises, inspections, and other control devices; initiate fitness reports and evaluation sheets, and review periodic marks; and make recommendations to the executive officer for meritorious masts and for disciplinary matters.

(6) Formulate and carry out a department training program within the framework of the command's training program.

(7) Implement and supervise the execution of PQS topics applicable to the department. Qualify personnel for watch

stations and for equipment/system operation and maintenance using PQS when appropriate.

(8) Review the eligibility of enlisted personnel in the department for advancement in rating.

(9) Forward special requests to the executive officer, with recommended action. In cases involving special privileges, comment on past conduct and performance of duty as appropriate.

(10) Formulate and submit budgetary requirements for the maintenance and operation of the department, and approve expenditures from the funds allocated by the commanding officer.

(11) Prepare the department organization manual and directives, and ensure proper dissemination and observance.

(12) Supervise the training of departmental personnel in damage control matters in coordination with the DCA.

c. **ORGANIZATIONAL RELATIONSHIPS**.
A head of department reports to the commanding officer for the operational readiness of his/her department; for the general conditions of the machinery and other installations, including the need for and progress on major repairs and any matters relating to his/her department whenever he/she believes such action necessary for the good of the department or the Naval Service. He/She reports to the executive officer for all administrative matters and keeps the executive officer appropriately informed of direct reports to the commanding officer.

Immediate subordinates within a department report directly to the head of department.

3104 DIVISION OFFICERS
The below areas apply to all division officers. Additional, and more specific, division officer requirements are set forth in this manual in the individual division concerned.

a. **BASIC FUNCTION**.
A division officer is one regularly assigned by the commanding officer to command a division of the command organization.

b. **DUTIES, RESPONSIBILITIES, AND AUTHORITY**.
(1) Responsible for the proper performance of the duties assigned to his/her division and for the conduct of assigned

subordinates, in accordance with regulations, the orders of the commanding officer, and other superiors.

(2) Direct the operation of the division through junior officers, Leading Chief Petty Officer(s), and/or Leading Petty Officers as prescribed in the organization manual.

(3) Report promptly to the head of department any repairs which may be required or other defects which need correction and which the division is unable to effect.

(4) Recommend improvements to department policies and procedures.

(5) Cooperate and work with division officers of other divisions.

(6) Be thoroughly familiar with all publications and directives in area of responsibility.

(7) Ensure prescribed security measures are strictly observed by personnel in the division (and in division spaces), and be alert for ways and means to improve internal security, forwarding recommendations as appropriate.

(8) Ensure optimum material conditions of readiness within the division in accordance with NWIP 50-3.

(9) Be familiar with operational procedures of equipment assigned to the division.

(10) Be responsible for all forms, reports, and correspondence originated or maintained by the division.

(11) By personal supervision and frequent inspection, ensure that the spaces, equipment, and supplies assigned are maintained in a satisfactory state of cleanliness and preservation.

(12) Ensure that all damage control equipment, fittings, and checkoff lists in assigned spaces are maintained in proper working condition and are properly labeled.

(13) Ensure the maintenance of an adequate amount of supplies in the division and inform the head of department well in advance of shortages that will have an adverse impact on current or anticipated operations.

(14) Supervise the administration and performance of designated work centers within the division in carrying out the shipboard maintenance and material management system (3M).

(15) Inventory and report on all equipment for which the division is responsible by (date) each year, or as directed by the head of department.

(16) Initiate disciplinary action when necessary in accordance with the Uniform Code of Military Justice (UCMJ) and other regulatory directives.

(17) Assign extra military instruction (EMI) within the guidance and direction set forth in this manual.

(18) Suppress any improper language or unseemly noise or disturbance.

(19) Maintain an up-to-date copy of OPNAVINST 3120.32 and other orders for the division, and ensure that pertinent parts thereof are kept posted where they will be accessible to subordinates.

(20) Maintain a division bulletin board, readily accessible to division personnel, on which will be posted the current Plan of the Day and other directives which directly affect the personnel of the division.

(21) Maintain the following notebooks and folders in accordance with the guidance and direction set forth in this manual:

(a) Division Officer's Notebook;

(b) Division Career Counseling Notebook;

(c) Division Sponsorship Folder; and,

(d) Billet Turnover Folder

(22) Carefully instruct subordinates in all applicable safety precautions, and require their strict observance.

(23) Ensure that watches and duties are stood in a correct and efficient manner.

(24) Make recommendations for personnel transfers and changes in division allowance.

(25) Monitor the performance of the division effort in accomplishing its mission to determine the adequacy of personnel allowances, billet assignments, operating procedures, and equipment and space configuration.

(26) Conduct periodic inspections, exercises, and musters to evaluate division individual and team performance.

(27) Supervise the administration of PQS within the division, providing personnel with guidance and incentives for the accomplishment of PQS. Select and designate petty officers qualified to authenticate completion of individual PQS qualifications.

(28) Ensure that Armed Forces Identification Cards and other identification tags and badges are correct and in good order.

(29) Ensure by periodic (at least quarterly) inspection that non-rated personnel have a full sea bag of regulation clothing, including appropriate medals and ribbons, and that the uniforms are in a good state of repair. Inspection will be conducted on petty officers if maintenance of a full sea bag is questionable.

(30) Conduct formal and informal personnel inspections, requiring at all times conformance with personal appearance standards, including a regulation haircut.

(31) Initiate enlisted performance evaluations in accordance with the requirements set forth in this manual.

(32) Assign personnel to watches and duties within the division, and develop rational programs for battle stations, watches, and general duties to ensure the training and proficiency of assigned personnel.

(33) Train subordinates in their own duties and in the duties to which they may succeed, and encourage them to qualify for advancement and to improve their education.

(34) Ensure the proper preparation for training exercises and drills within the division and for the submission of evaluation reports in connection with those exercises.

(35) Schedule and conduct training for division personnel within guidelines of the Department Training Plan/ Schedule. Phases of division training shall include:

(a) Indoctrination of new personnel;

(b) Preparation for advancement in rating, including correspondence courses and practical factors in both military and professional subjects;

(c) Individual instruction and drills in assigned duties;

(d) Team training to fulfill operational requirements of the division;

(e) Instruction in principles of effective leadership for petty officers; and,

(f) Individual training through off-duty educational sources.

(36) Keep informed of the capabilities and needs of each subordinate, and, within authority, take such action as may he necessary for the efficiency of the division and the welfare and morale of subordinates.

(37) Be available to personnel of the division who desire counsel and guidance, and take action to maintain the welfare and morale of the division.

(38) Coordinate with career counselors, and detailers if necessary, in conducting a meaningful career motivation program, ensuring that personnel are well aware of available career opportunities and benefits.

(39) Nominate the most qualified and deserving non-petty officer and petty officer in the division for department and command recognition as Sailor of the Month/ Quarter and Petty Officer of the Month/Quarter respectively, during each and every nominating period.

(40) Schedule liberty and leave periods in accordance with command and department policy.

(41) Evaluate the qualifications of division personnel and make recommendations for changes in their Navy Enlisted Classifications (NECs) as appropriate.

(42) Recommend individuals for advancement and special Navy programs and assignments when eligibility requirements have been met.

(43) Forward requests for leave, liberty, and other matters as prescribed in command instructions.

c. **ORGANIZATIONAL RELATIONSHIPS**.
Division officers report to their Head of Department. Junior personnel within the division report to the division officer.

3202 DIVISION LEADING CHIEF PETTY OFFICER
a. **BASIC FUNCTION**.
The function of the Division Leading Chief Petty Officer is to assist the division officer in coordinating and administering the division and develop a thorough understanding of the functions, directives, and equipment of the division in preparation for assuming the duties of the division officer.

b. **DUTIES, RESPONSIBILITIES, AND AUTHORITY**.
(1) Supervise the preparation and maintenance of the watch, quarter, and station bill and such other bills as may be necessary for the operation of the division.

(2) Aid in formulating and implementing policies and procedures for the operation of the division.

(3) Supervise the division in the performance of its daily routine, and conduct inspections to ensure that division functions are being properly executed.

(4) Aid in the administration of discipline within the division.

(5) Evaluate individual performances of division personnel, with the assistance of individual supervisors; and recommend periodic marks to the division officer.

(6) Provide counsel and guidance to division personnel.

(7) Ensure the maintenance of routine logs and records and in the preparation of reports required by the division.

(8) Act as division officer in the absence of the regularly assigned division officer as appropriate.

Specific duties shall include: (List specific duties)

c. **ORGANIZATIONAL RELATIONSHIPS**.
The Division Leading Chief Petty Officer reports to the division officer. Personnel report to the Leading Chief Petty Officer as designated in the division organization.

3207 WORK CENTER SUPERVISOR
a. **BASIC FUNCTION**.
The Work Center Supervisor is the senior petty officer assigned to a work center. He/She is responsible for the material condition and effective operation of the 3-M system within the work center.

b. **DUTIES, RESPONSIBILITIES, AND AUTHORITY**.
(1) Be PQS qualified for 3-M watch station "Work Center Supervisor," in accordance with ... of the command's 3-M Manual.

(2) Act as PQS Qualifier for cognizant personnel.

(3) Ensure that the work center's CSMP is maintained current and accurate so that it can be used to produce automated work requests.

(4) Maintain copies "One" and "Two" of the Deferred Maintenance Actions (OPNAV 4790/2K). Forward copy "One" as a "completed deferral" immediately after maintenance action completion, and destroy copy "Two" after the completion appears on the CSMP.

(5) Ensure that the Feedback Report system is correctly utilized to the maximum extent possible, in accordance with paragraph ..., Volume I, OPNAVINST 4790.4.

(6) Maintain the originator's copies of the Feedback Reports after they have been serialized by the 3-M Officer and returned to the work center.

(7) Conduct PMS walk-through reviews as required.

(8) Prepare the PMS weekly work center schedule.

(9) Ensure all required PMS actions are accomplished on schedule, and in accordance with MRCs.

(10) Advise the Head of Department, Division Officer, and Department 3-M Coordinator of any deviation from scheduled PMS action.

> *"There is no security on this earth.*
> *Only opportunity."* GEN DOUGLAS MACARTHUR
> From the book: *Successful Leadership Today*

c. **ORGANIZATIONAL RELATIONSHIPS**.
The Work Center Supervisor reports to the division officer and he/she works with other work center supervisors and the Department 3-M Coordinator. Personnel assigned to the work center, as detailed in the division organizational manual, report to the Work Center Supervisor.

3300 BOARDS, COMMITTEES, AND COLLATERAL DUTIES
a. **ASSIGNMENTS**.
Persons in the xxx Department may be assigned to boards, committees, and/or collateral duties by the command, department, or, as desired by division officers when it does not interfere with duties assigned by more senior personnel in the chain of command.

b. **COMMAND**.
Assignment to command collateral duties, or to membership on boards and committees will normally be by appointment letter, signed by the Commanding Officer.

Command board, committee, and collateral duty assignments take precedence and priority over department and division assignments.

A command notice is published periodically listing command collateral duty assignments.

c. **DEPARTMENT**
Persons within the xxx Department will be assigned to boards, committees, and/or collateral duties as necessary to meet department needs, obligations, and/or quotas.

Department board, committee, and collateral duty assignments take precedence and priority over division assignments.

Individuals assigned to fulfill xxx Department requirements will normally be appointed in writing by the xxx Officer.

d. **OBLIGATIONS**.
All persons assigned command or department duties, either as a board or committee member, or a collateral duty are required to attend all meetings and other events associated with that assignment. The inability to attend any meeting/event, for whatever reason, will be brought to the attention of the

appropriate division officer at the earliest opportunity. The division officer will ensure an alternate or other qualified substitute attends the meeting/event, or, notify the xxx Officer, PRIOR TO scheduled time. It is the responsibility of the division officer to assure compliance with these procedures by individuals within respective divisions.

For command functions, the person attending will deliver a verbal report of the highlights of meetings or events to the division officer who will determine if the information should be committed to print for distribution, and/or brought to the attention of the Head of Department.

e. **DIVISION**.
Division officers may assign collateral or other board or committee duties to individuals within their respective divisions to the extent desired so long as these assignments DO NOT interfere with command or department obligations and requirements.

5000 EXTRA MILITARY INSTRUCTION (EMI)
a. As noted in Chapter 1 of this manual, EMI may be assigned to correct minor infractions which DO NOT merit punishment under Article 15 of the UCMJ to correct deficiencies in a phase of military duty in which a subordinate may be deficient, or to direct completion of work assignments which may extend beyond normal working hours. Resort to imposition of withholding of privileges and EMI should be taken ONLY when counseling and normal instruction and training fail to accomplish the necessary objective. Excessive use of EMI within an organization may be an indication of improper leadership, guidance, and/or counseling.

b. **NAVY POLICY**. Basic policy guidance on EMI definition, implementation, and authority is contained in OPNAVINST 3120.32.

c. **COMMAND POLICY**. Command policy is that officers and Chief Petty Officers may, at the discretion of the Head of Department, impose EMI within the framework of OPNAVINST 3120.32.

d. **DEPARTMENT POLICY.**

(1) xxx Department personnel authorized to assign EMI is restricted to officers and Division Leading Chief Petty Officers. These individuals will read OPNAVINST 3120.32 as pertains to EMI prior to assigning EMI to personnel who work for them.

(2) EMI will be assigned in writing and will include the following:

(a) Reason assigned EMI;

(b) Date, time(s), and location to fulfill EMI responsibility, including person reporting to, if any; and,

(c) Signed by the person authorizing EMI and chopped by the xxx Officer PRIOR TO imposition of the actual EMI.

e. **DIVISION GUIDANCE**. Division officers will record in their Division Officer's Notebook all EMI imposed within their division. Information will include the paper noted in sub-paragraph d.(2) above. This information will be retained and submitted along with the division input when forwarding evaluations to the Head of Department for review. Once an evaluation is completed and signed by the individual and the approving official, EMI information assigned within the reporting period covered in the evaluation can be discarded/destroyed.

5060 AUTHORIZED READING MATERIAL IN xxx WORK SPACES

a. Authorized reading material in xxx work spaces is restricted to the following:

(1) PERSONAL MAIL (letters only). May be read during watch/duty hours in work spaces as authorized by the watch supervisor.

(2) NAVY CORRESPONDENCE COURSES. Supervisors will allow individuals to work on Navy correspondence courses required for advancement in rate at every opportunity, so long as operations are not hampered. Work on these courses during work hours is highly encouraged. Navy correspondence courses NOT required for advancement may be worked on under the same conditions set forth in sub-paragraph (3) below.

(3) CIVILIAN EDUCATIONAL CORRESPONDENCE COURSES AND SCHOOL TEXT BOOKS. Individuals enrolled in/attending civilian off-duty higher learning educational courses (i.e., high school, college classes, etc.) may, subject to watch

supervisor approval, work on this material during watch/duty hours. However, PQS, advancement courses, and other Navy training have top priority.

(4) NAVY ORIGINATED/ORIENTED MATERIAL. May be maintained in work spaces and read during watch/duty hours as approved by watch supervisors. Material in this area includes instructions, SOPs, All Hands, Navy Times, and the like.

b. No other reading material may be stored or read in xxx work spaces, this includes newspapers, magazines, novels, and the like.

c. If a question arises on what is/is not authorized, contact the division officer or division LCPO.

10000 DIRECTIVE ISSUANCE
The following official directive issuance system is prescribed for use within the xxx Department. (NOTE: Memorandums and the like are NOT official directives.)

10010 DEPARTMENTAL DIRECTIVE ISSUANCE
a. xxx DEPARTMENT ORGANIZATION AND REGULATIONS MANUAL (xxxDEPTINST 5400.1).
Lasting, UNCLASSIFIED, official directives within the xxx Department will normally be Articles/sub-Articles in the (command), xxx Department Organization and Regulations Manual. Articles and sub-Articles will be issued under a cover page signed by the xxx Officer.

b. **xxx DEPARTMENT NUMBERED INSTRUCTIONS**.
Lasting, UNCLASSIFIED, official directives within the xxx Department, when the Department O&R Manual is not considered appropriate. ALL CLASSIFIED official and lasting directives and instructions will be signed by the Head of Department.

c. **xxx DEPARTMENT STANDING ORDERS (SOs)**.
(1) Standing Orders (SOs) will be numbered sequentially starting with number 01 of each year (i.e., 01-93, 02-93, etc.). SOs may be issued by:
(a) xxx Officer
(b) Training Officer
(c) Supply Officer
(d) Department LCPO
(e) Department 3-M Coordinator
___ (others as required)

(2) SOs are authorized for issue to assure clarity, uniformity, and/or consistency of administration policy, or procedure across staff/division lines when not within the framework of a numbered instruction.

(3) All drafted SOs will be forwarded to the xxx Officer who will:

(a) Assign the next available SO number;

(b) Provide a properly formatted, smooth copy to the drafter for signature; and,

(c) Distribute signed copies to addressees.

(4) SOs will remain in effect until canceled. A self-cancellation date shall be included in SOs when possible.

(5) SOs will be retained as required. A complete file of effective SOs will be maintained by:

(a) xxx Officer

(b) Admin Officer

(c) Each Division Officer

10020 DIVISIONAL DIRECTIVE ISSUANCE

Divisional directives may be issued by division officers within the framework provided below.

a. SUBJECT MATTER DEFINITION.

(1) DIVISION ORGANIZATION AND REGULATIONS MANUAL.

Articles included will be of a constant and continuing nature, where routine updating or procedural change is not anticipated. Articles within an O&R Manual set forth WHAT TO DO policy (i.e., "Maintain a log.").

(2) STANDARD OPERATING PROCEDURES (SOPs)

SOPs are a set of instructions covering those features of operations which lend themselves to a definite or standardized procedure without loss of effectiveness. SOPs set forth HOW TO DO policy (i.e., Make the following log entries....").

(3) GENERAL DISTINCTION.

Some areas/subjects may be either an article in an organization and regulations manual or a SOP, depending on construction, intent, and purpose. Items that direct WHAT ACTION TO TAKE will be included in the O&R Manual. Items that direct HOW TO TAKE ACTION will be included in a division SOP. Billet and job descriptions shall be in the O&R Manual. Specific operator directions (i.e., log in here, take this there, etc.) shall be SOPs.

b. DIVISION ORGANIZATION AND REGULATIONS(O&R) MANUAL.

Format and construction in agreement with this department O&R Manual and OPNAVINST 3120.32. The manual and subsequent Articles will be issued under a cover letter, issued by the division officer and approved by the Head of Department.

c.   DIVISION STANDARD OPERATING PROCEDURES (SOPs).

(1)   Implemented in accordance with procedures in Article ... (included in this chapter).

(2) Each division will issue SOPs.

(3) A complete set of SOPs will be maintained by the division issuing the SOPs.

(4)   A copy of each SOP will be forwarded to the Department Admin Officer.

(5) SOPs will be issued by the respective division officers. Distribution will include the Head of Department and the Department Admin Officer, and other organizations as required by the contents of the SOPs.

"Be persuaded by someone's LOGIC and PROOF, not their enthusiasm."
From the book: **Successful Leadership Today**

The origin of a ship's commission pennant dates back to what century?   17TH CENTURY

"6P's of management: Proper Prior Planning Prevents Poor Performance."
From the book: **Successful Leadership Today**

CHAPTER 15

ESTABLISHING ORGANIZATION SOPs

After completing an organizational chart block diagram and job descriptions for each block on the chart, the next step is to establish organization policy through Standard Operating Procedures (SOPs).

WHAT IS POLICY?
1. Policy promotes uniform handling of similar activities.
2. Policy introduces a continuity of action and decision.
3. Policy acts as an automatic decision maker.
4. Policy predetermines answers to routine questions.
5. Policy serves as a major communications link.

General organization policy is usually set forth in an Organization and Regulations Manual (O&R Manual) and/or instructions.

Specific internal operating policy should be set forth in standard operating procedures (SOPs). All officers and chief petty officers should be well versed in writing SOPs.

GENERALLY ACCEPTABLE SOP CRITERIA.
1. Division SOPs should be signed by the division officer.
2. STRUCTURE:
    a. Structure of all SOPs should be in similar format.
    b. Easy for any E-2 to understand.
    c. Short words.
    d. Short sentences.
    e. Short paragraphs.
3. SUBJECT MATERIAL:
    a. Cover only one subject/procedure--and cover it completely.
    b. DO NOT refer reader to any other written source for needed information (quote any such necessary material in the SOP).

4. DISTRIBUTION:
    a. Head of Department (as appropriate)
    b. All division segments.
    c. Any organizations that might be interested/involved in any procedures spelled out in the SOP.
5. READING AND REVIEW:
    a. Each new/revised SOP should be passed through the organization with a signature cover sheet for signing. All hands should read and sign.
    b. Newly reporting personnel should read all effective SOPs and sign a cover sheet so noting.
    c. All SOPs should be reviewed periodically (monthly or quarterly is recommended). After review/update, all organization personnel should re-read the SOPs and sign a cover sheet.

SAMPLE SOP FORMAT

xxx DIVISION STANDARD OPERATING PROCEDURE NR. xx

Subj: Sample Standard Operating Procedure

Ref: (a) DEPT O&R Manual

1. **Purpose.** To establish the format for the preparation and promulgation of Standard Operating Procedures (SOPs) for the department.

2. **Discussion.** Reference (a) sets forth department policy and guidance for division SOPs. A SOP is defined as a "set of instructions covering those features of operations which lend themselves to a definite or standardized procedure without loss of effectiveness." Operations within divisions in this department meet the criteria for SOPs.

3. **Procedure.**
    a. Division officers will issue those SOPs necessary for the efficient operation of their respective divisions.
    b. Division SOPs will be read by all division personnel monthly. Division officers will monitor this requirement and maintain appropriate records.
    c. SOPs will contain basic paragraphing as described in the Navy Correspondence Manual, e.g., Title, Subject,

References (if any), Enclosures (if any), Purpose, Discussion/ Background, and Procedure/Action paragraphs. Sufficient detail shall be given to permit accomplishment of the described task/action without need for additional references or sources on a routine basis.

d. SOPs will not merely duplicate other directives, but may clarify or expand guidance contained in other directives.

e. SOPs may be modified, amended, or revised by Pass Down Log (PDL) entries. If such action is not permanent, the PDL entry can be effective no longer than the last day of the month following the month of issue. If permanent, it shall be incorporated into a changed, updated, or new SOP within two months.

f. SOPs will be reviewed quarterly to assess their effectiveness, validity, and completeness.

g. Each SOP will contain "Copy to" instructions, which will include as a minimum a copy to the Head of Department and other divisions or work groups affected by the involved SOP action.

Signature

PASS DOWN LOG

A division pass down log (PDL) should be used as a temporary supplement to division SOPs. Entries should be either printed or typed, not written out in long hand.

Normally, only the division officer, division chiefs, the LPO and section supervisors can make entries in a PDL.

All PDL entries should have a self-cancellation date (otherwise over a period of time the PDL entries become too numerous and make SOPs less effective).

"The best ideas are common property."
LUCIUS ANNAEUS SENECA
From the book: *Successful Leadership Today*

CHAPTER 16

DIVISION OFFICER'S NOTEBOOK

The information on the following pages is a continuation of the O&R Manual covered in a previous chapter. The paragraph numbering lends itself to be a part of the O&R Manual. However, by removing the paragraph numbering, this information can be used without reference to an O&R Manual.

DIVISION OFFICER'S NOTEBOOK

11000 DIVISION OFFICER'S NOTEBOOK
a.   OPNAVINST 3120.32 requires that each division officer maintain a Division Officer's Notebook.

b.   Each division officer shall maintain a Division Officer's Notebook using the criteria and requirements set forth in this chapter.

c.   A properly maintained Division Officer's Notebook allows division officers to record, or "track," past performance and to anticipate future requirements in people related matters.

11010 DIVISION OFFICER'S NOTEBOOK INSPECTIONS
The xxx Officer will inspect all Division Officer Notebooks at least quarterly.   The date/time of the inspection will be announced.

11020 DIVISION OFFICER NOTEBOOK REQUIREMENTS
a. Two separate actual notebooks will be maintained.
> (1) NOTEBOOK #1 will be locked-up when not in use.
> (2) NOTEBOOK #2 does not need to be kept under lock and key.

b. NOTEBOOK #1
Provide a tabbed section in the notebook for each enlisted person in the division.   This notebook should be the major source of information when drafting and writing enlisted

evaluations. The following minimum information will be maintained in this notebook.

(1) **DIVISION OFFICER'S PERSONNEL RECORD FORM (NAVPERS 1076/6)**. All possible blocks on this form shall be filled in (typewritten) as soon as an individual checks aboard and updated thereafter as changes occur.

(2) **INDIVIDUAL PERFORMANCE REPORTS (IPRs)** All individual performance reports (IPRs) occurring during any evaluation reporting period will be maintained in this notebook. These IPRs will be reviewed and considered when drafting enlisted evaluations.

(3) **MISCELLANEOUS ITEMS/FORMS** A copy of each individual's last rough evaluation as submitted by the department/division (if available). Other information to include: Request chits, promotion/frocking dates, courses/schools completed, inspection results, TAD tours, and any other information which might be of assistance either to the division officer or in the preparation of evaluations.

c. NOTEBOOK #2
(1) **PART I - ADVANCEMENT**. Using a Record Sheet of Advancement (see end of this section), list each person in the division and include information required to quickly and accurately determine all requirements necessary for advancement, distinguishing between the items completed and those not completed.

(2) **PART II - TRAINING.** This section DOES NOT encompass material required to be maintained in individual training records.
　　　(a) A copy of all division training reports submitted within the past year.
　　　(b) Attendance record sheets of classes attended by division personnel within the past year.
　　　(c) Individual damage control and 3-M PQS Status Report Sheets (see end of this section), listing all personnel in the division. Update monthly.
　　　(d) Progress chart listing all individuals in the division and recording the training/schools required by the command and those completed (see end of this section). Update monthly.
　　　(e) Division Record of Advancement Forms (see end of this section) listing individuals in the division and

recording advancement information as it is made available. Update monthly.

(f) Current notices/memos of upcoming schools and other training available to command personnel (i.e., damage control, 3-M, etc.).

(g) **NAVY ENLISTED CLASSIFICATIONS (NECs)**. Maintain a reproduced copy of the Manual of Navy Enlisted Manpower and Personnel Classifications and Occupational Standards of those sections that list NECs of billets authorized in the division.

NOTE: Division officers review this portion of the notebook to determine if personnel on board could earn NECs in present or anticipated NEC-deficient areas, or, if formal training is required.

(3) **PART III - DIVISION PERSONNEL ON-BOARD STRENGTH**
(a) Maintain appropriate portion of the command's Enlisted Distribution Verification Record (EDVR) and other manpower documents that relate to the division.
(b) A graph, updated monthly, depicting each of the following:
-Number of billets authorized in the division, broken down by rate/rating.
-Number of NEC billets authorized and on board.
-Other graphs as desired to afford tracking of on-board personnel and anticipated gains/losses. Retain these graphs for a two year period.

(4) **PART IV - MISCELLANEOUS.** Place ticklers in this section noting the location of:
(a) Division Officer's Billet Turnover Folder;
(b) Individual Training Records;
(c) Performance Appraisal Notebook; and,

(d) Other information as required/desired, such as copy of orders, sponsorship information, check-in sheet, security clearance information, security brief, etc.

> *"FORMULA FOR SUCCESS:*
> *Keep an ACTIVE MIND.*
> *Have a FERTILE IMAGINATION."*
> From the book: **Successful Leadership Today**

DIVISION RECORD SHEET
OF ADVANCEMENT E-1 TO E-5
(FILL IN MONTH/YEAR
EACH ITEM COMPLETED)

Division/Work Center: _____   Latest Update: _____

RATE/NAME	DATE REPORTED ACTIVE DUTY	DATE REPORTED COMMAND	E-1 DOR (DATE OF RANK)	E-2 DOR	E-3 BASIC MIL. RQMTS	E-3 CORR. COURSE	E-3 DOR	E-4 LEADERSHIP EXAM	PO3&2 PROF. CORR. COURSE	PO3&2 MIL REQ. COURSE	E-4 PARS/PERFOR. TEST	E-4 ELIG. EXAM DATE	E-4 DOR	E-5 LEADERSHIP EXAM	E-5 PARS/PERFOR. TEST	E-5 ELIG. EXAM DATE	E-5 DOR

144

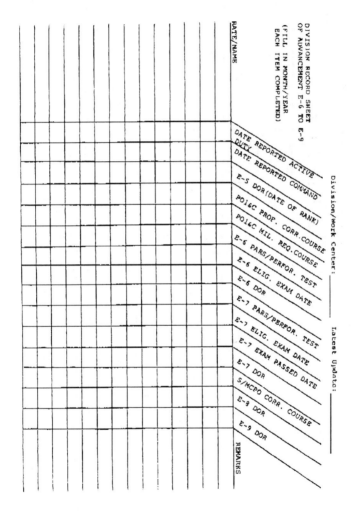

DIVISION RECORD SHEET
OF ADVANCEMENT E-6 TO E-9

(FILL IN MONTH/YEAR
EACH ITEM COMPLETED)

Division/Work Center: _____   Latest Update: _____

RATE/NAME

DATE REPORTED ACTIVE DUTY

DATE REPORTED COMMAND

E-5 DOR (DATE OF RANK)

PO1&C PROP. CORR. COURSE

PO1&C MIL. REQ. COURSE

E-6 PARS/PERFOR. TEST

E-6 ELIG. EXAM DATE

E-6 DOR

E-7 PARS/PERFOR. TEST

E-7 ELIG. EXAM DATE

E-7 EXAM PASSED DATE

E-7 DOR

S/MCPO CORR. COURSE

E-9 DOR

E-9 DOR

REMARKS

145

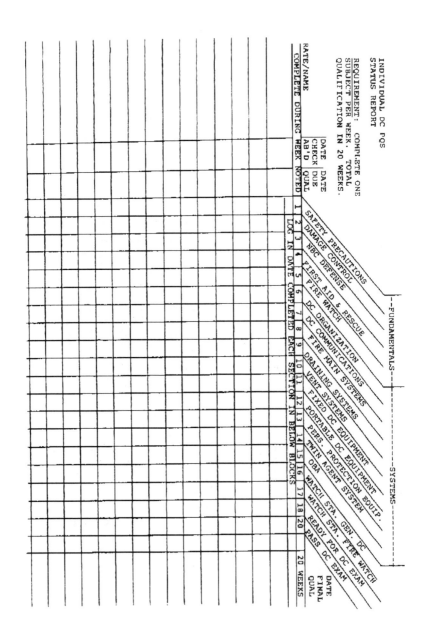

INDIVIDUAL DC PQS
STATUS REPORT

REQUIREMENT: COMPLETE ONE
SUBJECT PER WEEK. TOTAL
QUALIFICATION IN 20 WEEKS.

RATE/NAME

COMPLETE DURING WEEK NOTED

DATE CHECK AB'D | DATE DUE QUAL

1 2 3 4 5 6 7 8 9 10 11 12 13 14 15 16 17 18 20

LOG IN DATE COMPLETED EACH SECTION IN BELOW BLOCKS

SAFETY PRECAUTIONS
DAMAGE CONTROL
NBC DEFENSE
FIRST AID & RESCUE
FIRE WATCH
DC ORGANIZATION
DC COMMUNICATIONS
FIRE MAIN SYSTEMS
DRAINING SYSTEMS
VENT SYSTEMS
FIXED DC EQUIPMENT
PORTABLE DC EQUIPMENT
PERS. PROTECTION EQUIP.
TWIN AGENT SYSTEM
OBA
WATCH STA. GEN. DC
WATCH STA. FIRE WATCH
READY FOR DC EXAM
PASS DC EXAM

FUNDAMENTALS
SYSTEMS

DATE FINAL QUAL

20 WEEKS

INDIVIDUAL 3M PQS STATUS RECORD

Requirements must be completed within number of weeks indicated.

Division/Work Center: _____

Latest Update: _____

RATE/NAME	Complete During Week Noted	Required by Rates (Inclusive)	DATE CHECK AB'D	DATE DUE QUAL.	2 ALL 101-SHIP'S SYS	4 ALL 102-PMS	6 ALL 103-MDS	8 ALL 104-EQUIPMENT TAGOUT PROC.	10 ALL 201-PMS(SYS)	12 ALL 202-MDS(SYS)	14 ALL 301-MAINT. PERS.	16 E-6 302-WORK CEN/GROUP SUPVR	18 E-7 303-DIVISION OFFICER	20 DivO 304-DEPT HEAD	22 DivO 305-3M SYS COORD.

DIVISION QUALIFIED PQS PERCENTAGE RECORD

Division: _____   Year: _____

		OPERATORS			SUPERVISORS		
			NUMBER			NUMBER	
End of Month	TOTAL NUMBER ASSIGNED DIVISION	NUMBER FILLING BILLETS	PQS QUAL IN ONE POSITION	PERCENT QUAL	NUMBER FILLING BILLETS	PQS QUAL IN ONE POSITION	PERCENT QUAL
JAN	_____	_____	/	/	_____	/	/
FEB	_____	_____	/	/	_____	/	/
MAR	_____	_____	/	/	_____	/	/
APR	_____	_____	/	/	_____	/	/
MAY	_____	_____	/	/	_____	/	/
JUN	_____	_____	/	/	_____	/	/
JUL	_____	_____	/	/	_____	/	/
AUG	_____	_____	/	/	_____	/	/
SEP	_____	_____	/	/	_____	/	/
OCT	_____	_____	/	/	_____	/	/
NOV	_____	_____	/	/	_____	/	/
DEC	_____	_____	/	/	_____	/	/

SCHOOL/COURSE ATTENDANCE
RECORD-MILITARY SCHOOLS

FILL IN MONTH/YEAR
EACH ITEM COMPLETED
(PLACE "x" IN BLOCKS
NOT REQUIRED DUE TO
RATE/RANK, etc.).

Division/Work Center: _____   Latest Update: _____

RATE/NAME	DATE REPORTED	LOSS DATE (EST)	COMMAND INDOC.	DC PQS (3 DAYS)	3M OPERATOR CLASS	3M SUPVR CLASS	CNAL MGT SKILLS	CIAB	MIL. RIGHTS & RESPYS	CULTURAL EXPRESSION	NASAP	FIREFIGHTING	DCPO SCHOOL					

CHAPTER 17

BILLET TURNOVER FOLDER

The information on the following pages is a continuation of the O&R Manual covered in a previous chapter. The paragraph numbering lends itself to be a part of the O&R Manual. However, by removing the paragraph numbering, this information can be used without reference to an O&R Manual.

12000 BILLET TURNOVER FOLDER
A Billet Turnover Folder is an excellent tool for use in managing a Navy department or division, or any special unit within one of these organizations.

12010 BILLETS REQUIRED TO MAINTAIN A BILLET TURNOVER FOLDER
Individuals filling the following billets are required to maintain a Billet Turnover Folder:
> a. (list all division officer operations and all special independent unit operations.)
> b. ...
> c. ... etc....

12020 BILLET TURNOVER FOLDER INSPECTIONS
The xxx Officer will inspect Billet Turnover Folders once a quarter. The date/time of the inspection will be announced.

12030 BILLET TURNOVER FOLDER REQUIREMENTS
The Billet Turnover Folder will be maintained in sections and contain the below information, as applicable.

a. SECTION I - ORGANIZATION
CHAIN-OF-COMMAND BLOCK DIAGRAM. The below information may be combined.
> (1) Division organization (division officer down to and including each operator).
> (2) Department.
> (3) Command.
> (4) CO to CNO (to include administrative, tactical, and operational commanders).

b. SECTION II - MISSION, GOALS, AND TASKING
    (1) Established Navy goals and objectives.
    (2) Established command goals and objectives.
    (3) Established department goals and objectives.
    (4) Mission and tasking requirements from other sources.
    (5) Collateral duty assignments within the division as assigned by the command, department, and the division.

c. SECTION III - ASSIGNED SPACES
    (1) A listing, by compartment, of all spaces assigned to and maintained by the division/billet.
    (2) A copy of the command's zone inspection instruction.
    (3) A copy of zone inspection results of assigned spaces for last one (1) year.

d. SECTION IV - EQUIPMENT
    (1) A copy of equipment inventories, listing all major equipment assigned to the division/billet.
    (2) A copy of all correspondence concerning on-board equipment/systems; and, a copy of all correspondence on future equipment/systems to be installed in areas for which the division/billet is or will be responsible. If any material is classified and is not maintained in the Billet Turnover Folder, a tickler will be placed in this section noting the location of such information.

e. SECTION V - PROJECTS AND PROBLEMS. A copy of documents, correspondence, and point papers, separated by subject matter, which do not fall within the criteria set forth in Section IV above. If any material is classified and is not maintained in this section, a tickler will be placed in this section noting the location of such information.

f. SECTION VI - PERFORMANCE CRITERIA. A copy of the evaluation criteria for drills and exercises applicable to the division/billet.

g. SECTION VII - INSPECTIONS AND VISITS
    (1) Guides, instructions, and other criteria used in formal inspections and visits (FTGs, INSURVs, etc.).

(2) Copies of reports and results of inspections and visits noted above. To be retained for three (3) years, or until next inspection or visit, whichever is longer.

h. SECTION VIII - BILL AND ASSIGNMENTS
    (1) A working copy of the division's Watch, Quarter, and Station Bill.
    (2) A copy of all other bills and assignments not located elsewhere in this manual.

i. SECTION IX - PERFORMANCE HISTORY. A monthly summary of the performance and accomplishment of the division/billet (include any information which might be of historical interest, or information which might be useful in drafting fitness reports and/or enlisted evaluations). Retain this information for two (2) years.

j. SECTION X - DIVISION ORGANIZATION AND REGULATIONS MANUAL. A copy of the division O&R Manual, or a tickler noting the location of the manual will be placed in this section.

k. SECTION XI - DIVISION STANDARD OPERATING PROCEDURES. A Copy of the division Standard Operating Procedures (SOPs), or a tickler noting the location of the SOPs will be placed in this section.

l. SECTION XII - MISCELLANEOUS
    (1) A copy of billet relieving letters.
    (2) A copy of material/equipment signed for as billet incumbent.
    (3) Other information as required/desired.

"He who has never learned to obey,
cannot be a good leader." ARISTOTLE
From the book: *Successful Leadership Today*

CHAPTER 18

TICKLER FILE

GENERAL INFORMATION. Every organization in the Navy needs a "tickler file" of some sort to ensure that action due dates are met. A tickler file is a "reminder file." Any future event that requires action by your organization should be placed in your tickler file.

When reporting to a new organization, never assume that an existing tickler file is up to date. Start your own tickler file from scratch. When you have completed it, check the tickler file left by your predecessor to see if there is something you may have missed. You are held personally accountable if just one due date is missed, so why let someone else's error place you in an awkward position. Start and maintain your own tickler file for your organization.

STARTING A TICKLER FILE. One of the easiest ways to start or maintain a tickler file is to place the pertinent information on a 3x5 card and file the cards in a file box. Use tabs to identify card location and placement. For example, your first tabs might be "WEEKLY" and "MONTHLY," followed by the months of the year, "JAN," "FEB," etc.

TICKLER FILE INFORMATION. Include as much information on the 3X5 card as possible so that you don't have to keep referring to instructions and other sources of information to complete the action required. The following is an example of what kind of information to be placed on the 3x5 tickler file card.

15 JAN	15 FEB	ANNUAL
COMMENCE ACTION	FORWARD NLT	FREQUENCY
SUBJECT:	ANNUAL E-5 EVALUATIONS	
BILLET RESPY:	DIVISION OFFICERS	
REF/INST:	NMPC 1616.1 (series)	
FORM USED:	STD EVAL FORMS	
SUBMIT TO:	PERSONNEL OFFICER	
COMMENTS:	E-5 EVAL ENDING PERIOD	
	31 MARCH DivOs forward evals to	
	Dept Head NLT 15 FEB	

```
--------------------------------------------------------------------------------
```
15 FEB/15 MAY
15 AUG/15 NOV   25th OF MONTH   QUARTERLY
COMMENCE ACTION   FORWARD NLT   FREQUENCY

SUBJECT: QTLY SEA BAG INSPECTION
BILLET RESPY: DIVISION OFFICERS
REF/INST: COMMAND INST 1020.2
FORM USED: STD SEA BAG INSP. FORM
SUBMIT TO: DEPT HEAD & FILE
COMMENTS: Ref requires QTLY sea bag
                       inspection of non-rated pers,
                       and "as required" inspection of POs.
                       File completed forms in DivO Notebook.

TICKLER FILE SOURCES. Use every source available when constructing your tickler file. The first place to start is the command instructions and notices. Go through this material and look for any action, event, or report levied upon your organization. The following is a sample list of items to look for in your search.

    1. Enlisted Evaluation and Officer Fitness Report due dates.

    2. Navy-wide advancement examination dates.

    3. Cut-off dates for meeting advancement qualifications for every pay grade in your organization.

    4. Inspections - zone, personnel, seabag, admin, etc.

    5. Deployment, training schedules, etc.

    6. Qualification boards - Command qualification boards (EAWS, ESWS, SWO, SS, etc) usually have predetermined meeting times. Note these and ensure that your people are prepared for all qualification/certification boards.

    7. Collateral duties - Your organization will probably have some involvement in collateral duties. Most collateral duty assignments to boards or committees have regularly scheduled meeting times.

    8. Be sure to include TAD requirements like mess cook duties.

Read through each new instruction, notice, message, etc. to see if there is a future requirement for action by your organization. If there is, add that requirement to your tickler file.

TICKLER FILE ON PERSONNEL. Check the projected rotation date (PRD) of each person in your organization. Make out a 3x5 card on each person and file it in the month three months prior to transfer. Each 3x5 card should contain time frames for completing any necessary action. The below list is a sample of what your cards might look like.

90 DAYS PRIOR TO TRANSFER
* Start work on any award (Navy Achievement Medal, Navy Commendation Medal, etc.)
* If retiring, start setting up retirement ceremony.
* If the person's relief must have some special training or schooling, identify relief and arrange for training.

30 DAYS PRIOR TO TRANSFER
* Start work on transfer EVAL or FITREP
* Make necessary updates to watch bill(s)
* Identify and designate reliefs for collateral duties
* Another person sign for any equipment, publications or other material for which the transferring person is responsible.

LAST WEEK/DAY
* Complete and sign EVAL or FITREP
* Remove name from access lists
* Change safe combinations as necessary
* Security debrief (if necessary)
* Turn in any special badges
* Be sure to forward training record
* Remove from Watch, Quarter, and Station Bill

The above areas are samples of what might be used. Each command/organization should tailor the above list to the particular need of the organization and the individual maintaining the tickler file.

"If you don't have all the answers,
keep asking questions."
From the book: **Successful Leadership Today**

CHAPTER 19

WATCH, QUARTER, AND STATION BILL

For any ship to carry out its assigned missions and tasks, it must have an administrative organization wherein every person is assigned one or more tasks.

BATTLE BILL. The ship's organized plan for action is contained in the battle bill, which is based upon the organization manual and other pertinent publications and directives. Included in the battle bill are lists of stations that must be manned during battle and at other specified times.

WATCH, QUARTER, AND STATION BILL. Using the organization manual and the battle bill as references, each division is responsible for assigning personnel in the division to the stations, and for entering their names on the watch, quarter, and station bill. This bill displays in one place, the duties for each person in the division under various emergency and watch conditions.

BATTLE STATIONS. Under "battle stations," CONDITION I is general quarters, when all battle stations are manned, usually when surface or air action is imminent. Condition I is sometimes modified to permit a few persons at a time to rest on station or to permit designated personnel to draw rations for delivery to battle stations (Condition 1E).

CONDITION II is a special watch used by gunfire support ships for situations such as extended periods of shore bombardment.

CONDITION III is the normal wartime cruising watch. Normally, when cruising under Condition III, the ship's company stands watch on a regular rotation watch section basis.

SELF-DEFENSE FORCE. Assignments to the self-defense force vary according to ship type. The purpose of the self-defense force is to provide a capability for reacting to emergency security situations aboard ship and at pier side to protect the ship, its sensitive equipment, and the ship's personnel.

EMERGENCY GETTING UNDERWAY. This column is for use in port when most of the crew is ashore and the ship must get underway before personnel can be recalled.

WATCH DETAIL. Under "watch detail'" the LEFT COLUMN is for normal peacetime cruising, or CONDITION IV. The number of watch sections depends on the type of ship and the number of personnel aboard.

The RIGHT COLUMN lists the type of watch personnel will stand in port (CONDITION V). The time of the watch is posted on a separate in-port watch list.

SPECIAL SEA DETAIL. The "special sea detail" is manned whenever the ship leaves or enters port. Because of the critical nature of mooring or anchoring, getting underway, and maneuvering in restricted waters, only the most experienced persons are assigned to these details.

OTHER ASSIGNMENTS. The remaining columns of the watch, quarter, and station bill, except the last one, are for assignments to the ship's emergency bills (fire, rescue and assistance, collision, abandon ship, and man overboard). The last column is for assignments to such miscellaneous details as mess cooking, MAA duty, and side boys.

"I can give you a six-word formula for success: Think things through, then follow through."
EDDIE RICKENBACKER
From the book: ***Successful Leadership Today***

Which Navyman and future President served aboard submarines after World War II?
JAMES E. CARTER, JR.

WATCH, QUARTER & STATION BILL

SECTION __First__   DIVISION __First__

COMPT __A-303-L__

DATE: 7/14/—

BILLET	NAME	FRAME NO.	LWR BR.	RATE	CLEAN STATION	BATTLE STATIONS	Self Defense Force	GENERAL detail	WATCH DETAIL	SPECIAL SEA DETAIL	FIRE	RESCUE & ASSIST PARTY	COLLISION	ABANDON SHIP	MAN OVERBOARD	SPECIAL DETAIL
1101	King, K.K.	CPO 18		BMC/BMC												
1102	Johnson, J.J.	#1	1	BM2/BM2							OBA		G.Q.	Sta. E/1 Boat 1	Cong. Sec. I	
1103	Paterson, P.P.	2	2	GM1/GM1		MT3								Sta. E/ Boat 1		gtrs
1104	Smith, S.S.	6	6	G/GM3							OBA			Boat 1		
1105	Kato, K.K.	9	9	SN/SN		LBAT						Boat	scene	Boat 1		
1106	Brown, B.B.	4	4	SN/SN	GIG						scene CO₂		G.Q.	Boat 1		
1107	Oats, O.O.	8	8	SN/SN			BAR				scene appl.		G.Q.	Boat 1		
1108				SN	MT3		BAR				qtrs		G.Q.			
1109	Cook, C.C.	7	7	SN/SN							gtrs		G.Q.	Boat 1		
1110	Eng, E.E.	11	11	SN/SN	MT31						gtrs		G.Q.	Boat 1		
1111	Fox, F.F.	13	13	SN/SA							gtrs		G.Q.	Boat 1		
1112	Duffin, D.D.	5	5	SN/SA	A-300-L	MT E3 3c1	BAR				scene		G.Q.	Boat 1		

CHAPTER 20

LETTERS TO RELATIVES

Sending letters to relatives of your sailors on special occasions is a great way to tell the individual and the family that "we care." You can come up with a few sample letters and you won't have to re-invent the process each time an occasion arises. Simply change the name and the occasion on the sample letters. If you have a computer, save the sample letters and pull them up anytime they are needed.

Special occasions could include:
- -Advancement
- -Special Qualifications (EAWS, ESWS, SS, etc.)
- -PQS Qualifications
- -Sailor of the Month/Quarter/Year

The following sample letters can get you started.

> The Navy's first women nurses served aboard a hospital ship in which war?   CIVIL WAR

> *"Unrewarded acts can result in uninvolved people."*
> From the book: ***Successful Leadership Today***

> *"Ask open-ended questions and keep an open mind."*
> From the book: ***Successful Leadership Today***

Internal Codes
Date

(Name of next of kin)
(Street address)
(City, state, ZIP)

Dear (Next of kin name),

It is my pleasure to inform you of the advancement of your (son/daughter/ husband/wife) (name). It is certainly a noteworthy achievement and is indicative of (his/her) character and ability. With this advancement comes additional leadership responsibilities. We in (organization) have every confidence in your (relationship) ability to execute these additional duties in the same proven manner (he/she) exhibited in (his/her) previous position.

(Name) selection to (rate/rank) is impressive when one considers the large number of men and women competing for advancement. The Navy's advancement system is fair and extremely effective in selecting the best of those qualified for positions of higher responsibility. You may be assured that the Navy has many good men and women and that they all put forth their very best effort in anticipation of advancement. Therefore, to attain (his/her) advancement, your (son/daughter/ husband/wife) had to excel over many qualified individuals.

I speak for all of the officers and crew of (command/organization) when I say that we share with you the pride of (name) advancement.

Sincerely,

Signature
Typed name
Grade, U.S. Navy
Title

LETTER HEAD
COMMAND &
ADDRESS

Internal Codes
Date

(Name of next of kin)
(Street address)
(City, state, ZIP)

Dear (Next of Kin name),

It is with great pleasure that I take this opportunity to inform you that your (relationship, rate, name, USN) was advanced to (rate advanced to) on (day, month, year). This achievement was the result of much hard work that included many hours of individual study, good performance, and successfully passing the Navy-wide examination.

(First name) received authority for advancement at an official ceremony in the company of (his/her) peers and I'm sure (he/she) will always remember this special occasion.

I trust that you are equally proud as I am that (first name has achieved this hallmark in (his/her) Naval career and I join with you in recognizing (him/her) for (his/her) accomplishments and success in the United States Navy.

Sincerely,
Signature
Typed name
Grade, U.S. Navy
Title

"Recognizing the successes and accomplishments of others is easy and inexpensive."
From the book: ***Successful Leadership Today***

LETTER HEAD
COMMAND &
ADDRESS

Internal Codes
Date

(Name of next of Kin)
(Street address)
(City, state, ZIP)

Dear (Next of Kin name),

It is with great pleasure that I take this opportunity to inform you that your (relationship, name, rate, USN) was awarded the (type of award) for professional achievement in the superior performance of (his/her) duties while serving as (primary assignment) in/at/aboard (command/organization).

(First name) was presented the (type of award) at an official ceremony in the company of (his/her)peers and shipmates and I'm sure (he/she)will always remember this special occasion.

I trust that you are equally proud as I am that (first name) has achieved this hallmark in (his/her) Naval career and I join with you in recognizing (him/her) for (his/her) accomplishments and success in the United States Navy.

Sincerely,
Signature
Typed name
Grade, U.S. Navy
Title

In 1845, the 17th Secretary of the Navy established the U.S. Naval Academy (originally known as the U.S. Navy School). Who was this person?
GEORGE BANCROFT

162

CHAPTER 21

INDIVIDUAL PERFORMANCE REPORTS

Individual Performance Reports (IPRs) are an excellent management tool. The following passage from the *Navy Eval and Fitrep Writing Guide* is provided for information.

Subj: Individual Performance Reports (IPRs)

Encl: (1) Individual Performance Report Form
      (2) Individual Performance Report Samples

1. Purpose. To establish an effective program for reporting superior or substandard performance.

2. Discussion. Enlisted evaluations are the most important part of a servicemember's official record. Evaluations are used, in part, to determine eligibility for type of discharge, reenlistment, advancement, service school and duty assignment eligibility. It is important that superior or substandard performance be documented AS OCCURRING to assure it is not forgotten and that it is available for consideration at evaluation grading time. The following conditions and possibilities make it of paramount importance that superior and substandard performance be documented while it is fresh in memory.

   a. Long periods of time between evaluation reports.

   b. Individuals may transfer from one job to another or from one immediate supervisor to another one or more times during an evaluation period. Information not recorded is thus lost.

   c. An individual superior(s) may transfer during an evaluation period. Again, information not recorded is lost.

3. Action.

   a. Procedures & Responsibilities: Any superior in an individual's chain of command should complete an IPR whenever superior or substandard performance is observed in a subordinate.

b. Examples of when in IPR would be appropriate:

(1) Official award received.

(2) OUTSTANDING or UNSAT at any type of formal inspection.

(3) Individual instances of superior or substandard job performance.

(4) Volunteering for special assignments or projects (noting the results achieved).

(5) Significant off-duty time donated to job (note if voluntary).

(6) OUTSTANDING or UNSAT appearance at quarters, or as noted during the performance of duty.

(7) Late/UA instances.

(8) On other occasions as deemed appropriate.

c. Routing. When an IPR has been filled out and signed, it will be routed through the chain of command up to the division officer. The division officer will determine if the IPR should be reviewed by other personnel. (Note: Routing may be altered to reflect particular organization.)

d. Retention. Completed IPRs will be retained in the Division Officer's Notebook until the individual reported on is being evaluated. At that time, the person preparing the initial evaluation write-up will remove the IPRs from the notebook, consider the documents, and include such information as appropriate in the evaluation. As a reminder, isolated incidents or minor infractions should not be included in an evaluation write-up. One case of being ten minutes late for quarters and one haircut reminder in a twelve month period is not serious enough to be included in the narrative of an eval write-up. All IPRs will be forwarded up the chain of command along with the evaluation write-up. Once the evaluation is completed and signed by the appropriate personnel, all IPRs within the reported time frame should be destroyed unless some are being retained for other reasons.

> *"Failure is an education in learning."*
> From the book: *Successful Leadership Today*

EXAMPLE BLANK IPR FORM

(ORGANIZATION)	INDIVIDUAL PERFORMANCE REPORT (IPR)		
NAME	**RATE**	**DIVISION/WC**	**DATE**

PERFORMANCE

☐ MERITORIOUS   ☐ DEROGATORY   ☐ OTHER

REMARKS

SIGNATURE OF REPORTING SUPERIOR	SIGNATURE OF INDIVIDUAL BEING REPORTED ON

Routing:
Immed. Supvr _____ LPO _____ CPO _____ LCPO _____ DIV. OFFICER _____

EXAMPLE DEROGATORY IPR

(ORGANIZATION) **INDIVIDUAL PERFORMANCE REPORT (IPR)**

NAME	RATE	DIVISION/WC	DATE
A. B. SEAMAN	SKSN	S-1	5 JUN 19XX

PERFORMANCE

☐ MERITORIOUS   ☒ DEROGATORY   ☐ OTHER

REMARKS

SKSN SEAMAN WAS 15 MINUTES LATE FOR QUARTERS THIS DATE. (STATED CAR TROUBLES)

SIGNATURE OF REPORTING SUPERIOR	SIGNATURE OF INDIVIDUAL BEING REPORTED ON

Routing:
Immed. Supvr _____ LPO _____ CPO _____ LCPO _____ DIV. OFFICER _____

EXAMPLE MERITORIOUS IPR

(ORGANIZATION) **INDIVIDUAL PERFORMANCE REPORT (IPR)**

NAME	RATE	DIVISION/WC	DATE
W. T. HATCH	RM2	CR	1 MAR 19XX

PERFORMANCE

☒ MERITORIOUS   ☐ DEROGATORY   ☐ OTHER

REMARKS

PETTY OFFICER HATCH IDENTIFIED BY C.O. AS HAVING BEST PERSONAL APPEARANCE IN DIVISION AT C.O.'s PERSONNEL INSPECTION THIS DATE.

SIGNATURE OF REPORTING SUPERIOR	SIGNATURE OF INDIVIDUAL BEING REPORTED ON

Routing:
Immed. Supvr _____ LPO _____ CPO _____ LCPO _____ DIV. OFFICER _____

CHAPTER 22

PERSONNEL FILE

Many times during your career you are going to need to have some basic information on the personnel assigned to you immediately available. You might get a call from the CO or XO wanting to know something about someone who works for you. You might be at home and the OOD calls you for some information on someone. Or, it might be an individual calling you to ask for special liberty or emergency leave for any number of reasons. There are numerous other occasions where having readily available information on the people who work for you would be beneficial.

This information should be arranged in some sort of portable file. A file you can carry in your pocket or in your briefcase. A file with loose leaf, easily changeable pages is recommended. Use one sheet for each individual. Put any information you could possible need at a moment's notice in the file. The following is a sampling of information that could be useful to you.

This information should be arranged in some sort of portable file. A file you can carry in your pocket or in your briefcase. A file with loose leaf, easily changeable pages is recommended. Use one sheet for each individual. Put any information you could possible need at a moment's notice in the file. The following is a sampling of information that could be useful to you.

-Name
-Rank
-Date of Birth
-Date or Rank
-Date Qualified for Advancement
-Transfer Date
-Home Phone Number & Address
-Name, Phone Number & Address of Next of Kin
-Names & Ages of Children
-Amount of Leave on Books (as of certain date)
-Duty Section Assignment
-Qualifications Needed for Advancement
-Qualifications Needed for other areas (PQS, EAWS, ESWS, etc.)
-Other Personal Information as Desired

CHAPTER 23

TRAINING, SCHOOLS, AND EDUCATION

PERSONNEL QUALIFICATION STANDARD (PQS) SYSTEM

a.   The PQS program is one element in the Navy's overall training program.   The Handbook on Management and Implementation Procedures for Personnel Qualification Standards, NAVEDTRA 43001.1, provides information on the PQS concept and describes its implementation in the training program of naval units.

b.   The purpose of the program is to assist in qualifying the trainee to perform assigned duties.   The PQS program also helps to prepare individuals for advancement by referring them to applicable rate training manuals. To obtain the stock number for a particular PQS booklet, refer to the List of Training Manuals and Correspondence Courses, NAVEDTRA 10061.

c.   Each qualification standard has four main subdivisions in addition to a preface and introduction, glossary, bibliography, and feedback form. The four main subdivisions are:

(1) **100 SERIES - THEORY.** The theory section specifies the knowledge of theory necessary as a prerequisite to the study of the specific equipment or systems for which the PQS was written.

(2) **200 SERIES - SYSTEM**. The system section breaks the equipment or systems to be studied into functional sections. A study of this section provides the individual with the required information concerning what the system or equipment does, how it does it, and other pertinent aspects of operation. The answers must be extracted from the various maintenance and technical manuals covering the equipment or system in question.

(3)   **300 SERIES - WATCH STATIONS**.   The watch stations section includes questions regarding the procedures the individual must know before he/she can operate and maintain the equipment and/or system. The qualification process moves

beyond knowledge at this level by requiring the individual to demonstrate correct steps, procedures, and skills for specific equipment and systems. The individual must demonstrate these procedures during normal, abnormal, and emergency situations.

(4) **400 SERIES - QUALIFICATION CARDS.** The qualification cards provide accounting data used to record the individual's satisfactory completion of various items. The completion of part or all of the PQS provides a basis for the supervisor to certify completion of Personnel Advancement Requirements (PARs).

d. The Occupational Standards Manual, NAVPERS 18068, provides a list of the basic occupational skills for each Navy rating and pay grade. The PQS program will assist members in developing these skills; rate training manuals and nonresident career courses provide a method for acquiring the knowledge associated with these skills. The Navy advancement system is based on a competitive Navy-wide exam and an individual's demonstrated skills documented by the PARs program. The Manual of Advancement, BUPERSINST 1430.16 established enlisted personnel advancement requirements. The Bibliography for Advancement Study, NAVEDTRA 10052, lists the recommended rate training manuals and other materials for study prior to advancement exams.

NAVY SCHOOLS PROGRAM

a. The Navy's service schools are another major part of the overall education and training program. The Catalog of Navy Training Courses (CANTRAC), NAVEDTRA 10500, contains information on schools and courses. The CANTRAC is organized to provide a consolidated centrally produced catalog presenting courses in standardized form. It is divided into three volumes.

(1) VOLUME 1 - INTRODUCTION, GENERAL INFORMATION, AND QUOTA CONTROL NOTES. This volume includes all general information not subject to frequent changes. Volume I is published in hard copy annually. Volumes II & III are published quarterly in microfiche.

(2) VOLUME II - CANTRAC COURSE DESCRIPTIONS. All courses are arranged in numerical sequence by Course Identification Number (CIN).

(3) VOLUME III - CANTRAC CONVENING SCHEDULES. A numerical index of CINs that gives course short title and location, convening dates, and Course Data Processing number for each course.

KEYWORD INDEX. The keyword index of course long titles will be produced with each edition of the CANTRAC (Volumes II & III). Course titles are listed in alphabetical order by key words appearing in the title. Titles and related course numbers may appear five or six times in the index, depending on how many key words appear in the title.

SERVICE SCHOOLS

Service schools are grouped by class/type. Each class/type will be given a letter designation. The following is a brief description of the service school classes/types.

a. **CLASS "A"** - Class "A" schools provide basic technical knowledge and skills required to prepare for entry- level performance and further specialized training, including apprenticeship training. An NEC (Navy Enlisted Classification) or NOBC (Naval Officer Billet Code) may be awarded to identify the skill achieved. They also include some officer courses such as communication officer, ASW officer, etc.

b. **CLASS "C"** - Class "C" schools provide the advanced knowledge, skills, and techniques to perform a particular job in a billet. They may also be any course which awards or is a prerequisite to a skill awarding course (e.g., NEC, or NOBC) or is 13 calendar days or longer and does not conform to the definition for a Class "A" course.

c. **CLASS "E"** - Class "E" schools are designed to provide formal professional education instruction in a general or particular field of study which may lead to an academic degree.

d. **CLASS "F"** - Class "F" schools provide team training to fleet personnel, officers and enlisted, who normally are, or are enroute to duty as, members of ship's companies, and/or individual training such as refresher, operator, maintenance, and technical training of less than 13 calendar days established to meet the needs of the fleet or type commanders, an NEC or NOBC will not be awarded.

e. **CLASS "P"** - Class "P" schools are designed to provide undergraduate education and/or indoctrination and basic training in fundamentals, preliminaries, or principles to midshipmen, officer candidates, and other newly commissioned officers (except those acquired through Class "V" programs).

f. **CLASS "R"** - Class "R" schools provide training following initial enlistment or induction. "Boot Camp" provides general indoctrination and prepares the recruit for early adjustment to military life. Individuals receive training in the skills and knowledge of basic military subjects.

g. **CLASS "V"** - Class "V" schools provide the skills which lead to the designation as Naval Aviator (pilot) or Naval Flight Officer (NFO).

EDUCATIONAL ASSISTANCE - NAVY CAMPUS

Navy CHAMPUS is a Navy-wide network which implements and promotes off-duty voluntary education programs. It is comprised of the following programs and support services.

a. **NAVY CAMPUS EDUCATION SPECIALIST NETWORK -** Consists of civilian education specialists and education technicians located at all major Navy installations throughout the world. These personnel ensure the proper administration of off-duty education programs. Navy Campus education specialists function as installation and area voluntary education program coordinators. They serve in an additional duty status as the principal education advisor to base/station commanding officers, provide assistance and technical guidance to ESOs(Educational Services Offices) and career counselors, and offer individualized counseling and testing services to all Navy personnel.

b. **TUITION ASSISTANCE PROGRAM (TAP)** - TAP provides eligible personnel with a percentage of tuition costs for courses attended at accredited colleges, universities, and post-secondary trade, technical, and business schools and one hundred percent (100%) of tuition costs for credit courses applicable to the completion of a high school diploma or certificate. Tuition assistance is also offered for college-level correspondence courses.

ELIGIBLE PERSONNEL - Tuition Assistance is available to Regular Navy personnel, naval reservists on continuous active duty, naval reservists ordered to active duty for 120 days or more, and members of other U.S. military services assigned to duty with the Navy. Enlisted personnel must have sufficient active duty service time remaining to complete a course, or have approved extension or reenlistment authorization. Commissioned officers must agree to remain on active duty for at least two years following the end of the last course of instruction. Reserve officers on active duty are eligible for TA if they have two years active duty remaining upon completion of the last course.

c. **PROGRAM FOR AFLOAT COLLEGE EDUCATION (PACE)** - PACE is an integral part of the Navy Campus program. The Navy contracts with accredited colleges and universities to provide post-secondary courses to seagoing personnel. Shipboard personnel are provided off-duty collegiate education opportunities comparable to those provided personnel assigned to shore duty. The program may include instruction from civilian professors, videotapes, and correspondence courses.

d. **ENLISTED EDUCATION ADVANCEMENT PROGRAM (EEAP)** - This program provides an opportunity for selected personnel to earn either an associate or baccalaureate degree by attending college full-time while remaining in the Navy.

e. **BROADENED OPPORTUNITY FOR OFFICER SELECTION AND TRAINING (BOOST)** - This program prepares selected applicants for entry into the Naval Reserve Officers Training Corps (NROTC) Scholarship Program or the U.S. Naval Academy. This program is open to all eligible Navy enlisted personnel with a high school diploma or certificate.

> *"The superior man is firm in the right way, not merely firm."* CONFUCIUS
> From the book: *Successful Leadership Today*

f. **GRADUATE EDUCATION** - The need for effective use of officers educated beyond the baccalaureate level is clear. This program supports requirements for officers with a specific specialty skill. Funded graduate education programs are limited to providing sufficient officers with subspecialties for which valid billet requirements exist.

g. **COLLEGE DEGREE PROGRAM (CDP)** - The CDP provides an opportunity for active duty naval officers to earn baccalaureate degrees in approved service-related fields through full-time study at civilian educational institutions.

> *"Ambiguous goals and poor feedback can lead to confusion and frustration."*
> From the book: **Successful Leadership Today**

> The U.S. Navy submarine insignia ("dolphins") was adopted by the Navy in what year?   1924

> *"Most people will want to do a good job if they are properly motivated."*
> From the book: **Successful Leadership Today**

CHAPTER 24

ENLISTED RATINGS

AB Aviation Boatswain's Mate

AC Air Traffic Controller

AD Aviation Machinist's Mate

AE Aviation Electrician's Mate

AG Aerographer's Mate

AK Aviation Storekeeper

AM Av. Structural Mechanic

AO Aviation Ordnanceman

AS Av. Support Equip. Tech.

AT Av. Electronics Tech.

AW Aviation ASW Operator

AZ Av. Maint. Administration man

BM Boatswain's Mate

BU Builder

CE Construction Electrician

CM Construction Mechanic

CT Cryptologic Tech.

DC Damage Controlman

DK Disbursing Clerk

DM Illustrator-Draftsman

DT Dental Technician

EA Engineering Aide

EM Electrician's Mate

EN Engineman

EO Equipment Operator

ET Electronics Technician

EW Electronics Warfare Tech.

FC Fire Controlman

FT Fire Control Tech.

GM Gunner's Mate

GS Gas Turbine Systems Tech.

HM Hospital Corpsman

HT Hull Maint. Technician

IC Interior Comm. Electrician

IS Intelligence Specialist

JO Journalist

LI Lithographer

LN Legalman

MA Master-At-Arms

MM Machinist's Mate

MN Mineman

MR Machinery Repairman

MS Mess Management Specialist

MT Missile Technician

MU Musician

NC Navy Counselor

OS Operations Specialist

OT Ocean Systems Tech.

PC Postal Clerk

PH Photographer's Mate

PN Personnelman

PR Aircrew Survival Equipmentman

QM Quartermaster

RM Radioman

RP Religious Program Specialist

SH Ship's Serviceman

SK Storekeeper

SM Signalman

ST Sonar Technician

SW Steelworker

TM Torpedoman's Mate

UT Utilitiesman

YN Yeoman

CHAPTER 25

ENLISTED SERVICE RECORDS

The service record is the official history of an enlisted person's career in the Navy. It reveals basic aptitudes, education, special training, civilian and military experience, and disciplinary record. It also provides facts necessary to substantiate an individual's advancement progress and to measure overall performance and worth to the Navy.

TYPES OF RECORDS

1. ENLISTED MICROFICHE RECORD
a. Maintained at Naval Military Personnel Command (NMPC), Washington, D.C.
b. A permanent record of enlisted person's career.
c. May contain adverse information and copies of evaluations.

2. ENLISTED SERVICE RECORD
a. Maintained at local command.
b. Property of the government, not the individual.
c. May contain adverse information.
d. Authorized access includes the individual and his/her immediate chain of command.

LEFT SIDE OF ENLISTED SERVICE RECORD
Contains official and unofficial papers required for record and safe-keeping purposes. Completed in no particular order; latest information on top. Example of information included on left side:
a. Copies of orders
b. Educational documents
c. Special qualifications
d. Security clearance documents
e. Personal papers
f. Personnel advancement requirements (PARs)

RIGHT SIDE OF ENLISTED SERVICE RECORD
Pages are numbered in sequence from the bottom to top. Pages of primary importance are:
a. PAGE 1 - Enlistment/Reenlistment Document

b. PAGE IA - Agreement to Extend Enlistment

c. PAGE IB - Assignment to and Extension of Active Duty

d.   PAGE 2 - Dependency Application/Record of Emergency Data

e. PAGE 3 - Enlisted Classification Record

      -Lists civilian education and training prior to joining military

      -Armed Services Vocational Aptitude Battery (ASVAB) scores

f. PAGE 4 - Navy Occupation/Training and Awards

      -Enlisted Classification Codes (NECs) and designators.

      -Navy service schools attended

      -Navy training courses, PARs, other classes/courses completed.

      -Advancements, reductions, and changes in rate or rating

      -GED test, vocational/technical training, and off-duty study courses

      -Decorations and awards

g. PAGE 5 - History of Assignments

      -Also, record of extension, sea and shore duty commencement dates

h. PAGE 6 - Record of Unauthorized Absence

      -Any U/A in excess of 24 hours, and lost time due to confinement by civil authorities or sick misconduct

i. PAGE 7 - Court Memorandum

      -Used to record court-martial and NJP actions which affect pay

j. PAGE 9 - Enlisted Performance Record

      -Chronological record of enlisted members performance evaluations and career milestones. Includes evaluations, meritorious mast, courts-martial, changes in rating, advancement, and reduction in rate

k. PAGE 10 - Administrative Remarks

      -To record significant miscellaneous entries not provided for elsewhere in record, or where more detailed information may be required to clarify entries on other pages of the service record.

"Almost nothing is more treasured than LOYALTY.
Loyalty is a two-way street, you have to give it to get it."
From the book: ***Successful Leadership Today***

CHAPTER 26

DAILY QUARTERS

Division Chief Responsibilities (before arrival of Division Officer):
-Muster All Hands
-Read command Plan of the Day (POD)
-Inspect personnel for proper uniforms and haircuts
-Go over day's work schedule
-(Periodic) Check all ID Cards
-Other areas as required

Division Officer Responsibilities:
-Pass along any recent information
-(As required) Discuss upcoming special events (Inspections, operations, etc.)
-(Weekly) Inspect personnel for proper uniforms and haircuts
-(Periodic) Discuss special interest areas (Safety, PQS, etc.)

MORNING QUARTERS ITEMS TO DISCUSS

1) Advancement Program
2) Career Incentives
3) Medical Benefits
4) Chain of Command
5) Classified Material
6) Code of Conduct
7) Damage Control
8) Education Benefits
9) Financial Responsibility
10) Firefighting
11) First Aid
12) Saluting
13) Navy History
14) Inspections
15) Leave & Earnings Statement
16) Liberty/Conduct Ashore
17) Command Organization
18) Command Mission
19) Physical Training
20) PQS Training
21) Maintenance System
22) UCMJ
23) Collateral Duties
24) Personal Hygiene
25) Reenlistment Benefits
26) Uniforms
27) Uniform of the Day
28) Grooming Standards
29) Watch, Quarter & Station Bill
30) Watchstanding
31) Special Request Chit Procedures
32) Schools & Training Available
33) Navy customs & traditions
34) Commission Opportunities
35) Recreation Facilities Available
36) Sea Bag Inspections & clothes markings

CHAPTER 27

PRESENTING DIVISIONS AT PERSONNEL INSPECTIONS

There is much that a division officer can do to make a division personnel inspection a success. Remember, the division officer is the first person to be inspected. First impressions are important. The division officer should have an inspection uniform set aside for such special occasions. The division officer should present the division in a snappy, alert, and military manner. The exact method of presentation of a division varies little throughout the Navy. Personnel will be formed in ranks according to height with the tallest people in each rank at the end of the division which the inspecting party will first approach. Junior division officers and chief petty officers will form a rank or file in the rear of the division.

The division stands at parade rest while waiting for the inspecting party to arrive. When the inspecting party approaches the division, the division officer should give the command, ".... Division, attention." After the inspecting party has departed, the division officer will place the division at parade rest. It is a good idea for the division officer to place the division at "Attention" every few minutes when there is a long time delay before or after the inspection, and before "fall out." This affords the people in ranks to loosen up a bit. It is a comforting relief to be able to reposition one's self from time to time. This action also lessens the chance that someone in ranks will faint.

The division officer will fall in so that the inspecting party will approach from the right side. When the inspecting party approaches, the division will be called to attention. When the inspecting officer is within six paces, the division officer will order, "Hand...Salute." The inspecting officer will be greeted with, "Good morning, Captain(etc.)." After the inspecting officer returns the salute, the division officer will give the division the command, "Two."

The division officer will then address the inspecting officer: "... Division, standing by for your inspection, sir. (Number) personnel assigned, no unauthorized absentees (or number of absentees)."

As the inspecting officer and his/her party inspect, the division officer will fall in just behind the inspecting officer, on the side away from the rank under inspection.

At the request of the inspecting officer, the division officer may be called upon to give the division the command to make an "about face" and "uncover."

Upon completion of the inspection, the division officer will place the division at "parade rest."

"People want to believe they made a difference, that they contributed something someone else might not have contributed."
From the book: **Successful Leadership Today**

The Navy's Supply Corps was established in 1871. What was the original name of the Supply Corps?
PAY CORPS

"Leadership is the ability to get men to do what they don't want to do, and like it." Harry Truman
From the book: **Successful Leadership Today**

CHAPTER 28

POINT PAPER

A point paper is a brief summary of information and facts on a single subject. Point papers may be used to:
-Assist in developing policy
-Assist in stating policy
-Determining courses of action
-Used in briefings and conferences

Point papers should be:
-Accurate
-Complete (but not overly detailed)
-Concise
-Current
-Brief (routinely not more than one page)

POINT PAPER FORMAT
1. Concept or Purpose. A brief statement of the concept, idea or purpose of the paper.

2. Background. A brief description of issue, topic or program and generating factors. Salient, factual information. Ensure clear understanding.

3. Status or Discussion. Concise, factual statement of current status. Relation to established guidelines, goals, steps, predictions, recent or proposed positions, and any conflict with other positions. State anticipated or desired solution.

4. Problems. The impact of the unresolved problems, critical decision dates, contingent requirements, etc. State recommended organization position . Avoid broad, non-specific recommendations or requests for action.

5. Other Paragraph Titles as Required. Every attempt should be made to include all pertinent information within the standard paragraphs above. The basic paper should be one page. Put detailed discussion, rationale, etc. in a TAB, not the basic paper.

CHAPTER 29

MEETINGS

1. How often depends on problems to discuss.

2. Schedule at regular time day/week.

3. Length of meeting depends on knowledge of persons present and task at hand.

4. New meeting groups may require more frequent meetings than established groups.

5. Ideal group can meet without the normal leader present.

6. Begin on time, even if someone is late.

7. End at a specific time.

8. Normal meeting should be no longer than 30 minutes. No meeting should exceed two hours.

9. Meeting should have priority over other events. DO NOT DISTURB.

10. Distribute agenda or items to be discussed if possible. Members should have options formulated by meeting time.

11. Do not conduct meetings during meals.

12. Conduct in private, quiet, and comfortable location.

13. Each person should be able to be seen by all others.

14. Coffee/Refreshments available?

15. Chalkboard or other required materials available?

16. Provide recorder to record highlights.

17. Written reports should contain only decision actions taken. Do not include discussions and differences.

18. Develop START and FINISH agenda. Prioritize items - most important items discussed first.

19. If an item doesn't effect all members of the group, don't discuss it at general meeting.

20. Strive for unanimous agreement if possible.

21. Any decision should be made primarily by those who are responsible for the outcome of the decision.

22. Take some definitive action on every item on the agenda. Don't leave undecided decisions until the next meeting.

23. Type and publish meeting minutes at earliest opportunity.

24. If decisions made that affect others, notify them as quickly as possible. Don't let rumors get started.

25. Continually evaluate effectiveness, and need, of group meetings.

CHAPTER 30

ADMINISTRATION

STANDARD SUBJECT IDENTIFICATION NUMBERS. The Department of the Navy Standard Subject Identification Codes, SECNAVINST 5210.11, provides a single, standard subject scheme. This classification system is used for numbering Navy and Marine Corps documents by subject throughout the Department of the Navy. This instruction contains a list of standard subject identification numbers and a list of name-title subject identification codes.

Except at activities with an exceptionally large volume of correspondence, files normally are established by subject identification numbers. However, files may be established by name-title codes or a combination of both.

For the purpose of identification and filing, standard subject identification numbers classify Navy correspondence and directives under 13 major series groups. These major series groups are further subdivided by the use of the last three digits in the major series. The 13 major series groups consist of the following:
1000 Series - Military Personnel
2000 Series - Communications
3000 Series - Operations and Readiness
4000 Series - Logistics
5000 Series - General Administration and Management
6000 Series - Medicine and Dentistry
7000 Series - Financial Management
8000 Series - Ordnance Material
9000 Series - Ships Design and Ships Material
10000 Series - General Material
11000 Series - Facilities and Activities Ashore
12000 Series - Civilian Personnel
13000 Series - Aeronautical Management

The 13 major subject groups are subdivided into primary, secondary, and sometimes tertiary breakdowns, as indicated in the following example.

4000 - Indicates the major subject group - Logistics
4400 - Indicates the primary breakdown - Supply Control
4440 - Indicates the secondary breakdown - Inventory Control
4441 - Indicates the tertiary breakdown - Allowances

DOCUMENT ORIGINATION. Each office identifies the directives which it originates by the following:
1. The originator's abbreviation.
2. The type of directive.
3. The subject identification number.
4. A consecutive number, preceded by a decimal point (applies to instructions only).
5. A consecutive letter, indicating the revision.
The following example is an identifying symbol assigned to an instruction issued by the Office of the Secretary of the Navy.

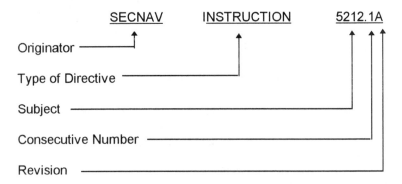

Consecutive numbers are assigned to instructions having the same subject identification number to show the order of issuance. For example, the subject number of contract financing is 7800. An originating office would assign numbers to the first, second, and third instructions which it issues on contract financing as follows: 7810.1, 7810.2, and 7810.3, respectively. The number 7810.1A indicates the first revision of the instruction 7810.1.

Notices are not assigned consecutive numbers because of their one-time nature or brief duration.

The subject identification number assigned as the file number of a letter is not assigned a consecutive number.

The security classification of Confidential or Secret instructions and notices is indicated by prefixing the subject number by "C" for Confidential and by "S" for Secret.

FILES. File arrangement within any office depends upon the mission of the office and on the volume of its official correspondence. Normally, general correspondence is stored in metal file cabinets. This includes letters, speedletters, and memorandums received or originated by the office.

Folders are used to keep correspondence orderly in the files. The total number of folders and the appropriate primary, secondary, or tertiary subject identification numbers, or the name-title symbols, to be used are determined by the volume of written matter in each category to be filed. There may be no need to establish any folders on some major series groups, while others may require several folders broken down to primary, secondary, or tertiary numbers. The subject identification numbers or name-title symbols should be printed on each folder.

The subject identification number placed on the correspondence by the originator assists in determining the correct folder in which to file the correspondence. This number, however, may not be appropriate for the particular office concerned, thereby requiring reclassifying. The proper method of classifying a document for the purpose of selecting the appropriate file is to read it carefully and analyze it, considering the following factors:
1. The most important, definite, or concrete subject mentioned.
2. The purpose or general significance of the document.
3. The manner in which similar documents are requested by users of the files.
4. The subject identification code under which previous documents of a similar nature are filed.

Directives are not placed in the general correspondence files except when copies of instructions and notices are attached to or interfiled in such files when needed to complete a record or document. Instructions are filed in standard three-ring binders and are arranged as follows:
1. In numerical order of subject identification number.
2. By the originating office within each subject identification number.
3. By consecutive number (suffix number) for each originating office.

Notices ordinarily need not be filed because of their brief duration. In cases in which the recipient believes it necessary to file some notices temporarily, they may be interfiled with instructions.

Messages are filed by date/time group number. Normally, two files are maintained--one containing incoming messages and the other outgoing messages.

DISPOSITION OF CORRESPONDENCE AND RECORDS

Retention of obsolete and inactive correspondence and records is costly. Such correspondence and records should be destroyed or transferred in accordance with approved records disposal instructions. If this is not performed periodically, the volume of file space required becomes excessive and the files become inefficient.

The destruction of records is governed by law which requires authorization by proper authority. The authority for destruction of Navy records is contained in SECNAVINST 5215.5, Disposal of Navy and Marine Corps Records.

The provisions of SECNAVINST 5215.5 are normally amplified by the issuance of local instructions outlining the procedures as they apply locally.

LOCAL DISPOSITION. Not all materials in the files have a record characteristic. In fact, most print matter in general files fall in the category of nonrecord material. This includes documents that are copies of those filed in the ship's office or station administrative department or material accumulated in the process of producing records, but which never acquire a record characteristic themselves.

SECNAVINST 5212.5 (Part II for shore stations, and Part III for ships) contains the retention standard for naval records. Record materials are listed by broad subject and the retention period is furnished. Nonrecord material may be destroyed locally as soon as it has served its purpose. Records material may be destroyed upon completion of the retention period.

Unclassified records or nonrecords materials authorized for destruction may be placed in wastebaskets and disposed of in the normal manner for trash. Classified matter authorized for destruction should be destroyed by burning in the presence of two designated witnesses. All persons witnessing the destruction of classified material must have security clearances at least as high as the category of material being destroyed. Classified matter may also be destroyed by pulping, provided destruction of the classified material is complete and reconstruction impossible.

NAVY DIRECTIVES. Navy directives are issued in accordance with the Department of the Navy Directives Issuance System, SECNAVINST 5215.1, which sets forth the policies, responsibilities, and standards for the administration of the Navy Directives System.

PURPOSES. Use of a single Navywide numbering system for directives enables each naval activity receiving directives to:
1. Group directives by subject and combine related subjects.
2. Distinguish between directives of a continuing nature and those of a brief duration.
3. Obtain complete sets of instructions upon activation or commissioning.
4. Determine, by use of periodic checklists, the current status and completeness of its set of directives.
5. Determine, by use of subject indexes, what directives are in effect on a subject.
6. File directives and describe them as references by one easy method.
7. Use the same numbering system for correspondence files as for directives.

CRITERIA. A document shall be issued in the directives system when it meets one or more of the following criteria:
1. Regulates or is essential to effective administration.
2. Establishes policy.
3. Delegates authority.
4. Assigns responsibility.
5. Establishes an organizational structure.

TYPES. The directives system provides for two types of directives.

189

1. INSTRUCTION
a. For information of a continuous reference value or requiring continuous action.

b. Remains in effect until canceled by the originator or is superseded.

2. NOTICE.
a. For information of a one time or temporary nature.

b. Self-canceling, usually remains in effect for less than six months, but not more than one year.

CHANGE TRANSMITTAL. The medium used to transmit changes to an instruction, or under extenuating circumstances, a notice.

Each transmittal describes the nature of the changes it transmits and gives directions for making them.

TYPES.
1. PEN AND INK CHANGES - For correcting a word or sentence. A pen change will not be issued when the time required for all changes on a single sheet (two sides) of paper would exceed that required to remove a superseded sheet and insert a new one.

2. PAGE CHANGES - Replaces entire pages. Usually preferred over a pen and ink change.

NAVAL LETTERS

Within the Navy, official letters are usually prepared in naval format as stated in the Department of the Navy Correspondence Manual. This format is also used when writing to certain other agencies of the U.S. Government or the U.S. Coast Guard. Various components and guidelines of a naval letter are discussed in the following paragraphs. Some examples are located at the end of this chapter.

STATIONERY. Letterhead stationery of the activity responsible for signing the correspondence is used for the first page of a naval letter. If printed letterhead stationery is not available, the letterhead is typed or stamped in the center of the page, four lines from the top of the page.

Second and subsequent pages are typed on plain bond paper similar to the letterhead in size, color, and quality. For carbon copies, white and colored tissues are used. The official file copy is prepared on green tissue.

COPIES. Before beginning to type a letter, determine the number of copies needed. Requirements for copies of naval letters are determined by such factors as subject of the letter, type and number of addressees, and local filing practices. Although the necessary number of copies must be determined separately for each letter, the following copies are generally standard:

    1. One green (or designed reproduced copy) for originator's official files.
    2. One white copy for each "Via" addressee.
    3. One white copy for each "Copy to" addressee.

MARGINS. On the first page of all naval letters, the left margin and the right margin are 1 inch, and the bottom margin at least 1 inch. On the second and succeeding pages, the margin at the top is 1 inch. The other margins are the same as on the first page.

GENERAL STYLE. No salutation or complimentary closing appears on a naval letter. Major paragraphs are typed in block style; that is, without indenting.

Periods do not follow the parts of the heading or the closing.

Abbreviations are used in the following items of the heading:
    1. Subject (Subj)
    2. Reference (Ref)
    3. Enclosure (Encl)

When referred to in the text of the letter, these are spelled out.

A heading entry that is too long to be completed on one line is carried over to the next line, flush with the first word following the colon.

"Progress comes from the intelligent use of experience." ELBERT HUBBARD
From the book: *Successful Leadership Today*

IDENTIFICATION SYMBOLS

Three types of identification symbols may be used on correspondence for reference and record purposes. One or more may appear on a letter, depending on local practice.

1. ORIGINATOR'S CODE - is a system of letters, numbers, or a combination of both, used for the sake of brevity to indicate the organizational unit within the activity preparing the correspondence.

An originator's code is formed according to local instructions and must appear on all outgoing correspondence. Since the "From" line appears on all naval letters, the originator's code should not contain the activity code. It should, except in the case of ships, identify the department or organizational unit within the activity preparing the letter. The hull number of a ship may be used instead of an originator's code.

The originator's code should appear one line below the last line of the letterhead and commence 2 inches from the right of the page.

2. FILE NUMBER - is used to indicate the subject under which the letter is to be filed. A file number is not mandatory, but when used it consists of a four- or five-digit numeric code selected from the list of standard subject identification numbers, which is contained in the Department of the Navy Standard Subject Identification Codes, SECNAVINST 5210.11.

A file number, when used, should appear one line below and blocked with the originator's code.

3. SERIAL NUMBER - is one of a consecutive group of Arabic numerals assigned to a specific piece of correspondence for identification purposes.

Classified correspondence must be serially numbered each calendar year by the originator. Unclassified mail may be serially numbered if desired.

The serial number, when used, should appear one line below the preceding line of type and blocked with the originator's code.

On continuation pages the originator's code begins 2 inches from the right margin and 6 lines from the top of the page. The other identification symbols are blocked as they are on the first page.

DATE. The date is always placed on the right side of the page, blocked one line below the last line of the identification symbols and arranged as follows:
1. The day, month, and year are expressed in the order named.
2. The day is always expressed in numerals.
3. The month is either spelled out or abbreviated by using the first three letters of the word. If abbreviated, it is not followed by a period.
4. The year is expressed in four digits.
5. No punctuation is used between the month and the year.

Correspondence is dated with the date on which it is signed. The date may be typed or stamped according to local practices.

"FROM" LINE. Use of the "From: line is optional, except where there is specific need to include it. In cases where it is omitted, copies provided for "Copy to" and "Via" addressees must have a printed, stamped, or typed letterhead to indicate the originator of the correspondence. When it is used, it must not unnecessarily duplicate the printed letterhead, and should include only that information which, together with the letterhead, will provide sufficient title and address for reply without reference documents having to be consulted.

If it is used, the "From" line is typed on the third line below the designation of postal service or of classification (which follows the date information listed above). If there is no such designation, the "From" line is on the seventh line below the last line of the letterhead address.

Two spaces are allowed between the colon after "From" and the beginning of the addresser's title.

The "From" line identifies by title the official in authority over the activity or other organizational unit having cognizance of the subject covered by the letter. As the addresser of the letter, he is the official to whom reply, if necessary, is directed. Sufficient information is given in connection with the title to enable the recipient of a copy not on letterhead to identify the letter as to origin.

An activity, except a mobile unit, which uses an FPO number in lieu of a geographical location in its envelope address, must use its geographical location in the letter head, and in the "From" line (if used).

Titles in the "From" line follow the form shown in Section 2 of the Catalog of Naval Shore Activities, OPNAV PO9B3-105 and Standard Navy Distribution List, Part 1 (Operating Forces of the Navy), OPNAV PO9B3-107.

If a window envelope is to be used for transmitting a letter, the position of the heading entries on the letter should be adjusted to meet the spacing requirements of the envelope.

On a letter to be enclosed in a window envelope, the "From" entry is typed on the 2nd line below the seal or on the 11th line from the top of the page.

"TO" LINE. The "To" line is placed on the line below the "From" entry, if used, on letters to be mailed in regular envelopes (three lines below for window envelope). If there is no "From" line, the "To" line is placed in the same position as that prescribed above for the "From" entry.

There are four spaces from the colon after "To" to the beginning of the title of the addressee.

When the functional title does not clearly distinguish the addressee, sufficient information is given as to his activity to assure that the letter is correctly delivered. If the complete mailing address is shown, the ZIP Code or FPO number is included.

The title of the addressee may be followed by the title or the code designation (in parentheses) of the office having immediate responsibility for the subject matter. The word "Attention" is normally not used.

If the letter is to be transmitted in a window envelope, special care in placing the address is necessary. The "To" line on letters for window envelopes is 14 lines from the top of the page, or 3 lines below the "From" line. Often, letterhead carries a printed dot indicating the point on which the "T" in "To" is based.

No line of the address may extend more than 3 1/4 inches. Nothing except the title and the address should appear in the window.

"VIA" LINE. "Via" addressees are indicated when it is necessary for another addressee to endorse (approve, disapprove, or comment on) the document before it is received by the ultimate addressee.

The "Via" line is placed on the line below the "To" line. If there is more than one "Via" addressee, each is numbered with an Arabic numeral enclosed in parentheses. The numerals indicate the sequence through which the correspondence is to be sent, the official numbered (1) being the first "Via" addressee to receive the letter, and so on.

When there is only one "Via" addressee, three spaces are left between the colon after "Via" and the beginning of the title of the addressee. If two or more "Via" addressees are to be included, three spaces are left between the colon and the beginning of the numbering of the first addressee.

"SUBJECT" LINE. The abbreviation "Subj" is used to introduce a topical statement of the subject of the correspondence. The "Subj" line is two lines below the preceding line of typing. There are two spaces from the colon after "Subj" to the beginning of the subject.

The subject is stated briefly and specifically, with key words first, and followed by necessary explanatory words. Only the first word and proper nouns are capitalized. If the explanatory words break the normal sequence of words in the subject, they are separated from the key phrases by a semicolon.

EXAMPLE: Naval letters; instructions for preparation and use of.

A letter of reply usually repeats the subject of the incoming letter.

"REFERENCE" LINE. The abbreviation "Ref" (without an "s" even though there is more than one reference) is used as the caption when previously prepared material is cited.

The "Ref" line is two lines below the last line of the subject; each reference citation begins on a new line. Three spaces intervene between the colon after "Ref" and the beginning of the first reference.

References are listed in the order in which they are discussed in the text of the letter. They are designated by small letters enclosed in parenthesis ((a), (b), (c), etc.). An enclosure is never listed as a reference.

When a letter is cited as a reference, the reference line should include the following identifying information:
1. The abbreviated title of the originator of the referenced letter.
2. The location of the activity.
3. The abbreviation "ltr."
4. All identification symbols assigned to the referenced letter.
5. The date of the referenced letter preceded by the preposition "of."
6. The functional title of the addressee of the referenced letter if the letter was not addressed to the originator of the letter being prepared. The functional title is preceded by the preposition "to."
7. If no identification symbols appear on the letter, the subject is given instead. The subject is introduced by the abbreviation "Subj" followed by a colon and is added at the end of the reference.

When documents other than letters are listed as references, they are fully identified as to origin, type, title, or subject, symbol or number, and date.

"ENCLOSURE" LINE. The abbreviation "Encl" (without an "s" even though there is more than one enclosure) is used to introduce a listing of materials forwarded with the letter. The "Encl" line is two lines below the preceding line of type, with each enclosure notation beginning on a new line. Two spaces follow the colon after "Encl."

Enclosures are numbered with Arabic numerals in parentheses. They are identified in the same manner as references are in the "Ref" line. When material must go under separate cover, the designation "(SC)" is placed between the number and the description of the enclosure.

Each enclosure that accompanies the letter is identified by typing or stamping, and a copy of the covering letter is sent with the material being forwarded.

Copies of enclosures are provided to all "Via" addressees. Copies are also provided to "Copy to" addressees unless they are known to be holders or unless providing copies is impractical. An enclosure is never listed as a reference.

Ordinarily, a transmittal of multiple copies of the same material is considered a single enclosure, and only one copy is labeled. The number of copies should be indicated on the "Encl" line.

TEXT. The text (or body) of the letter begins two lines below the preceding line of type.

Major paragraphs are numbered at the left margin with Arabic numerals followed by a period. Two spaces are allowed between the period and the beginning of the first word. The text of the letter is single spaced, with double spacing between paragraphs and subparagraphs.

Subparagraphs are indented four spaces from the left margin and are lettered with small letters, followed by a period. The second and succeeding lines extend from left to right margins.

Each further degree of subdivision is indented correspondingly. Sub-subparagraphs are marked by numerals in parentheses, the next degree by small letters in parentheses, after which come numerals underscored, and then letters underscored.

EXAMPLE: 1.
       a.
          (1)
             (a)
               $\underline{1}$
                 $\underline{a}$

SIGNATURE. The signature information is typed or stamped in block style, four lines below the last line of the text, beginning at the center of the page. All names are typed in capitals at the end of a letter.

Neither the grade, nor, as a rule, the functional title of the signing official is shown in the signature, except that a functional title is added for a chief of staff, a deputy, an assistant chief, or a similar official authorized to sign correspondence without the use of the phrase "By direction," and also for executive officers or similar officials authorized to sign orders affecting pay and allowances.

"COPY TO" LINE. The "Copy to" line is placed at the left margin, two lines below the last line of the signature information. "Copy to" is not abbreviated. Officials receiving copies are listed, with titles abbreviated, below the words "Copy to," even with the left margin.

If copies of any of the enclosures listed in the heading are sent to "Copy to" addressees, the words "with encl" and the enclosure numbers assigned in the heading are added in parentheses after the title of each recipient.

PAGING. The first page of a letter is not numbered. Second and succeeding pages are numbered consecutively with Arabic numerals, beginning with "2," centered 1/2 inch from the bottom of the page. The numerals are typed without parentheses or dashes.

The signature page of a letter exceeding one page in length should contain a minimum of two lines of text.

A paragraph is not begun near the end of a page unless there is space for at least two lines of text on the initial page and unless at least two lines are carried over to the next page.

IDENTIFYING PAGES. For identification of second and succeeding pages, the originator's code and the file or serial number, if any, are repeated at the top of the page. They are typed, block style if both are used on the right side, 1 inch from the top and beginning 2 inches from the right edge. When a file number is not used, the serial number, if any, may be used instead of the file number. When neither a file number nor a serial number is used, the date is added below the originator's code and the subject (introduced by the abbreviation "Subj") is repeated, beginning at the left margin, two lines below the date.

The text of the letter is continued two lines below the subject, or the symbols, as the case may be.

ENDORSEMENTS. The endorsement is used to approve, disapprove, or comment on the content of a letter which is forwarded through one or more addressees before reaching its final destination.

When there is adequate space remaining on the page, the first and subsequent endorsements may be placed on the same page containing the basic letter or prior endorsement. Letterhead paper is used for the original of an endorsement and manifold (tissue) paper is used for carbon copies.

When an endorsement is typed below the preceding basic letter or endorsement, a dash line is placed one line below the last line in the preceding communication. The originator's code is placed one line below the dash line. If endorsements are started on a new page where no dash line is required, the originator's code is typed six lines from the top of the paper.

Endorsements may be typewritten, stamped, or handwritten.

Stamped or handwritten endorsements may be used when comment is brief and no record copies are needed.

The format of an endorsement is much the same as that of an official letter except for the heading.

> *"To build on teamwork and secure loyalty,*
> *allow key subordinates a voice in policy decisions."*
> From the book: **Successful Leadership Today**

> Commodore became a fixed grade in the
> U.S. Navy in what year?   1862

> *"Losers lose opportunities.*
> *Winners create opportunities."*
> From the book: **Successful Leadership Today**

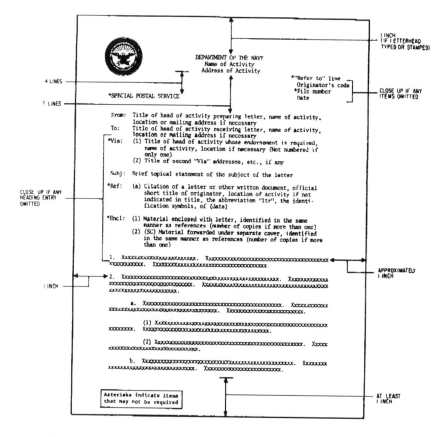

Fig 1. First Page of an Unclassified Letter (Example).

200

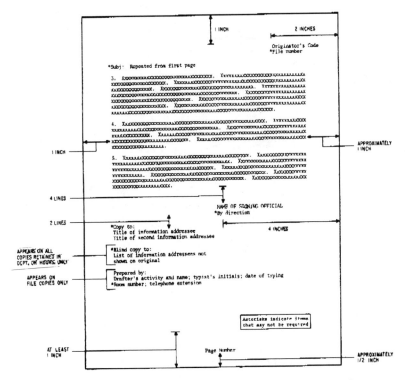

Fig 2. 2nd & Succeeding Pages of Unclas Naval Letter.

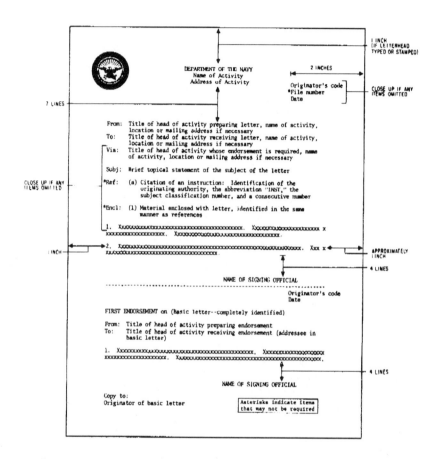

Fig 3. An Endorsement (Typed on Same Page as Basic Letter).

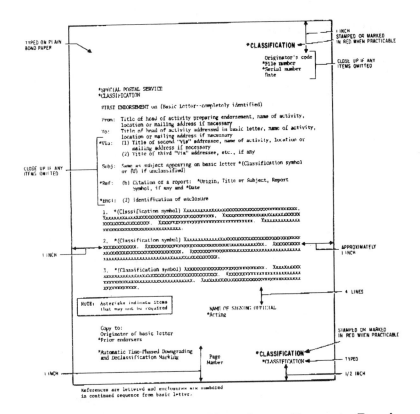

Fig 4. An Endorsement (Typed on a Separate Page).

203

CHAPTER 31

CORRESPONDENCE

The following tips are provided for Naval correspondence. For specific drafting and format rules, consult the Navy Correspondence Manual, SECNAVINST 5216.5.

PERSONAL CONTACT. Preparing correspondence is time-consuming and expensive. Don't write unless you must. Whenever possible, official business should be transacted through personal contact. A conversation in person or by phone often saves you at least two letters. Conversations are better than letters for working out details that require give and take. Try to use written correspondence only when record communications is necessary. In this case, work out all of the details in person or on the phone and use official correspondence to put forth the end result of these personal communications efforts.

RESPONDING. Give prompt attention to incoming correspondence that requires action or answers. Normally, answer written correspondence in no more than 15 working days, or in the time set by the incoming correspondence. Naval messages are normally answered within 5 working days if an earlier deadline is not directed. Congressional correspondence must be answered within 5 working days of receipt.

CHAIN OF COMMAND. All correspondence to higher authority must go through the chain of command to the commanding officer.

SIGNATURE AUTHORITY. A commanding officer may delegate signature authority to military or civilian personnel and may authorize those subordinates to delegate signature authority further. Delegation of signature authority must be in writing, to titles rather than names, and must include a brief outline of the type of documents involved. When subordinates sign documents under this delegated authority, they usually sign "By direction."

The commanding officer, officer in charge, or person "acting" in either position must personally sign documents that:

1. Establish policy

2. Center on changes to the command's mission and are addressed to higher authority

3. Deal with certain aspects of military justice

4. Are required by law or regulation (e.g., ship's deck log).

"Energy and persistence conquer all things."
BENJAMIN FRANKLIN
From the book: **Successful Leadership Today**

Who was the first Secretary of the Navy?
BENJAMIN STODDERT

"Leadership is something you do
WITH people, not TO people."
From the book: **Successful Leadership Today**

CHAPTER 32

WRITING AND SPEAKING

Mastery of self-expression is one difference between the competent and the exceptional. All things being equal, the officer who has expended the effort to master the skills of writing and speaking will rise more rapidly, be a more effective leader and contribute more to the military service and the nation.

Ability to impart information in a clear, concise manner is a blessing for both superiors and subordinates. Superiors already overburdened with a mass of sometimes conflicting information welcome the discovery of an officer who can present an oral or written case that is logical, brief and to the point. For the subordinate, it is a blessing to find a superior who can provide clear information in an understandable manner. Most people neither need nor want long, detailed expositions of grand strategy. They simply want to know what they are supposed to do now.

In the Armed Forces, command is exercised through written and oral communication that must be articulate and understandable at all levels. Superior qualification in the use of the written and spoken word is as essential to military leadership as the knowledge of the whole technique of weapons handling and the use of complex systems.

It is a matter of personal decision whether an officer will develop the communications skills necessary for exceptional leadership or will hide behind the excuse offered by too many, "I have no gift for writing or speaking."

Anyone who has the brains to gain a commission has the brains to become a good writer. It requires work. It doesn't come easily or quickly. It demands time and effort to master the language. It demands practice and more practice. Extensive practice creates the ability to look at a problem, define its important parts and discover the possible solutions. Before one can write, one has to think. What an officer thinks will be reflected in the structure, the choice of words and the logic of the writing. This does not mean that the task will ever become easy. Good writing always will require more perspiration than inspiration.

Lastly, the writer must have something to say. The task is to deliver the message of substance in the clearest possible way. Almost always this means the shortest way. A person who reads a lot soon finds that writing is almost as easy as reading. Most effective officers read a lot, and not just instruction manuals.

Formal education is not a prerequisite for writing ability and having something to say. What is required is an interest in development of the skills and of the surrounding world. A few simple rules are helpful:

-The more simply a thing is said, the more powerfully it influences those who read it.

-There is always one best word to convey a thought or feeling. The use of a weaker substitute will deprive the writing of force and impact.

-Economy of words strengthens the writing.

According to Carl Sandburg, adverbs are better tools than adjectives because they enhance the verb and are active. Adjectives simply load down the noun.

Verbs make language live. The verb is the operative word; it gives the sentence meaning. Strength in sentence structure comes from emphasis on the verb.

An outline is imperative. It may exist only in the mind of the writer, but it must exist. Each piece of writing must have three things: a beginning, a middle and an end. Writing is similar to a journey. The destination--the conclusion--must be known before the effort is begun.

One must write with the words that most accurately express his/her thoughts. The words must be understandable to the audience. Anything else misses the point.

In conclusion, the important points are to master the language, practice the skills and have something to say.

CHAPTER 33

WRITING TIPS

1. When writing, don't tell the reader what you know. Tell the reader only what he or she needs to know, what it means, and why it matters.

2. When responding to someone, start with what concerns that person the most. When writing on your own, start with what concerns you most.

3. Most writers try to impress readers. The size of your words is less important than skill in manipulating the words you already know.

4. Written communications should follow the newspaper pattern. Open with the most important information and add the supplemental information later. Don't bury the main point somewhere in the middle.

5. Placement:
> -Put requests <u>before</u> justifications
> -Put answers <u>before</u> explanations
> -Put conclusions <u>before</u> discussions
> -Put summaries <u>before</u> details
> -Put general <u>before</u> specific

6. Written words should be in the same language as you might use in speaking. The most readable writing sounds like people talking to people.

7. When constructing sentences, vary sentence length. If you write a couple of 10-15 word sentences, follow up with a much shorter sentence, perhaps 4-6 words. This makes reading and understanding easier.

8. Short paragraphs are especially important at the start of correspondence. Long first paragraphs discourage reading. Call attention to lists of items or instructions by placing them in subparagraphs. Again, keep them simple.

9. Put the main point in the first paragraph, and keep that paragraph short and to the point.

10. The longer you take to get a point across, the weaker you come across and the more you risk masking important ideas.

11. Each paragraph should cover only one specific point. Use additional paragraphs as necessary. One sentence paragraphs are acceptable.

12. Use short paragraphs. Long paragraphs conceal ideas. Cover one topic completely before starting on another topic. A single topic may take more than one paragraph, but keep them short and simple.

13. Paragraphs with more than 10-12 sentences generally have to be read over more than once to ensure all the information is collected by the reader. Again, use short paragraphs.

14. Use personal pronouns. "We," "us," and "our" are more personal and are generally more accepted than stating a command or a billet position. When writing to a particular individual use "you."

15. Avoid words ending in "ion" and "ment" where possible.

16. Be sure to mention in the text any reference cited in the reference block. The first textual reference should be "reference (a)," the second would be "reference (b)" etc.

17. Remember, most "no" communications need some explanation. "Yes" answers need little explanation.

18. When you reach the end--STOP. When writing to persuade rather than just inform, you may want to end strongly--with a forecast, appeal, or implication. When feelings are involved, you may want to exit gracefully--with an expression of good will.

"Self-discipline is doing what NEEDS to be done, not what you WANT to do."
From the book: ***Successful Leadership Today***

Avoid these	Try these	Avoid these	Try these
accompany	go with	accorded	given
accordingly	so	adjacent to	next to
advantageous	helpful	allocate	divide, give
a number of	some	apparent	clean, plain
appreciable	many	approximately	about
ascertain	find out	attain	meet
attempt	try	benefit	help
capability	ability, can	close proximity	near
comply with	follow	component	part
consequently	so	contains	has
disclose	show	eliminate	cut, end
encounter	meet	endeavor	try
equivalent	equal	expeditious	fast, quick
expend	spend	facilitate	ease, help
feasible	workable	finalize	complete, finish
forward	send	frequently	often
furnish	give, send	however	but
identical	same	immediately	at once
inasmuch as	since	inception	start
incumbent upon	must	inform	tell
initiate	start	in order to	to
in the amount of	for	in the event that	if
in the near future	soon	in view of	since
is applicable to	applies to	is authorized to	may
limited number	few	magnitude	size
methodology	method	not later than	by
numerous	many	observe	see
perform	do	portion	part
promulgate	issue, publish	provided that	if
remain	stay	remainder	rest
requests	ask	set forth in	in
sufficient	enough	terminate	end, stop
transmit	send	utilization	use
with reference to	about		

Who uttered the now-famous words:
"We have met the enemy and they are ours?"
COMMODORE OLIVER HAZARD PERRY

CHAPTER 34

DRAFTING & WRITING EVALUATIONS & FITREPS

The Navy Eval & Fitrep Writing Guide, and its predecessor the *Enlisted Eval & Officer Fitrep Writing Guide*, has become the guide to use in writing evaluations and fitness reports since its first printing in 1984. Most of the information in this chapter comes from these books. *The Navy Eval & Fitrep Writing Guide* is a must for those individuals who want to give and receive the best evaluations possible. SEE INFORMATION IN THE BACK OF THIS BOOK TO ORDER THIS WRITING GUIDE.

PRIMARY OBJECTIVES OF GIVING ENLISTED EVALUATIONS
- Identify advancement, retention and future duty potential.
- Provide feedback to the evaluee.

PERFORMANCE MEASURED
- **PERSONAL TRAITS** - How something is done (for example, the leadership, initiative, etc. used or applied to accomplish something).
- **JOB PERFORMANCE** - What and how much is done.
- **JOB BEHAVIOR** - Appearance, adaptability, behavior, etc.

OBJECTIVE AND SUBJECTIVE ANALYSIS

- **OBJECTIVE ANALYSIS** should be used whenever possible to document an individual's performance. Objective analysis means to quantify performance results. How much was done? What was done" Use hours, time, percent, dollars, etc.

- **SUBJECTIVE ANALYSIS** is the evaluator's perceptions, beliefs, or thoughts on how something was accomplished. This is an analysis of a person's "inner" qualities (or personality) and must be based on observation over a period of time. Subjective analysis is used to describe what prompted or caused an individual to do something (personal traits such as leadership, imagination, etc.).

PREPARATION CHECK-LIST

The more knowledge and tools an evaluator has at his/her disposal the better. The following information should be reviewed PRIOR TO committing a subordinate's performance to print.

1. All performance appraisals should be handled discretely. They should be worked on in private.

2. Rough copies of past performance appraisals should be retained on file for reference in the next reporting period.

3. Insofar as practicable, reporting seniors should grade all evaluations of the same competitive category at one time. This will facilitate comparative grading.

4. Endeavor to obtain a just and equitable spread in the marks assigned to a comparative group.

5. Do not gravitate toward either a gratuitously high or rigidly severe policy of grading. The Navy is plagued by general over-assessment of average performers and occasional under assessment of "top performers." This serves to reduce the advancement opportunities of the "best qualified."

6. Exercise care to mark objectively, avoiding any tendency which might allow general impressions, a single incident or a particular trait, characteristic, or quality to influence other marks unduly.

7. When uncertain, due to limited observation, as to the appropriate evaluation of any rating area, mark the "Not Observed" block rather than assign a "middle-of-the-road" mark.

8. Avoid marking a new person somewhat lower than he/she deserves in order to reflect improved performance in subsequent evaluations. This malpractice can result in unjust advancement or assignment actions.

9. Before beginning to write, check over available performance data and determine which category you are going to place an individual being reported on:

a. Head and shoulders above contemporaries--promote now.
b. Above many contemporaries--promote above most.
c. Good performer - promote with majority of contemporaries.
d. Behind peer group performance - do not promote.

When a decision has been reached, write an evaluation that will support and justify your position.

10. The "head and shoulders" performers should be immediately identified at the start of the narrative. The remaining write-up must justify and reinforce your position.

11. Ensure that realistic marks are assigned to individuals whose performance of duty has been manifestly unsatisfactory. Impersonal grading and concise statements of fact best serve overall interests under such circumstances.

12. Conversely, ensure that due recognition is accorded when an individual demonstrates truly outstanding or exceptional professional competence and potential. In such cases accentuate the positive. State major accomplishments that have been achieved. More importantly, comment constructively on capacity or potential for future increased responsibility and advancement.

13. If the command has made an outstanding performance during the reporting period, an individual's contribution to this effect should be included in the write-up. Of course, the converse is true.

14. After completion of an evaluation, review previous worksheets on the same person, if available, to ensure that any changes in the marks on the current evaluation are intended. Any significant shift of marks in reports signed by the same reporting senior must be substantiated by the narrative.

15. When marking subsequent reports on the same person, guard against repetitive phraseology, as this will reflect lack of thought.

16. Before submitting a smooth evaluation, analyze the narrative to make sure that what is meant to be said is, in fact, actually being said, giving careful thought not only to what

chosen words mean to the evaluator, but also how they may be construed by a selection board.

17. When the evaluation is finished, review it to ensure that:
      - All parts are consistent (marks & narrative agree).
      - The trend in performance (increase or decrease) is correctly conveyed.

18. Bear in mind that evaluations reflect the degree and extent in which evaluators measure up to their moral obligation. And, an evaluator's write-up may be used to judge his/her evaluation.

19. Remember, words are both valuable and dangerous tools. Choose them carefully.

DO CHECK LIST

-DO submit evaluations on time and in correct format.
-DO write evaluations directed TO selection boards.
-DO write on how someone contributed above or below what is normally expected.
-DO write to express, not impress.
-DO be fair, honest, and objective.
-DO comment on growth potential and qualifications for promotion and future duty assignments.
-DO write on hard, pertinent facts, not "faint praises" without substance.
-DO use short, concise "bullets" or complete sentences with proper grammar.
-DO use underline to highlight key areas only.
-DO include specific extracurricular activities.

> *"Leadership is a function of interpersonal relationships."*
> From the book: **_Successful Leadership Today_**

> Who uttered the now-famous words:
> "I have not yet begun to fight?"
> JOHN PAUL JONES

DON'T CHECK LIST

-DON'T assign marks that are inconsistent with the narrative.

-DON'T write evaluations directed TO the individual.

-DON'T assign exceptionally high/low marks without comments in the narrative that clearly distinguish the performance.

-DON'T include minor, isolated, or insignificant imperfections which do not affect performance. Someone can be "Five-O" without being perfect.

-DON'T use glittering generalities which go on and on without saying anything useful.

-DON'T use long words when shorter words will do.

-DON'T be verbose or redundant.

-DON'T restate the job description in the narrative. That space is too valuable.

-DON'T write "During the period of this report," or words to that effect. It is understood, unless otherwise stated, that all actions and events in an evaluation occurred during the reporting period being covered. Again, narrative space is too valuable.

-DON'T start too many sentences with the same: Petty Officer... He...He...Petty Officer...He... etc. Reading becomes sluggish and boring and shows lack of attention or ability on the part of the drafter.

-DON'T use a person's name without associated rank. For example, do not write "Jones is..."' instead, it should be "Petty Officer Jones is..." An evaluation is an official document and an individual's rank should always accompany his/her name.

-DON'T use the term "ratee." It is too impersonal and impresses no one.

> *"Focus on results, not activity."*
> From the book: ***Successful Leadership Today***

> *"Leadership also means to stay out of the way."*
> From the book: ***Successful Leadership Today***

DRAFTING THE NARRATIVE

1. OBJECTIVE.   Evaluations should be drafted with two objectives in mind. These objectives are:

a. To document, in SPECIFIC terms, what an individual contributed to Navy, command, and department/division mission effectiveness and accomplishment; and,

b. To document the SUBJECTIVE "inner" qualities demonstrated by an individual on how performance was accomplished.

2. GUIDANCE.

a. BE POSITIVE. Any shortcoming or deficiency mentioned in the narrative should be significant, either in terms of performance or potential. At any level in an organization some occasional, routine guidance is necessary. If the comment is made that someone requires occasional instruction or guidance, that means he/she requires more instruction or guidance than would normally be expected. In effect, comments on minor deficiencies are automatically magnified when they are included in the narrative.

b. BE CONCISE. A direct hard-hitting write-up is better than an elegant one--concentrate more on content and specific accomplishments.

c. BE FACTUAL. Quantify individual achievement and accomplishments when possible.

d. BE SPECIFIC. A few well worded phrases or sentences on individual accomplishment and achievement mean much more than pages on billet description, command employment, etc.

e. BE OBJECTIVE. To the maximum extent possible, comment on quantifiable "objective" accomplishments, not on "subjective" personal notions.

3. STRUCTURE. The following evaluation structure has won wide acceptance in the Navy and is highly favored by Navy selection boards. Format in order given.

a. OPENING FORMAT
b. JOB ACCOMPLISHMENT
c. PERSONAL AND BEHAVIORAL TRAITS
d. CLOSING FORMAT

EVALUATION SAMPLE #1

Superior leader, manager, and organizer. Virtually unlimited potential. Continually supports and enforces command goals and policy. Mature, articulate, and dedicated, meets or exceeds all deadlines.

Accomplishments include:
- Reenlisted 7 of 8 eligible personnel.
-All personnel in (organization) qualified for advancement.
- Received Letter of Appreciation for outstanding work on, and support of command 3M duties.
- Qualified OOD (Inport) in 3 months. OOD Underway in 6 months. Less than half average time. Runs taut watch team and enjoys my complete confidence and support.
- Excels in self-directing and self-pacing.
- Attains quality results at any tasking level.
- Uses penetrating and objective analysis in arriving at decisions.
- Immaculate personal appearance.
- Cheerful, witty, and friendly, asset to high morale.
- Maintains articulate and up-to-date records.
- Active in community: Vice President PTA; Editor local VFW chapter newsletter; Church leader.

Unequaled ability to obtain maximum results of available material and manpower resources. Unyielding dedication and loyalty. Analytical in thought, reasoned in mind. Humane and compassionate. Seasoned counselor. Demanding yet fair, impressive leader and organizer. Strong moral fiber, respected by subordinates and superiors. Top achiever of boundless potential and ability.

> *"A man who is always ready to believe what is told him will never do well."* GAIUS PETRONIUS
> From the book: *Successful Leadership Today*

EVALUATION SAMPLE # 2

(Name) is a top performer. unlimited potential. Totally professional, poised, mature, and dedicated.

Significant achievements include:
-Awarded Navy Achievement Medal for ...
-Awarded Letter of Commendation from... for sustained superior performance during (period).
-Awarded Letter of Appreciation for off-duty assistance in civic functions.

Self-starter. Can plan, coordinate, direct, and finish job right the first time. Highlights of specific accomplishments include:

-Established superb supply system within (organization) that affords complete and accurate stock control management and auditing capabilities.

-(Organization) keyperson in Navy Relief, Combined Federal Campaign, and special Red Cross Drive. 100% participation.

-Drafted two command instructions and fifteen (organization) SOPs. All excellently researched, documented, and accurate.

-Managed and led 15-man "tiger team" in installation of new (equipment) and systems package. Completed three months ahead of schedule and $10,000 under budget.

Neat, trim, and fit. Immaculate "recruit poster" quality appearance. Articulate in speech, polite in manner. Submits timely and accurate paperwork. Enjoys loyalty, cooperation and support of subordinates. Intelligent and dedicated, always volunteers for additional work to help shipmates and increase own knowledge, skill, and worth. A rising star of unlimited potential. Highly qualified and recommended for any demanding and challenging billet within or two pay grades above present rate.

(Name) does not believe in idle time or unfinished projects. Manages own time and that of others to best possible advantage. Possesses managerial and organizational expertise rarely observed in contemporaries. Completes large volume of work each day, frequently working extra hours.

CHAPTER 35

DRAFTING & WRITING PERSONAL AWARDS

The following information was taken from the **_NAVY AND MARINE CORPS PERFORMANCE WRITING GUIDE._** See information in the back of this book for ordering this 300+ page writing guide.

In this section, PERSONAL AWARDS includes Navy Commendation Medals, Navy Achievement Medals, and other individual award medals. The drafting of all personal awards and most Letters of Commendation is a two-document process. A CITATION and a SUMMARY OF ACTION draft is required. The following guidance is offered for these two distinctly different drafts.

CITATION

The CITATION must meet strict, rigid requirements of uniformity and consistency.

NAME HEADING

Type complete name and rate in capital letters. Although the exact number of lines used to list this information is not mandated at Department of the Navy level, the information is routinely displayed on three lines for enlisted members and two lines for officers.

ENLISTED HEADING EXAMPLES

RADIOMAN FIRST CLASS
JOHN FITZGERALD KENNEDY
UNITED STATES NAVY

SENIOR CHIEF YEOMAN (SUBMARINES)
JOHN FITZGERALD KENNEDY
UNITED STATES NAVY

CITATION NARRATIVE

GENERAL RULES

1. DO NOT USE - "YOU." (Write in THIRD PERSON, i.e. HE, SHE.)

2. DO NOT USE - names, terms, etc., that are not readily and easily understandable to people not in the military.

3. DO NOT USE - "Petty Officer Second Class" Kennedy (use "Petty Officer Kennedy").

4. DO NOT USE - abbreviations such as LT, SN, etc. (use "Lieutenant," "Seaman" etc.).

5. DO NOT USE - information not included in the Summary of Action.

6. Local directives usually dictate the maximum number of typewritten lines allowed in the narrative. The general range is 15-20 lines. Check local reference material to assure conformance.

CITATION NARRATIVE PARTS

The citation narrative can be broken down into three distinct parts with specific information required in each part.

PART ONE

Part ONE gives standard wording for a particular award, the job/billet held, the command (and location if appropriate), and the inclusive period of the award. The Navy and Marine Corps Awards Manual provides specific wording which is to be used for each award. As an example, the Navy Achievement Medal may be awarded for either PROFESSIONAL ACHIEVEMENT or LEADERSHIP ACHIEVEMENT. ALL Navy Achievement Medals awarded for PROFESSIONAL ACHIEVEMENT require the wording: "For professional achievement in the superior performance of his duties..."

EXAMPLE:

"For professional achievement in the superior performance of his duties while assigned to (job/billet), (division, department, branch, etc.), (command), from (starting date) to (ending date).

PART TWO - FIRST SENTENCE

Part TWO starts with a single sentence which identifies the recipient by name and lists the outstanding personal attributes displayed. Following this first sentence note highlights of actual accomplishment/performance. The amount of space (total typewritten lines) available normally limits this information to 3-4 sentences).

EXAMPLE:

"...Displaying consistently high qualities of technical skill, resourcefulness, and dedication in the execution of his duties, (Name) demonstrated exceptional performance in a position of great responsibility."

PART TWO - AFTER FIRST SENTENCE

After the first sentence highlight the actual performance.

EXAMPLE:

"...He planned and directed implementation of the ... program, managed ..., and personally devised an ingenious ... plan. His diligent efforts and unending resourcefulness inspired all who observed him and contributed significantly to the mission of the command."

PART THREE

Part THREE ends the citation by naming the recipient and listing the personal attributes mentioned or implied in Part TWO, followed by:

"... reflected great credit upon himself and was/were in keeping with the highest traditions of the United States Naval Service."

EXAMPLE:

"...(Name) exceptional professional ability, initiative and loyal dedication to duty reflect great credit upon himself and the United States Naval Service."

SUMMARY OF ACTION

The Summary of Action is what reviewing/approving authorities scrutinize closely to determine if approval of an award is justified based on the criteria set forth in the Navy and Marine Corps Awards Manual.

Before attempting to write the Summary of Action, the drafter should know exactly all requirements stipulated for the award. For example, to be eligible for a Navy Achievement Medal for "professional achievement," the Award Manual states that an individual must:

"(a) clearly exceed that which is normally required or expected, considering the individual's grade or rate, training, and experience", and

"(b) be an important contribution which is of benefit to the United States and the Naval Service."

The Summary of Action MUST contain sufficient information to overpoweringly convince reviewing/awarding authorities that the individual being recommended for the award is fully deserving. This section MUST contain specific, and where appropriate, quantifiable, information (i.e. saved the Navy $30,000; reduced manpower requirements by 30,000 man hours, etc.).

There is no minimum or maximum length of the Summary of Action, so long as sufficient evidence is presented to justify approval of the award. Three pages of "glittering" generalities (i.e. top performer, limitless potential, etc.) will not carry as much convincing evidence as a single page of well documented "fact" on what was accomplished and how the individual directly contributed to the accomplishments.

> *Ask a different person for a new idea or suggestion—every day."*
> From the book: **Successful Leadership Today**

SUMMARY OF ACTION EXAMPLE

(Name) displayed outstanding professional performance from (starting date) to (ending date) while serving on (organization). During this period he made valuable and lasting contributions to command operational readiness and effectiveness. In his first assignment as ... he was faced with developing and implementing a training program that would prepare an inexperienced crew of ... personnel for full-scale... operations. He launched himself into his new and unaccustomed duties with uncommon zeal and vitality, working almost around the clock developing ... standards for virtually every supervisory and operational position in (organization). Within ... months qualifications were established and specific individual objectives were mandated. The program was such a success that in the next ... months (organization) received (number) performance evaluations with a grade of "OUTSTANDING" by (organization). His ... program enjoyed similar success. Overall qualification increased dramatically from ... percent to ... percent in less than ... months. As a final measure of his comprehensive training effort, (number) out of (number) were advanced during his tenure in this demanding billet.

During ... operations (Name) was cited in official correspondence by (organization) and (organization) for his professionalism and sterling performance.

As manning decreased significantly during ... period, (Name) volunteered and was assigned more responsibilities, including those of ... Within a short time he had assumed no fewer than (number) of primary and collateral duties, more than any other person in (organization). Each area of responsibility received his full attention and he labored long hours before and after the normal work day ensuring all tasks and projects were completed on or ahead of schedule. His assignment to ... duties proved immensely successful; (number) of (number) accomplished ...

> *"Spread the good news around.*
> *Keep bad news under wraps."*
> From the book: ***Successful Leadership Today***

(Name) mastery of any and all assignments ultimately led to his selection to one of the most demanding billets at (organization). As (billet title) he was tasked with the enormous duty of ... and he proved more than equal to the challenge. As a direct result of his diligent, untiring efforts, (organization) accomplished...

(Name) professional performance, initiative, and devotion to duty throughout his tour cannot adequately be reflected in a performance appraisal and is unquestionably worthy of recognition for this special award.

> What President and ex-Navyman was an
> All-American college football player? GERALD FORD

> *"One of the worst advisors a leader*
> *can have is a flatterer."*
> From the book: *Successful Leadership Today*

> *"Every man loves what he is good at."*
> THOMAS SHADWELL
> From the book: *Successful Leadership Today*

CHAPTER 36

WRITING SYMBOLS & SIGNS

APOSTROPHE

TO CREATE POSSESSIVE FORMS OF CERTAIN NOUNS.
-Add an apostrophe s when nouns do not end with an s.
-Add only the apostrophe to nouns that end in s or with an s sound.

officer's rank (singular)
officers' clubs (plural)
Smith's duty section (singular)
Jones' duty section (singular)

To show possession of compound nouns, add an apostrophe s to the final word.

secretary-treasurer's report
mother-in-law's car

To show joint possession for two or more nouns, add the apostrophe or apostrophe s to the last noun. Add only the apostrophe to plural nouns ending in s and apostrophe s to singular nouns.

girls and boys' club
Doug and Jan's son Ken

To show separate possession, place the possession indicators on each noun or pronoun identifying a possessor.

Doug's and Jan's cars
sailors' and soldiers' uniforms

TO FORM PLURALS OF CERTAIN LETTERS.
-Make lower-case letters plural by adding an apostrophe s.
-Upper-case letters are made plural by adding s alone unless confusion would result.

dotting the i's
crossing the t's
COs   XOs   SOS's

ASTERISK

An asterisk is used to refer the reader to footnote(s) at the bottom of a page.
Two asterisks** identify a second footnote.
Three asterisks*** identify a third footnote.

When more than three footnotes are used, numbered footnotes should be used.

BRACKETS

Brackets are used:...
TO CLARIFY OR CORRECT MATERIAL WRITTEN BY OTHERS.

She arrived on the 3rd (4th) of August.
The statute (sic) was added to the book of statutes.

NOTE: The word "sic" in brackets tells the reader that something is probably wrong with the word immediately in front of the first bracket but the word is reproduced exactly as it appeared in the original.

TO INSERT EXPLANATORY WORDS OR PHRASES WITHIN QUOTED MATERIAL.

"Tell them (the sailors) to report to their duty stations."

TO ENCLOSE A PHRASE THAT FALLS WITHIN PARENTHESES.

(It was noted that everyone attending (including the sailors) wore uniforms.)

TO INSERT EDITORIAL COMMENTS.

"Please welcome (audience rises) Commodore Jones."

"Consistent leadership removes much confusion, doubt, and misunderstanding."
From the book: **Successful Leadership Today**

COLON

The colon is used:

TO SEPARATE AN INTRODUCTORY STATEMENT FROM EXPLANATORY OR SUMMARIZING MATERIAL THAT FOLLOWS WHEN THERE IS NO COORDINATING CONJUNCTION OR TRANSITIONAL EXPRESSION.

> *They requested two documents: the O&R Manual and the ACT.*
> *We had only one place to go: over the side.*
> *The board consists of three officers: president, vice president, and secretary-treasurer.*

WHEN A SENTENCE CONTAINS AN EXPRESSION SUCH AS "THE FOLLOWING" OR "AS FOLLOWS" AND IS FOLLOWED DIRECTLY BY THE ITEMS.

> *Results were as follows: better morale, less work, and improved relations.*
>
> *The following pertain:*
> *1. A Navy ship.*
> *2. A Navy captain.*
> *3. At sea.*

NOTE: capitalization and punctuation above.

AS A FULL STOP WITH ENUMERATIONS.

> *He selected four people: Doug, James, Wayne, and Ken.*

WITH A QUOTATION WHEN THE WORD "SAY" OR A SUBSTITUTE FOR "SAY" HAS BEEN OMITTED.

> *The captain turned: "Who gave that order?"*

Do not use a colon...

WHEN THE ITEMS SHOWN IN ENUMERATION COMPLETE THE SENTENCE THAT INTRODUCES THEM.

> *Liaison officers must*
> *a. become familiar with the situation,*
> *b. know the mission, and*
> *c. arrange for communications.*

NOTE PUNCTUATION

WHEN AN EXPLANATORY SERIES FOLLOWS A PREPOSITION OR A VERB.

> *The committee consists of LT Jones, LT Frank, Chief Turner, and PO1 Jeffrey.*

TO INTRODUCE AN ENUMERATED LIST THAT IS A COMPLEMENT OR THE OBJECT OF AN ELEMENT IN THE INTRODUCTORY STATEMENT.

> *Our goals are to (1) learn the basic first aid elements, (2) apply the basic elements, and (3) save lives.*

COMMA

USE A COMMA...

-WITH THE COORDINATING CONJUNCTIONS "AND," "BUT," "OR," OR "NOR" WHEN THEY JOIN TWO OR MORE INDEPENDENT CLAUSES.

> *It was a good choice, but the other choices deserve future consideration.*

-TO SEPARATE THREE OR MORE WORDS IN A SERIES, INCLUDING THE WORD BEFORE THE FINAL "AND," "OR," OR "NOR."

> *He issues food, equipment, and clothing.*
> *The captain neither laughed, swore, nor joked.*

-WITH PARALLEL ADJECTIVES THAT MODIFY THE SAME NOUN.

> *If the order of the adjectives can be reversed or if "and" can stand between them, the adjectives are parallel and should be separated by a comma.*
> *a long, dry trip*
> *a cold, wet winter*

If the first adjective modifies the idea expressed by the combination of the second adjective and the noun, do not use a comma.

> *a heavy winter overcoat*

-WITH PARALLEL PHRASES OR CLAUSES.

> *The officer should be aware constantly that debts, personal health, or any one of many problems may destroy a person's peace of mind....*

-TO INDICATE OMISSION OF WORDS IN REPEATING A CONSTRUCTION.

> *We had a tactical reserve; now, nothing.*
> *The comma takes the place of "we have."*

-WITH WORDS, PHRASES, OR CLAUSES THAT EXPLAIN, DESCRIBE, OR IDENTIFY THE NOUN.

> *If nonessential, they are set off by commas.*
> *The executive officer, CDR Jones, was in a foul mood.*
> *This book, a writing guide, is an indispensable aid.*

If essential or restrictive in nature, they are not set off by commas.

> *My son Robert was the first to leave home.*
> *The aircraft carrier GEORGE WASHINGTON was away from its home port.*

-TO SET OFF INTERRUPTING WORDS, PHRASES, OR CLAUSES WHEN THEY BREAK THE FLOW OF THE SENTENCE.

> *The lieutenant, after all, was an experienced pilot.*
> *This, indeed, was exactly what they wanted.*

-AFTER INTRODUCTORY SUBORDINATE CLAUSES.

> *When the captain entered the wardroom, everyone came to their feet.*

-TO SEPARATE TWO OR MORE COMPLEMENTARY PHRASES THAT REFER TO A SINGLE WORD THAT FOLLOWS.

> *The coldest, if not the most severe, winter we have had was in 1991.*

-TO SET OFF DATES, ADDRESSES, PLACE NAMES, AND WORDS IDENTIFYING A TITLE OR POSITION FOLLOWING A PERSON'S NAME.

> *The date of the party, 4 August 1996, was the turning point.*
> *We visited 10 Downing Street, London, England in 1987.*
> *The address was 2348 Main street, Wichita, Kansas 33042.*

NOTE: DO NOT place a comma between a state and ZIP code.

-TO SET OFF CONTRASTING ELEMENTS INTRODUCED BY "NOT" OR "BUT."

> *He was a captain, not a commander.*
> *I am willing to sell, but only on my terms.*

-TO SET OFF STATEMENTS SUCH AS "..SAID," OR "...REPLIED."

> *The admiral said, "Welcome to the U.S. Navy."*
> *He replied, "I have to leave by noon."*

-WITH THE ADVERB "TOO."

When the adverb "too" (meaning also) occurs at the end of a sentence or clause, do not use a comma before "too."

> *You should try to improve your typing too.*
> *When "too" occurs elsewhere in the sentence,*
> *particularly between subject and verb, set it off.*
> *You, too, can save money by shopping selectively.*

-AFTER INTRODUCTORY WORDS SUCH AS "YES," "NO," OR "OH."

> *Yes, I'll do it.*
> *Oh, I see.*

-WITH AFTERTHOUGHTS (WORDS, PHRASES, OR CLAUSES LOOSELY ADDED TO THE END OF A SENTENCE)

> *Send the flowers as soon as possible, please.*

-TO PREVENT CONFUSION OR MISREADING.

> *To John, Smith was an honorable man.*
> *For each group of 20, 10 were rejected.*
> *Soon after, the meeting was interrupted abruptly.*

-TO SEPARATE REPEATED WORDS.

> *That was a long, long time ago.*
> *Well, well, look who's here.*

"Honesty is the trait most favored by others."
From the book: **Successful Leadership Today**

DASH

A dash is used...

-TO INDICATE A SUDDEN BREAK OR ABRUPT CHANGE IN THOUGHT THAT CAUSES AN ABRUPT CHANGE IN SENTENCE STRUCTURE.

> *He is going--no, he's turning back.*
> *The publication update should be--no, will be-- completed by the end of the month.*

-TO GIVE SPECIAL EMPHASIS TO THE SECOND INDEPENDENT CLAUSE IN A COMPOUND SENTENCE.

> *That restaurant is great--it's economical too.*
> *This plan will double our productivity--and I can prove it.*

-TO EMPHASIZE SINGLE WORDS.

> *Dan--he's all she ever talks about.*
> *They're after one thing--money--nothing else matters.*

-TO EMPHASIZE OR RESTATE A PREVIOUS THOUGHT.

> *Last week one day--Wednesday, I think--we went to lunch.*

-BEFORE SUMMARIZING WORDS SUCH AS "THESE," "THEY," AND "ALL" WHEN THEY SUMMARIZE A SERIES OF IDEAS OR LIST OF DETAILS.

> *A bat, ball, and tennis racket--these are the only recreational items you'll need for the weekend.*
> *Faculty, staff, and students--all are invited.*

-IN PLACE OF COMMAS TO SET OFF A NONESSENTIAL ELEMENT THAT REQUIRES SPECIAL EMPHASIS.

> *There is a typo in one of these paragraphs--the fourth one.*
> *We will see that all staff officers--as well as members of the ship--have a chance to play in the game.*

-TO SET OFF A NONESSENTIAL ELEMENT WHEN THE NONESSENTIAL ELEMENT CONTAINS INTERNAL COMMAS.

> *All of these subjects--accounting, calculus, and speech--are required courses.*

-INSTEAD OF PARENTHESES WHEN A NONESSENTIAL ITEM REQUIRES STRONG EMPHASIS (DASHES EMPHASIZE; PARENTHESES DE-EMPHASIZE).

> *Call Lieutenant Jones--he's the expert--and get his opinion.*

HYPHEN

A hyphen is used...

-TO INDICATE THE CONTINUATION OF A WORD DIVIDED AT THE END OF A LINE.

> *Use a hyphen to indicate the contin-*
> *uation of a word divided at the end of a line.*

-TO CONNECT THE ELEMENTS OF CERTAIN COMPOUND WORDS AND WHEN "EX" IS ATTACHED TO A NOUN.

> *She exhibited great self-control.*
> *The ex-mayor was in town.*
> *We shopped at the duty-free store.*

-TO INDICATE TWO OR MORE RELATED COMPOUND WORDS HAVING A COMMON BASE (SUSPENDED HYPHEN).

> *A 12- to 15-page document.*
> *Long- and short-term money rates are available.*

-WHEN DESCRIBING FAMILY RELATIONS INVOLVING GREAT- AND -IN-LAW.

> *great-grandfather*   *great-uncle*
> *father-in-law*   *sister-in-law*

-TO HYPHENATE PHRASES USED AS COMPOUND ADJECTIVES BEFORE A NOUN.

> *an up-to-date report*
> *a question-and-answer session*
> *a first-come-first-served basis*

-WHEN EXPRESSING THE NUMBERS 21 THROUGH 99 IN WORDS AND IN WORDS WITH A NUMERICAL FIRST ELEMENT.

> *twenty-one people were there*
> *eighty-nine miles from here*
> *3-years old*
> *a 10-minute delay*

-TO LINK NUMBERS THAT REPRESENT A CONTINUOUS SEQUENCE WHEN THEY ARE NOT INTRODUCED BY THE WORD "FROM" OR "BETWEEN."

during the years 1988-1993   from 1988 to 1993
on pages 15-30 of ...   between pages 15 and 30 of

-TO JOIN SINGLE CAPITAL LETTERS TO NOUNS OR PARTICIPLES.

T-square   U-boat   X-ray   H-bomb

PARENTHESES

Are used...

-TO ENCLOSE MATERIAL THAT IS INDEPENDENT OF THE MAIN THOUGHT OF THE SENTENCE.

Our car (Mercedes-Benz) will arrive today.
The results (see Figure 3) were surprising.

-TO SET OFF ELEMENTS WHEN COMMAS WOULD BE INAPPROPRIATE OR CONFUSING.

The committee will meet two days a week (Monday and Wednesday).
Contact Commander Jones (if you want another opinion) and ask his advice.

-TO ENCLOSE LETTERS OR NUMBERS WITHIN A SENTENCE.

My aim is to (1) rewrite the 0&R Manual, (2) update the SORM, and (3) go on early liberty.

PERIOD

The period is used...

-TO END A SENTENCE.

Commander Jones went to work.

-TO INDICATE AN OMISSION WITHIN A SENTENCE OF FRAGMENTED SPEECH. (In these cases use 3 spaced periods)

In broad terms, work measurement is . . . to work produced.
(In the case of omission at the end of a sentence, use 4 spaced periods.)
In broad terms....

QUESTION MARK

A question mark is used...

-TO INDICATE THE END OF A DIRECT QUESTION.

What did Commander Jones call you about?

QUOTATION MARKS

Quotation marks are used...

-TO ENCLOSE THE EXACT WORDS OF A DIRECT QUOTATION.

Commander Jones said, "Will the ship arrive on schedule."

-TO ENCLOSE A SLOGAN OR MOTTO.

He had a "do or die" attitude.
It was a "gentlemen's agreement."

-TO ENCLOSE WORDS OR PHRASES USED TO INDICATE HUMOR, SLANG, IRONY, OR POOR GRAMMAR.

They serve "fresh" seafood all right--fresh from the freezer.
For whatever reason, she just "ain't talkin'."

-WITH WORDS AND PHRASES THAT ARE INTRODUCED BY SUCH EXPRESSIONS AS "MARKED," "SIGNED," DESIGNATED," AND "CLASSIFIED," WHEN THE EXACT MESSAGE IS QUOTED.

The card was signed "Your friend."
The package was stamped "fragile."
The report is classified "secret" and will not be distributed.

SEMICOLON

A semicolon is used...

TO SEPARATE INDEPENDENT CLAUSES NOT CONNECTED BY A COORDINATING CONJUNCTION (AND, BUT, FOR, OR, NOR, SO), AND IN STATEMENTS THAT ARE TOO CLOSELY RELATED IN MEANING TO BE WRITTEN AS SEPARATE SENTENCES.

The students were ready and it was time to go.
The students were ready; it was time to go.
It's true in peace; it's true in war.

-BEFORE WORDS AND PHRASES SUCH AS "HOWEVER," "THEREFORE," "HENCE," "FURTHERMORE," "AS A RESULT," "CONSEQUENTLY," "MOREOVER,"

"NEVERTHELESS," "FOR EXAMPLE" WHEN THEY CONNECT TWO COMPLETE BUT RELATED THOUGHTS. (These words and phrases are followed by a comma.)

> *Our expenses have increased; however, we haven't received an increase in our budget.*
> *The admiral had heard the briefing before; thus, he chose not to attend.*

-TO PRECEDE WORDS OR ABBREVIATIONS THAT INTRODUCE A SUMMARY OR EXPLANATION OF WHAT HAS GONE BEFORE IN THE SENTENCE.

> *There are many things you must arrange for before leaving on vacation; for example: mail pickup, pet care, yard care.*

"*Enhance relationships and you enhance teamwork.*"
From the book: ***Successful Leadership Today***

"**Be just and fear not.**" WILLIAM SHAKESPEARE
From the book: ***Successful Leadership Today***

In what year did Congress give the Secretary of the Navy authorization to name all Navy ships.?
1819

CHAPTER 37

ARMED FORCES CHAIN-OF-COMMAND

(OPERATIONAL)

AT THE HIGHEST LEVELS.
I. The President of the United States is Commander in Chief of the U.S. Armed Services.

2. The Secretary of Defense (SECDEF) is the next person in the operational chain-of-command of U.S. military forces.

At this point in the chain-of-command the operational responsibilities and support/administrative responsibilities go in different directions.

The Secretary of the Navy (SECNAV) has support responsibilities, but not operational authority or responsibility.

The Chairman of the Joint Chiefs of Staff, and Joint Chiefs of Staff (heads of military services) have no independent operational control of the military services. However, the Chairman of the Joint Chiefs of Staff functions within the chain of command by transmitting communications to the commanders of the combatant commands from the President and Secretary of Defense. Neither the Chairman nor the Joint Chiefs have executive authority over any combatant command.

3. **COMBATANT COMMANDS.** U.S. combatant commands include UNIFIED COMMANDS and SPECIFIED COMMANDS.

a. **UNIFIED COMMAND.** The unified command is a command with a broad, continuing mission and is composed of forces from two or more military departments under a single commander. Currently there are eight (8) unified commands.
      (1) U.S. EUROPEAN COMMAND (CINCEUR)
      (2) U.S. PACIFIC COMMAND (CINCPAC)
      (3) U.S. ATLANTIC COMMAND (CINCLANT)
      (4) U.S. SOUTHERN COMMAND(CINCSOUTH)
      (5) U.S. CENTRAL COMMAND (CINCCENT)
      (6) U.S. SPACE COMMAND (CINCSPACE)

(7) U.S. TRANSPORTATION COMMAND (CINCTRANS)
(8) U.S. SPECIAL OPERATIONS (CINCSOC)

b. **SPECIFIED COMMAND.** The specified command is a command with a broad, continuing mission and is composed of forces from a single military department under a single commander. There are currently two (2) specified commands.
(1) FORCES COMMAND (FORSCOM) - U.S. Army only
(2) STRATEGIC AIR COMMAND(SAC) - U.S. Air Force only

4. **COMPONENT COMMANDS.** The Navy (and the Army and Air Force) have component commands within each unified command. These component commands have both operational and administrative control over assigned forces. Administratively Navy component commanders report to the Chief of Naval Operations (CNO). Operationally they report to the appropriate unified commander.

The Navy has three (3) major component commanders.
a. COMMANDER IN CHIEF U.S. ATLANTIC FLEET (CINCLANTFLT)
b. COMMANDER IN CHIEF U.S. PACIFIC FLEET (CINCPACFLT)
c. COMMANDER IN CHIEF U.S. NAVAL FORCES, EUROPE (CINCUSNAVEUR)

NOTE: CINCPAC (Unified Command) and CINCPACFLT (Component Command) are two commands headed by the same four- star admiral; and, CINCLANT (Unified Command) and CINCLANTFLT (Component Command) are two commands headed by the same four-star admiral. These two admirals are said to wear "dual hats."

5. **NUMBERED FLEETS.** The next breakdown of the operating forces is into numbered fleets. The commanders of these numbered fleets have responsibilities that encompass the oceans of the world. There are four numbered fleets.

"Having a voice in the decision stimulates the action."
From the book: ***Successful Leadership Today***

---

a. **COMMANDER THIRD FLEET** (COMTHIRDFLT)
b. **COMMANDER SEVENTH FLEET**   (COMSEVENTHFLT)

The above commanders report to the Commander-in- Chief Pacific Fleet.   Their areas of responsibility encompass the Pacific and Indian Oceans.

c. **COMMANDER SECOND FLEET (COMSECONDFLT).** This commander reports to the Commander-in- Chief Atlantic Fleet. Areas of responsibility encompass the Atlantic, the Caribbean and the Pacific Oceans adjacent to the west coast of Central and South America.

d.   **COMMANDER SIXTH FLEET (COMSIXTHFLT)**. The Commander Sixth Fleet reports to the Commander-in-Chief United States Naval Forces Europe.   Areas of responsibility encompass the Mediterranean Sea and the Black Sea.

6. **TASK FORCE.** The level below numbered fleets is TASK FORCE. A task force is a subdivision of a fleet composed of several types of ships, submarines and aircraft according to the operational necessity.   There is no set size of composition of a task force. The specific "task" determines size and composition.

Several task-oriented groups that have commonly used titles are:
   a. CARRIER BATTLE GROUPS
   b. AMPHIBIOUS TASK FORCES
   c. UNDERWAY REPLENISHMENT GROUPS
   d. CONVOY ESCORT GROUPS

Naval forces must control the multi-dimensional threat posed by enemy forces in the there naval warfare areas: the air, the surface, and the subsurface.

Each naval platform (ship, submarine, or aircraft) is designed to accomplish a specific naval warfare task, often while performing other warfare tasks simultaneously. These tasks include:
   a. ANTI-AIR WARFARE (AAW)
   b. ANTI-SUBMARINE WARFARE (ASW)
   c. ANTI-SURFACE SHIP WARFARE (ASUW)
   d. STRIKE WARFARE
   e. AMPHIBIOUS WARFARE
   f. MINE WARFARE

and supporting warfare tasks such as:
    g. ELECTRONIC WARFARE (EW)
    h. COMMAND, CONTROL, & COMMUNICATIONS (C3)
    i. INTELLIGENCE
    j. SPECIAL OPERATIONS
    k. LOGISTICS
    l. OCEAN SURVEILLANCE
All of the above factors are taken into account when assembling a task force.

7. **TASK GROUP.** A task force is divided into TASK GROUPS. A task group may include an aircraft carrier, a cruiser, a submarine, amphibious craft, and various auxiliary vessels.

8. **TASK UNIT.** Task groups are further divided in to TASK UNITS. Task units normally consist of a small number of individual operational commands.

9. **TASK ELEMENT.** A TASK ELEMENT is the smallest unit of a task force. A task element will be an individual detachment, ship, submarine, or aircraft squadron.

10. **TASK NUMERICAL DESIGNATION.** Each level of command in a task force has a corresponding number designation which is used for communications and coordination purposes.

Example:
TF 21   is a task force of the 2nd Fleet
TG 21.1   is a task group of Task Force 21
TU 21.1.2   is a task unit of Task Group 21.1
TE 21.1.2.3 is a task element of Task Unit 21.1.2

SUMMARY. If you were on a ship with the above designation of TE 21.1.2.3, from top to bottom, your chain-of command for operational purposes would be as follows.
    a. PRESIDENT OF THE UNITED STATES
    b. SECRETARY OF DEFENSE (SECDEF)
    c. CINCLANT (UNIFIED COMMANDER)
    d. CINCLANTFLT (COMPONENT COMMANDER)
    e. COMSECONDFLT
    f. COMMANDER TASK FORCE 21
    g. COMMANDER TASK GROUP 21.1
    h. COMMANDER TASK UNIT 21.1.2
    i. COMMANDING OFFICER (TE 21.1.2.3)

NAVY CHAIN-OF-COMMAND

(ADMINISTRATIVE)

The Navy's operating forces are supported by the administrative chain of command which oversees the training, readiness, administration, and logistical support functions.

1. **SECRETARY OF THE NAVY (SECNAV).** The Secretary of the Navy is the head of the Department of the Navy. Under the direction, authority, and control of the Secretary of Defense, he is responsible for the following.

a. The functioning and efficiency of the Department of the Navy.

b. The formulation of policies and programs by the Department of the Navy that are fully consistent with national security objectives and policies established by the President or the Secretary of Defense.

c. The effective and timely implementation of policy, program and budget decisions and instructions of the President or Secretary of Defense relating to the functions of the Department of the Navy.

d. Carrying out the functions of the Department of the Navy so as to fulfill (to the maximum extent practicable) the current and future operational requirements of the unified and specified combatant commands.

e. Effective cooperation and coordination between the Department of the Navy and the other military departments and agencies of the Department of Defense to provide for more effective, efficient and economical administration and to eliminate duplication.

f. The presentation and justification of the position of the Department of the Navy on the plans, programs and policies of the Department of Defense.

g. The effective supervision and control of the intelligence activities of the Department of the Navy.

h. Such other activities as may be prescribed by law or by the President of Secretary of Defense.

2. **CHIEF OF NAVAL OPERATIONS (CNO).** The Chief of Naval Operations is the professional head of the Navy. In the performance of duties within the Department of the Navy, the CNO takes precedence above all other officers of the naval service, except an officer of the naval service who is serving as Chairman or Vice Chairman of the Joint Chiefs of Staff. He is a member of the JCS and the principle advisor to the President, SECDEF, and SECNAV on naval matters. Except where responsibility rests with the Commandant of the Marine Corps, he exercises overall authority throughout the Department of the Navy. The CNO is assisted by the Vice Chief of Naval Operations (VCNO), by several deputy chiefs (DCNO's) and assistant chiefs (ACNO's), and by a variety of program directors. These officers and their staffs make up the Office of Chief of Naval Operations (OPNAV). In operational matters CNO has no direct operational/executive authority over naval forces that are under command of a unified or specified commander. His voice/input in operational matters for unified or specified commands is a function of his role as a member of the JCS.

3. **NAVAL COMPONENT COMMANDS.** Component commands have both operational and administrative control over assigned forces. The Navy's major component commands are:
>   a. COMMANDER IN CHIEF U.S. ATLANTIC FLEET (CINCLANTFLT)
>   b. COMMANDER IN CHIEF U.S. PACIFIC FLEET (CINCPACFLT)
>   c. COMMANDER IN CHIEF U.S. NAVAL FORCES EUROPE (CINCUSNAVEUR)

4. **TYPE COMMANDS.** The Atlantic and Pacific fleets are organized into administrative commands by type. The major type commands are fleet training commands, submarine forces, surface forces, and naval air forces. Type commands administratively own ships, submarines and aircraft and are responsible for making assignments to operational commands.

Examples of type commands:

COMMANDER SUBMARINE FORCES ATLANTIC (COMSUBLANT)

COMMANDER NAVAL SURFACE FORCES PACIFIC (COMNAVSURFPAC)

COMMANDER NAVAL AIR FORCES ATLANTIC (COMNAVAIRLANT)

5. **GROUP COMMANDS.** Under each type command, ships, submarines and aircraft are under a group commander. Group commands usually control units within a given geographic location. They are responsible for assisting the type command in carrying out assigned administrative tasks.

Examples of group commands:

COMMANDER CRUISER-DESTROYER GROUP 12 (COMCRUDESGRU 12)

COMMANDER SUBMARINE GROUP EIGHT (COMSUBGRU 8)

COMMANDER CARRIER GROUP TWO (COMCARGRU 2)

COMMANDER PATROL AIR GROUP, ATLANTIC (COMPATWINGSLANT)

6. **SQUADRON/AIR WING COMMANDS.** Group commands are further divided into ship/ submarine squadrons and/or air wing commands. Squadrons and air wings usually control similar vessels or aircraft within a specific geographic location (homeport/air station).

Examples of squadron/air wing commands:

COMMANDER DESTROYER SQUADRON EIGHT (COMDESRON 8)

COMMANDER SUBMARINE SQUADRON TEN (COMSUBRON 10)

COMMANDER TRAINING WING SIX (COMTRAWING 6)

7. **INDIVIDUAL UNIT COMMANDS.** Each individual command (ship/submarine or aircraft squadron) represents an administrative and operational unit, with the commanding officer exerting administrative and operational control over the personnel and equipment assigned.

Examples of individual unit commands:
USS WASP (LHD-1)
FITRON 201 (VF-201)
PATRON 5 (VP-5)

"Anyone who stops learning is old, whether at twenty or eighty. Anyone who keeps learning stays young."
HENRY FORD
From the book: **Successful Leadership Today**

"So much of what we call management consists of making it difficult for people to work." PETER DRUCKER
From the book: **Successful Leadership Today**

In what year did women first attend the U.S. Naval Academy?   1976

"When you betray someone else, you also betray yourself." ISAAC SINGER
From the book: **Successful Leadership Today**

CHAPTER 38

UNITED STATES NAVY ORGANIZATION

PRIMARY FUNCTIONS

1. To organize, train, and equip Navy and Marine Corps forces to conduct prompt and sustained combat operations at sea. These operations include those of sea-based aircraft and land-based naval air components. Specifically, these forces seek out and destroy enemy naval forces, suppress enemy sea commerce, and gain and maintain naval supremacy. They control vital sea areas and protect vital sea lines of communication. They establish and maintain naval and air superiority in an area of naval operations. They seize and defend advanced naval based and conduct land and air operations as needed to carry out naval campaigns.

2. To coordinate with other U.S. military services to provide, organize, and equip naval forces (including naval close air-support forces) to conduct joint amphibious operations.

3. To furnish adequate, timely, and reliable intelligence for the Navy and Marine Corps.

4. To organize, train, and equip naval forces for naval reconnaissance, antisubmarine warfare, protection of shipping, and mine laying (including air and controlled mine field operations).

5. To provide air support essential for naval operations.

6. To provide sea-based air defense and sea-based means for coordinating control for defense against air attack, coordinating with other U.S. military services in matters of joint concern.

7. To provide naval forces, including naval air forces, for defense of the United States against air attack.

OVERALL MISSION. The Navy's overall mission is: "...to be prepared to conduct prompt and sustained combat operations at sea...." The following four naval missions support the accomplishment of this overall mission:

1. Strategic Deterrence
2. Peacetime Presence
3. Power Projection
4. Sea Control (keeping the sea lanes open)

DEPARTMENT OF THE NAVY. The Department of the Navy is made up of the U.S. Navy and the U.S. Marine Corps. Individual commands within the Department of the Navy are divided into three functional components:
1. Navy Department
2. Shore Establishment
3. Operating Forces

NAVY DEPARTMENT. The Navy Department as the central executive authority refers to the central executive offices of the Department of the Navy located at the seat of government. The Navy Department includes:
1. Under Secretary of the Navy
2. Assistant Secretaries
3. Chief of Naval Operations
4. Commandant of the Marine Corps
5. Office of Legislative Affairs
6. Office of Information
7. Office of the Judge Advocate General
8. Office of the Auditor General

The Navy Department assists the Secretary of the Navy (SECNAV) in carrying out the responsibilities of that office. SECNAV is responsible, under the Secretary of Defense (SECDEF), for the policies and control of the Navy. These include its organization, administration, operation, and efficiency.

The Navy Department functions to establish policy, provide direction, and exert control over the operations of the other two components of the Department, that is, the Shore Establishment and the Operating Forces of the Navy.

SHORE ESTABLISHMENT. The Shore Establishment encompasses shore activities with defined missions approved for establishment by the SECNAV. The function of the Shore Establishment is to supply, maintain, and support the Operating Forces through the furnishing of required materials, services, and personnel. A representative list of such activities includes:

1. Naval Air Stations
2. Naval Facilities
3. Reserve Training Centers
4. Computer & Telecommunications Stations
5. Recruiting Stations
6. Shipyards
7. Naval Bases
8. Naval Stations
9. Naval Supply Centers

OPERATING FORCES. The Operating Forces of the Navy are combat or combat-support oriented. Combat forces and certain supporting forces are assigned for duty under the commander of a unified or specified command. The Operating Forces of the Navy include those forces assigned to:

1. CINCLANTFLT
2. CINCPACFLT
3. CINCUSNAVEUR
4. FLEET MARINE FORCES
5. MILITARY SEALIFT COMMAND
6. MINE WARFARE COMMAND
7. NAVAL RESERVE FORCE
8. OPERATIONAL TEST AND EVALUATION FORCE
9. U.S. NAVAL FORCES CENTRAL COMMAND
10. U.S. NAVAL FORCES SOUTHERN COMMAND
11. Shore activities assigned to the Operating Forces.

"All problems become smaller if you don't dodge them but confront them." ADM WILLIAM F. HALSEY
From the book: **Successful Leadership Today**

What future President was the youngest man in Naval history to earn his "Wings of Gold," at age 18?
GEORGE BUSH

CHAPTER 39

NAVY SHIPS

SHIP CLASSIFICATIONS

The U.S. Navy has used letter symbols to identify the different types of ships since the 1920s. The following ship classifications are provided:

AD	Destroyer Tender
AE	Ammunition Ship
AFS	Combat Store Ship
AGSS	Auxiliary Research Submarine
AH	Hospital Ship
AOE	Fast Combat Support Ship
AOR	Replenishment Oiler
AR	Repair Ship
ARS	Salvage Ship
AS	Submarine Tender
ASR	Submarine Rescue Ship
ATF	Fleet Ocean Tug
BB	Battleship
CG	Guided Missile Cruiser
CGN	Guided Missile Cruiser (Nuclear)
CV	Multi-Purpose Aircraft Carrier
CVN	Multi-Purpose Aircraft Carrier (Nuclear)
DD	Destroyer
DDG	Guided Missile Destroyer
DSRV	Deep Submergence Rescue Vehicle
FF	Frigate
FFG	Guided Missile Frigate
LCC	Amphibious Command Ship
LCM	Landing Craft, Mechanized
LCU	Landing Craft, Utility
LCVP	Landing Craft, Vehicle Personnel
LHA	Amphibious Assault Ship/General Purpose Assault Ship
LHD	Multipurpose Assault Ship
LKA	Amphibious Cargo Ship
LPD	Amphibious Transport Dock
LPH	Amphibious Assault Ship (Helicopter)
LSD	Landing Ship, Dock
LST	Landing Ship, Tank

MCM	Mine Countermeasures Ship
MHC	Mine Hunter, Coastal
PB	Patrol Boat
PBR	Patrol Boat, River
PHM	Guided Missile Patrol Combatant (Hydrofoil)
SS	Submarine
SSBN	Submarine, Ballistic Missile (Nuclear)
SSN	Submarine (Nuclear)

BALLISTIC MISSILE SUBMARINES

OHIO CLASS (SSBN-726)
Displacement: 18,700 tons submerged
Length: 560 feet
Beam: 42 feet
Speed: 20-plus knots
Power Plant: 1 nuclear reactor, 2 geared turbines, 1 shaft
Armament: 24 tubes for Trident I and II missiles
4 torpedo tubes
Complement: 165

BENJAMIN FRANKLIN, LAFAYETTE, AND JAMES MADISON
CLASS
Displacement: 18,700 tons submerged
Length: 425 feet
Beam: 33 feet
Speed: 20-plus knots
Power Plant: 1 nuclear reactor, 2 geared turbines, 1 shaft
Armament: 16 tubes for Poseidon or Trident I Missiles,
4 torpedo tubes
Complement: 139

ATTACK SUBMARINES

SEAWOLF CLASS (SSN-21)

The SSN 21-class submarine is designed to be a quiet, fast and
well-armed submarine with advanced sensors. It is designed to
be capable of deploying to forward ocean areas to search out
and destroy enemy submarines and surface ships and attack
land targets. The many new features of this submarine
represent a dramatic improvement over earlier designs.

LOS ANGELES CLASS (SSN-688)
Displacement: 6,900 tons submerged
Length: 360 feet
Beam: 33 feet
Speed: 20-plus knots
Power Plant: 1 nuclear reactor, 2 geared turbines, 1 shaft
Armament: Harpoon and Tomahawk Missiles, MK-48 Torpedoes, with 4 torpedo tubes
Complement: 142

STURGEON CLASS (SSN-637)
Displacement: 4,640 tons submerged
Length: 292 feet
Beam: 32 feet
Speed: 20-plus knots
Power Plant: 1 nuclear reactor, 2 steam turbines, 1 shaft
Armament: Harpoons, Tomahawks, Torpedoes (4 tubes)
Complement: 140

AIRCRAFT CARRIERS

NIMITZ CLASS (CVN-68)
Displacement: 92,000-97,000 tons (full load)
Length: 1,040 feet
Beam: 134 feet
Flight Deck Width: 252 feet
Speed: 30-plus knots
Power Plant: 2 nuclear reactors, 4 geared steam turbines, 4 shafts
Aircraft: 85
Armament: Sea Sparrow Missiles, Phalanx Close-In Weapons Systems (3 on CVN-68/69) (4 on CVN-70-75)
Complement: 3,200 ship's company, 2,480 air wing

ENTERPRISE CLASS (CVN-65)
Displacement: 89,600 tons (full load)
Length: 1,040 feet
Beam: 133 feet
Flight Deck Width: 252 feet
Speed: 30-plus knots

Power Plant: 8 nuclear reactors, 4 geared steam turbines, 4 shafts
Aircraft: 85
Armament: Sea Sparrow Missiles
3 Phalanx Close-In Weapons Systems
Complement: 3,350 ship's company, 2,480 air wing

JOHN F. KENNEDY CLASS (CV-67)
Displacement: 82,000 tons (full load)
Length: 1,052 feet
Beam: 130 feet
Flight Deck Width: 252 feet
Speed: 30-plus knots
Power Plant: 8 boilers, 4 geared steam turbines, 4 shafts, 280,000 shaft horsepower
Aircraft: 85
Armament: Sea Sparrow Missiles
3 Phalanx Close-In Weapons Systems
Complement: 3,117 ship's company, 2,480 air wing

CRUISERS

TICONDEROGA CLASS (CG-47)
Displacement: 9,600 tons (full load)
Length: 567 feet
Beam: 55 feet
Speed: 30-plus knots
Power Plant: 4 gas turbines, 2 shafts,
80,000 shaft horsepower total
Aircraft: 2 SH-60 (LAMPS III)
Armament: Standard Missile (MR); Anti-Submarine Rocket (ASROC); Tomahawk ASM/LAM; 6 MK-46 Torpedoes (2-triple tube mounts); 2 5-inch/54 caliber MK-45 lightweight guns; 2 Phalanx Close-In Weapon Systems.
Complement: 364 (24 officers, 340 enlisted)

VIRGINIA CLASS (CGN-38)
Displacement: 11,000 tons (full load)
Length: 585 feet
Beam: 63 feet
Speed: 30-plus knots
Power Plant: 2 nuclear reactors, 2 geared turbines, 2 shafts

Aircraft: none
Armament: Standard Missile (MR); 8 Harpoons, 8 Tomahawks, 6 MK-46 Torpedoes, 2 5-inch/54 MK-45 lightweight guns; 2 Phalanx Close-In Weapon Systems
Complement: 578 (39 officers, 539 enlisted)

CALIFORNIA CLASS (CGN-36)
Displacement: 10,450 tons (full load)
Length: 596 feet
Beam: 61 feet
Speed: 30-plus knots
Power Plant: 2 nuclear reactors, 2 geared turbines, 2 shafts
Aircraft: none
Armament: Standard Missiles (MR), 8 Harpoons, ASROC (MK-16 box launcher; 4 MK-46; 2 5-inch'54 caliber MK-45 lightweight guns; 2 Phalanx Close-In Weapon Systems
Complement: 584 (40 officers, 544 enlisted)

TRUXTUN CLASS (CGN-35)
Displacement: 9,127 tons (full load)
Length: 564 feet
Beam: 58 feet
Speed: 30-plus knots
Power Plant: 2 nuclear reactors, 2 geared steam turbines, 2 shafts
Aircraft: 1 SH-2 (LAMPS)
Armament: Standard Missile(ER), 8 Harpoons, ASROCs, 4 MK-46 Torpedoes, 1 5-inch'54 caliber lightweight gun; 2 Phalanx Close-In Weapon Systems.
Complement: 567 (37 officers, 530 enlisted)

BAINBRIDGE CLASS (CGN-25)
Displacement: 8,590 tons (full load)
Length: 565 feet
Beam: 58 feet
Speed: 30-plus knots
Power Plant: 2 nuclear reactors, 2 geared turbines, 2 shafts
Aircraft: none
Armament: Standard Missiles (ER), 8 Harpoons, ASROCs, 6 Mk-46 Torpedoes, 2 Phalanx Close-In Weapon Systems
Complement: 558 (42 officer, 516 enlisted)

LONG BEACH CLASS (CGN-9)
Displacement 17,525 tons (full load)
Length: 721 feet
Beam: 73 feet
Speed: 30-plus knots
Power Plant: 2 nuclear reactors, 2 geared turbines, 2 shafts
Aircraft: none
Armament: Standard Missiles (ER), 8 Harpoons, 8 Tomahawks, ASROCs, 6 MK-46 Torpedoes, 2 5-inch 38 caliber guns, 2 Phalanx Close-In Weapon Systems
Complement: 825 (55 officer, 770 enlisted)

BELKNAP CLASS (CG-26)
Displacement: 7,930 tons (full load)
Length: 547 feet
Beam: 55 feet
Speed: 32 knots
Power Plant: 4-1200 psi boilers, 2 geared turbines, 2 shafts, 85,000 shaft horsepower
Aircraft: 1 SH-2F(LAMPS);(CG-26 SH-3)
Armament: Standard Missile (ER), 8 Harpoons, ASROCs, 6 MK-46 Torpedoes, 1 5-inch'54 caliber MK-42 gun, 2 Phalanx Close-In Weapon Systems
Complement: 477 (27 officer, 450 enlisted)

DESTROYERS

ARLEIGH BURKE CLASS (DDG-51)
Displacement: 8,300 tons (full load)
Length: 466 feet
Beam: 59 feet
Speed: 31 knots
Power Plant: 4 gas turbines, 2 shafts, 100,000 total shaft horsepower.
Aircraft: None
Armament: Standard Missiles, Harpoons, Tomahawks, ASROCs, 6 MK-46 Torpedoes, 1 5-inch/54 caliber MK-45, 2 Phalanx Close-In Weapon Systems
Complement: 323 (23 officer, 300 enlisted)

KIDD (DDG-993) and SPRUANCE (DD-963) CLASS
Displacement:
KIDD - 8,300 tons (full load), SPRUANCE - 7,865 tons (full load)
Length: 563 feet
Beam: 55 feet
Speed: 33 knots
Power Plant: 4 gas turbines, 2 shafts, 80,000 shaft horsepower
Aircraft:
KIDD - 1 SH-2F (LAMPS)
SPRUANCE - 2 SH-60 (LAMPS III)
Armament: 8 Harpoons, Tomahawks, ASROCs, 6 MK-46 Torpedoes
2 Phalanx Close-In Weapon Systems
KIDD - Standard Missiles
SPRUANCE - Sea Sparrow AAW Missiles
Complement:
KIDD - 339 (21 officer, 318 enlisted)
SPRUANCE - 334 (20 officer, 314 enlisted)

HYDROFOILS

Displacement: 255 tons (full load)
Length: 133 feet (foils extended)
145 feet (foils retracted)
Beam: 28 feet
Speed: foilborne - 40-plus knots
hullborne - 12 knots
Power Plant:
Foilborne - 1 gas turbine, 18,000 shaft horsepower, waterjet propulsion units.
Hullborne - 2 diesels, 1,600 brake horsepower, waterjet propulsion units
Armament: 8 Harpoon Missiles, 1 76mm gun
Complement: 25

---

*"STRESS: What people place on themselves
to make something more difficult."*
From the book: **Successful Leadership Today**

AMPHIBIOUS TRANSPORT DOCK

AUSTIN CLASS (LPD-4)
Displacement: 17,000 tons (full load)
Length: 570 feet
Beam: 84 feet
Speed: 21 knots
Power Plant: 2 boilers, 2 steam turbines, 2 shafts, 24,000 shaft horsepower
Aircraft: Up to 6 CH-46 Sea Knight helicopters
Armament: 1 or 2 twin 3-inch/50 caliber guns, 2 Phalanx Close-In Weapon Systems
Complement: 425 ship's company 900 troops

RALEIGH CLASS (LPD-1)
Displacement: 13,600 tons (full load)
Length: 522 feet
Beam: 84 feet
Speed: 21 knots
Power Plant: 2 boilers, 2 steam turbines, 2 shafts, 24,000 shaft horsepower
Aircraft: landing only
Armament: 6 3-inch/50 caliber buns
Complement: 429 ship's company
930 troops

AMPHIBIOUS ASSAULT SHIPS

WASP CLASS (LHD-1)
Displacement: 40,500 tons (full load)
Length: 844 feet
Beam: 106 feet
Speed: 22-plus knots
Power Plant: 2 boilers, 2 geared turbines, 2 shafts, 70,000 total shaft horsepower
Aircraft: Assault: 45 CH-46 Sea Knights   20 AV-8B Harrier 6 ASW Helicopters
Landing Craft: 3 LCAC
Armament: 2 8-cell Sea Sparrow launchers, 8 50-caliber machine guns, 3 Phalanx Close-In Weapon Systems
Complement: 1,081 ship's company (98 officer, 983 enlisted), 1,875 troops

TARAWA CLASS (LHA-1)
Displacement: 39,400 tons (full load)
Length: 833 feet
Beam: 106 feet
Speed: 24 knots
Power Plant: 2 boilers, 2 geared turbines, 2 shafts, 70,000 total shaft horsepower
Aircraft: 9 CH-53 Sea Stallion, 12 CH-46 Sea Knight, 10 AV-8B Harrier (LHA 2-5)
Armament: 2 8-cell NATO Sea Sparrow, 3 5-inch/54 caliber MK-45 lightweight guns, 1 Phalanx Close-In Weapon System, 6 20mm MK-67 single barrel AA guns
Complement: 940 ship's company (58 officer, 882 enlisted), 1,900-plus troops

IWO JIMA CLASS (LPH-2)
Displacement: 18,000 tons (full load)
Length: 602 feet
Beam: 84 feet
Flight Deck Width: 104 feet
Speed: 23 knots
Power Plant: 2 boilers, 1 geared turbine, 1 shaft, 22,000 total shaft horsepower
Aircraft: 11 CH-53 Sea Stallions 20 CH-46 Sea Knights
Armament: 2 8-cell NATO Sea Sparrow Launchers, 4 3-inch/50 caliber machine guns 2 Phalanx Close-In Weapon Systems
Complement: 685 (47 officer, 638 enlisted),
2000 Troops

LANDING CRAFT AIR CUSHION
The landing craft air cushion (LCAC) is a fully amphibious air cushion vehicle capable of operating from ship's well decks. Their mission is the transport of weapons systems, equipment, cargo and personnel of the assault elements of the Marine Air/Ground Task Force both from ship to shore and across the beach.
Displacement: 200 tons (full load)
Length: 88 feet
Beam: 47 feet
Speed: 40-plus knots with payload
Cargo Capacity: 60-75 tons

Power Plant: 4 gas turbines, 12,280 bhp, 2 shrouded reversible-pitch propellers, 4 double-entry fans for lift
Armament: 2 M-60 MG
Range: 200 miles at 40 knots with payload
Complement: 5

DOCK LANDING SHIPS

WHIDBEY ISLAND CLASS (LSD-41)
Displacement: 15,700 tons (full load)
Length: 609 feet
Beam: 84 feet
Speed: 20-plus knots
Power Plant: 4 16-cylinder diesels, 2 shafts, 33,600 shaft horsepower
Landing Craft: 4 LCAC (Landing Craft Air Cushion)
Armament: 2 25mm machine guns, 2 Phalanx Close-In Weapon Systems
Complement: 342 ship's company (21 officer, 321 enlisted), 500 troops

ANCHORAGE CLASS (LSD-36)
Displacement: 14,000 tons (full load)
Length: 553 feet
Beam: 85 feet
Speed: 22 knots
Power Plant: 2 600-psi boilers, 2 geared turbines, 2 shafts, 24,000 total shaft horsepower
Landing Craft: 3 LCAC, or 3 LCUs, or 9 LCMs, or 52 AAV/LVTP-7 amphibious tractor
Armament: 4 3-inch/50 cal MK-33 AA guns, 2 Phalanx Close-In Weapon Systems
Complement: 358 (18 officer, 340 enlisted) 330 troops

"The best test of a man is authority." PROVERB
From the book: ***Successful Leadership Today***

LANDING SHIP TANKS

NEWPORT CLASS (LST-1179)
Displacement: 8,450 tons (full load)
Length: 522 feet
Beam: 69 feet
Speed: 20 knots
Power Plant: 6 diesels, 2 shafts, 16,000 brake horsepower
Armament: 4 3-inch/50 caliber guns, Phalanx Close-In Weapon Systems
Complement: 290 ship's company, 400 troops

AMPHIBIOUS COMMAND SHIP

BLUE RIDGE CLASS (LCC-19)
Displacement: 19,000 tons (full load)
Length: 620 feet
Beam: 82 feet
Speed: 23 knots
Power Plant: 2 boilers, 1 geared turbine, 1 shaft, 22,000 horsepower
Aircraft: Utility helicopter can be carrier
Complement: 720 (40 officer, 680 enlisted)

MINE COUNTER MEASURES SHIPS

AVENGER CLASS (MCM-1)
Displacement: 1,312 tons (full load)
Length: 224 feet
Beam: 39 feet
Speed: 13.5 knots
Power Plant: 4 Aluminum block diesels, 2 shafts, 2,280-2,600 bhp
Armament: Mine Neutralization System
Complement: 74 (6 officer, 68 enlisted)

OSPREY CLASS (MHC-51)
A total of 17 MHCs are planned
Displacement: 840 tons (full load)
Length: 188 feet
Beam: 36 feet
Speed: 15 knots

Power Plant: 2 Aluminum block diesels
Armament: 2 .50-caliber machine guns, Mine Neutralization System, and other countermeasures systems
Complement: 45 (4 officer, 41 enlisted)

FAST COMBAT SUPPORT SHIP

SACRAMENTO CLASS (AOE-1)
Displacement: 53,000 tons (full load)
Length: 793 feet
Beam: 107 feet
Speed: 26 knots
Power Plant: 4 boilers, geared turbines, 2 shafts, 100,000 shaft horsepower
Aircraft: 2 CH-46 Sea Knight helicopters
Armament: Sea Sparrow Missiles, 2 Phalanx Close-In Weapon Systems
Complement: 615

REPLENISHMENT OILERS

WICHITA CLASS (AOR-1)
Displacement: 38,100 tons (full load)
Length: 659 feet
Beam: 96 feet
Speed: 20 knots
Power Plant: 3 boilers, steam turbines, 2 shafts, 32,000 shaft horsepower
Aircraft: 2 CH-46 Sea Knight helicopters
Armament: 2 Phalanx Close-In Weapon Systems, Sea Sparrow Missiles
Complement: 460

AMMUNITION SHIPS

KILAUEA CLASS (AE-26)
Displacement: 18,100 tons (full load)
Length: 564 feet
Beam: 81 feet
Speed: 20 knots
Power Plant: 3 boilers, geared turbines, 1 shaft, 22,000 shaft horsepower

Aircraft: 2 CH-46 Sea Knight helicopters
Armament: 4 3-inch/50-caliber guns, 2 Phalanx Close-In Weapon Systems
Complement: 410

SURIBACHI (AE-21) AND NITRO (AE-23) CLASS
Displacement: 15,000 tons (full load)
Length: 512 feet
Beam: 72 feet
Speed: 20 knots
Power Plant: 2 boilers, geared turbines, 1 shaft, 16,000 shaft horsepower
Armament: 4 3-inch/50-caliber guns
Complement: 390

FLEET OILERS

CIMARRON CLASS (AO-177)
Displacement: 27,500 tons (full load)
Length: 592 feet
Beam: 88 feet
Speed: 20 knots
Power Plant: 2 boilers, 1 steam turbine, 1 shaft, 24,000 shaft horsepower
Armament: 2 Phalanx Close-In Weapon Systems
Complement: 215

ASHTABULA CLASS (AO-51)
Displacement: 34,750 tons (full load)
Length: 644 feet
Beam: 75 feet
Speed: 18 knots
Power Plant: Steam turbine, 4 boilers, 2 shafts, 13,500 shaft horsepower
Armament: 2 3-inch/50-caliber anti-aircraft weapons
Complement: 372

> *"There are no bad soldiers, only bad officers."* NAPOLEON
> From the book: *Successful Leadership Today*

COMBAT STORES SHIPS

MARS CLASS (AFS-1)
Displacement: 16,000 tons (full load)
Length: 581 feet
Beam: 79 feet
Speed: 20 knots
Power Plant: 3 boilers, steam turbines, I shaft, 22,000 shaft horsepower
Aircraft: 2 UH-46 Sea Knight helicopters
Armament: 4 3-inch/50-caliber guns, 2 Phalanx Close-In Weapon Systems
Complement: 438

SUBMARINE TENDERS

L.Y. SPEAR AND EMORY S. LAND CLASSES
Displacement: 23,000 tons (full load)
Length: 644 feet
Beam: 85 feet
Speed: 20 knots
Power Plant: 2 boilers, steam turbines, 1 shaft
Armament: 2 40mm guns, 4 20mm guns
Complement: AS 36-37 - 605
               AS 39-41 - 617

SIMON LAKE CLASS (AS-33)
Displacement: AS-33: 19,934 tons (full load)
                AS-34: 21,090 tons (full load)
Length: 644 feet
Beam: 85 feet
Power Plant: 2 boilers, steam turbines, 1 shaft
Armament: 2 20mm guns
Complement: 601

HUNLEY CLASS (AS-31)
Displacement: 19,000 tons (full load)
Length: 599 feet
Beam: 83 feet

Speed: 19 knots
Power Plant: Diesel electric, 1 shaft
Armament: 4 20mm guns
Complement: 603

DESTROYER TENDERS

YELLOWSTONE (AD-47) AND SAMUEL GOMPERS (AD-37)
Displacement: 22,500 tons (full load)
Length: 644 feet
Beam: 85 feet
Speed: 20 knots
Power Plant: 2 boilers, steam turbines, 1 shaft, 20,000 shaft horsepower
Complement: 1,400

DIXIE CLASS (AD-38)
Displacement: 18,000 tons (full load)
Length: 530 feet
Beam: 73 feet
Speed: 18 knots
Power Plant: 4 boilers, geared turbines, 2 shafts 12,000 shaft horsepower
Complement: 1,000

RESCUE, SALVAGE AND TOWING SHIPS

SAFEGUARD CLASS (ARS-50)
Displacement: 2,880 tons (full load)
Length: 255 feet
Beam: 50 feet
Speed: 14 knots
Power Plant: Diesels, 2 shafts, 4,200 shaft horsepower
Armament: 2 20mm guns
Complement: 91
Diving: Manned diving operations to 190 feet using air

There have been four Naval officers to hold the rank of Fleet Admiral. Only one person has ever held the special rank of "Admiral of the Navy." Who was this officer? GEORGE DEWEY

EDENTON CLASS (ATS-1)
Displacement: 2,930 tons (full load)
Length: 282 feet
Beam 50 feet
Speed: 16 knots
Power Plant: 4 diesels, 2 shafts, 6,000 brake horsepower
Armament: 2 20mm guns
Complement: 129
Diving: Manned diving operations to 300 feet using mixed gas

SUBMARINE RESCUE SHIPS

PIGEON CLASS (ASR-21)
Displacement: 4,200 tons (full load)
Length: 251 feet
Beam: 86 feet
Speed: 15 knots
Power Plant: 4 diesels, two shafts
Armament: 2 20mm guns
Complement: 240 ship's company,   24 submersible operations

> *"Obstacles are those frightening things you see when you take your eyes off the goal."* HANNAH MOORE
> From the book: ***Successful Leadership Today***

> *"Good leadership comes from the heart."*
> From the book: ***Successful Leadership Today***

> In what year did the President direct that all American commissioned ships be titled "United States Ship."   1907

CVN - Nuclear Aircraft Carrier

CG - Ticonderoga Class Cruiser

CGN - Virginia Class Nuclear Cruiser

DD - Spruance Class Destroyer

DDG - Arleigh Burke Class Guided Missile Destroyer

FFG - Guided Missile Frigate

LCC - Amphibious Command Ship

LHA - Amphibious Assault Ship

LHD - Amphibious Assault Ship

LPH - Amphibious Assault Ship

LPD - Amphibious Transport Dock

LSD - Dock Landing Ship

LST - Tank Landing Ship

AE - Ammunition Ship

AO - Oiler

AS - Submarine Tender

AD - Destroyer Tender

AFS - Combat Stores Ship

SSBN - Ohio Class Submarine

SSN - Nuclear Attack Submarine

PHM - Patrol Hydrofoil

MCM - Mine Countermeasures Ship

CHAPTER 40

SHIPBOARD COMPARTMENTS

COMPARTMENT: 03-24-3-L

1. DECK NUMBER. The first part of a compartment number is the deck number. The main deck is deck number 1. The first deck below the main deck is the second deck, and so forth. The first deck above the main deck is the 01 deck. The next deck up is the 02 deck, etc. Below the lowest complete deck are "platform decks." Platforms are numbered downward, as first platform, second platform, and so forth. In the above example, the compartment is on the 03 deck or 03 level.

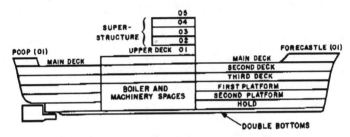

Decks of a Ship

2. FRAME NUMBER. The second part of a compartment number is in relation to the bow of the ship. Compartments near the bow of a ship have very low numbers. Compartments near the stern of a ship have higher numbers. In COMPARTMENT 03-24-3-L, the compartment is located near the forward part of a ship.

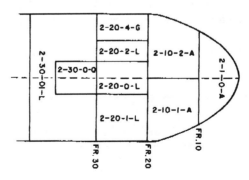

Frame Numbers

3. RELATION TO CENTERLINE OF SHIP. The third part of a compartment number is the compartment in relation to the centerline of a ship. A compartment located so that the centerline of a ship passes through it carries the number zero (0). Compartments located to the port side have odd numbers. The first compartment to port would be 1, the next compartment outboard would be 3, and so forth. Compartments located to the starboard side have even numbers. The first compartment to the starboard of the centerline would be 2, the next compartment outboard would be 4, and so forth. In the example COMPARTMENT 03-24-3-L, the compartment is the second compartment outboard of the centerline on the port side of the ship.

4. COMPARTMENT USAGE. The fourth and last part of a compartment number is a capital letter that identifies the assigned primary use of the compartment. In the example COMPARTMENT 03-24-3-L, the letter "L" identifies the compartment as a living space. The following is a list of compartment usages and the associated letter designation.

In what year was the Navy's
first Destroyer commissioned?   1902

---

*"Good words are worth much,
and cost little."* GEORGE HERBERT
From the book: ***Successful Management Today***

"Success and hard work share the same bed."
From the book: ***Successful Leadership Today***

SHIPBOARD COMPARTMENTS

LETTER	TYPE COMPARTMENT	USES
A	Stowage Spaces	Stores & Refrigerated Items
AA	Cargo Holds	
C	Control Centers and Fire Control Operations	Pilot House, CIC, Communications, etc.
E	Engineering Control Centers	Machinery Spaces, Evaporators, Steering Gear Rooms, etc.
F	Oil Stowage (For use by ship)	Diesel, Lubricating & Fuel
FF	Oil Stowage (for cargo)	
G	Gasoline Stowage (For ship use)	Cofferdams, Gasoline, etc.
GG	Gasoline Stowage (for cargo)	
J	JP-5 Fuel (for ship use)	Jet Fuel
JJ	JP-5 Fuel (for cargo)	
K	Chemicals & Other Dangerous Materials	
L	Living Spaces	Berthing, Messing Spaces, Staterooms, Sickbay, etc.
M	Ammunition Spaces	Magazines
Q	Miscellaneous	Galley, Laundry, Shops, etc.
T	Vertical Access Trunks	Escape Trunks
V	Voids	
W	Water Stowage Spaces	Freshwater, Feedwater, etc.

"Successful people see opportunities, not problems."
From the book: *Successful Leadership Today*

In what year did the Navy's first night carrier landing take place?   1925

CHAPTER 41

DAMAGE CONTROL

The ship's engineering officer is responsible for the operational readiness of the damage control (DC) organization. A ship's Damage Control Assistant (DCA) works for the engineering officer. The DCA coordinates the efforts of repair parties in the control of damage, which includes the control of the ship's stability, fighting fires, repairing damage, and NBC defense measures.

The DCA's operating location is Damage Control Central (DCC), the ship's nerve center. From here the DCA directs the entire damage control organization of the ship. Representatives of various departments and divisions are also assigned to DCC. Repair parties receive their instructions from DCC. Repair parties keep DCC up to date on repair activities. Under the direction of the DCA, graphic records of damages are made on various damage control diagrams and status boards as the reports are received.

REPAIR PARTIES

Repair parties work for the ship's Damage Control Assistant (DCA). Repair parties receive direction from, and report progress to, Damage Control Central (DCC).

All ships have at least one repair party. Most ships have three or more repair parties. The make up of each repair party depends upon the type of ship, the section of the ship assigned to the repair party, and the number of personnel available. The following chart lists the repair parties and their assigned area of responsibility:

"You may pardon much to others, nothing to yourself." AUSONIUS
From the book: ***Successful Leadership Today***

REPAIR PARTY	LOCATION OR FUNCTION
Repair 1	Main Deck Repair
Repair 2	Forward Repair
Repair 3	After Repair
Repair 4	Amidship Repair
Repair 5	Propulsion Repair
Repair 6	Ordnance
Repair 7	Gallery Deck/Island Structure
Repair 8	Electronics

In addition to the above, aircraft carriers and ships equipped for helicopter operations have aviation fuel repair and crash and salvage teams. Carriers also have an ordnance disposal team.

The specific purpose of each repair party depends on its area of responsibility. Each repair party must be capable of performing the following functions:

1. Make repairs to electrical and sound-powered telephone circuits.

2. Give first aid and transport injured personnel to battle dressing stations without seriously reducing the party's damage control capabilities.

3. Detect, identify, and measure radiation doses and dose rate intensities. Decontaminate the affected areas of nuclear, biological, and chemical attacks.

4. Control and extinguish all types of fires.

5. Evaluate and report correctly the extent of damage in its area of responsibility.

> In World War II this type of ship was known as a Destroyer Escort (DE). What is this type of ship known as today?   FRIGATE (FF)

WATERTIGHT INTEGRITY

SPECIAL CLASSIFICATIONS FOR FITTINGS

MARKINGS   **PURPOSE**

W (William)   Classification **W** is applied to sea suction valves that supply water to the condensers and fire pumps, and to other fittings and equipment necessary for fire protection and mobility. These fittings are normally open or running.

CIRCLE W   Ventilation fittings and certain access openings are marked (W) (circles are black). Normally open, these fittings are closed only to prevent NBC contamination or smoke from entering a vent system.

RED CIRCLE Z   Special fittings marked (Z) (circles are
(Zebra)   red) may be opened during long periods of general quarters to allow for preparation and distribution of food or for cooling vital spaces such as magazines. When open, these fittings are guarded so that they can be closed immediately if necessary.

BLACK CIRCLE   Fittings marked with (X) or (Y)
X & Y   permit access to battle stations, are used for transfer of ammunition, or are part of vital systems. They may be opened without special permission, but must be kept closed when not actually in use.

DOG ZEBRA   (Z) is applied to accesses to weather decks that are not equipped with light traps or door switches that will turn lights off when the access is opened during darkened ship conditions.

MATERIAL CONDITIONS OF READINESS

The degree of watertight integrity protection aboard a ship depends on the material condition of readiness in effect at any given time. The Navy has three material conditions:

-CONDITION XRAY - Provides the least protection
-CONDITION YOKE - Provides medium protection
-CONDITION ZEBRA -Provides maximum protection

> *"Good deeds must be supported by good rewards."*
> From the book: ___Successful Leadership Today___

> Fighter aircraft armed with machine guns made their debut in war in what year?   1915

> *"Want some new answers?*
> *Ask someone else, not yourself."*
> From the book: ___Successful Leadership Today___

> *"All good ideas don't come from the top."*
> From the book: ___Successful leadership Today___

CONDITION	CIRCUMSTANCES	CLOSED FITTINGS
XRAY	In well-protected harbors; at home base during regular hours.	X, (X) These fittings are kept closed at all times except when actually in use.
YOKE	**At sea; in port outside of regular working hours.**	X, (X) Y, (Y) Circle **X** and **Y** may be opened for access, to pass ammo, for inspections, etc.
ZEBRA	General Quarters; fire, flooding; when entering or leaving port in wartime.	X, (X) Y, (Y) Z, (Z) , ⟨Z⟩ : Circle Zebra fittings may be opened to permit distribution of food, use of sanitary facilities, and ventilation of vital spaces. Must be guarded when open.

SHIPBOARD FIRES

FIREFIGHTING AGENTS

1. Water (in its various forms: Fog, steady stream, etc.)
2. Aqueous Film Forming Foam-(AFFF)
3. Purple Potassium (chemical element K) - PKP
4. Carbon Dioxide - CO_2

CLASSES OF FIRE

CLASS A. Encompasses fires of solid materials that leave an ash, such as wood, cloth, and paper. Explosives such as dynamite are also placed in the CLASS A category.

MATERIAL	**EXTINGUISHING AGENT**
WOOD	- Water Sprinkler System
	- High-velocity Fog
CLOTH	- Solid Water Stream
PAPER	- Foam (AFFF for example)
	- Dry Chemical (PKP)
	- CO_2
EXPLOSIVES	- Solid Water Stream
	- High-velocity Fog
	- Foam (AFFF for example)

CLASS B. Encompasses fires of flammable liquids, **NEVER** use a solid water stream on a CLASS B fire.

MATERIAL	**EXTINGUISHING AGENT**
PAINTS	- CO_2
	- Foam (AFFF)
	- Installed Sprinkler System
	- High-Velocity Fog
	- Dry Chemical (PKP)
GASOLINE	- Foam (AFFF)
	- CO_2
	- Water Sprinkler System
	- Dry Chemical (PKP)
FUEL OIL	- Foam (AFFF)
JP-5	- Dry Chemical (PKP)
Diesel	- Water Sprinkler System
Oil	- High-Velocity Fog
Kerosene	- CO_2

CLASS C. Includes electrical or electronic equipment. ALWAYS deenergize equipment before attempting to fight the fire. **NEVER** use FOAM or SOLID WATER STREAM on a CLASS C fire.

MATERIAL	EXTINGUISHING AGENT
ELECTRICAL	- CO_2
ELECTRONICS	- High-Velocity Fog

CLASS D	EXTINGUISHING AGENT
MAGNESIUM	- Jettison Overboard
TITANIUM	- Low-Velocity Fog

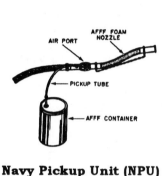

Navy Pickup Unit (NPU) Nozzle

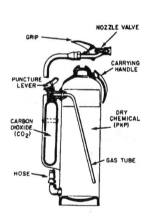

PKP Extinguisher

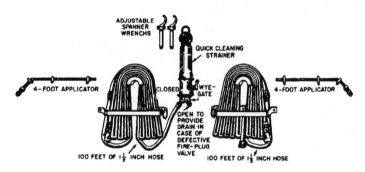

Display of Firestation Equipment

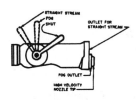

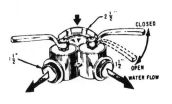

All-Purpose Nozzle

Wye Gate

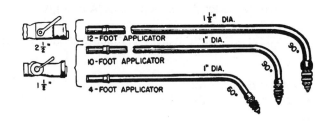

Applicators

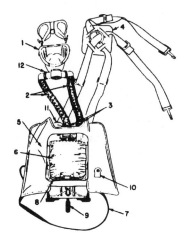

1. FACEPIECE
2. BREATHING TUBES
3. BREATHING TUBE COUPLINGS
4. BODY HARNESS AND PAD
5. BREATHING BAG
6. BREASTPLATE
7. WAIST STRAP

8. BAIL ASSEMBLY HANDLE (STANDBY POSITION)
9. CANISTER RELEASE STRAP
10. PRESSURE RELIEF VALVE AND PULL TAB
11. TIMER
12. VALVE HOUSING

Oxygen Breathing Apparatus (OBA)

CHAPTER 42

SHIPBOARD CIRCUITS

Shipboard Sound-Powered Circuits

Primary sound-powered circuits are designated JA through JZ, and include such circuits as engineering, damage control, maneuvering, etc. Auxiliary circuits maintain vital communications in the event of damage to primary circuits. Auxiliary circuits carry the same designator as primary circuits, except preceded by the letter "X," such as XJA or X1JV.

Below is a listing of some typical shipboard sound-powered circuits:

JA	Captains Battle Circuit
JC	Weapons Control Circuit
JL	Lookout Circuit
21JS	Surface Search Radar Circuit
22JS	Air Search Radar Circuit
61JS	Sonar Information Circuit
JV	Maneuvering & Docking Circuit
JZ	Damage Control Circuit
JW	Navigator's Circuit
JX	Communicator's Circuit

SHIP ANNOUNCING SYSTEMS

The purpose of the announcing systems aboard ship is to transmit orders and information between stations. Some examples of announcing systems found on U.S. Navy ships are listed below:

Circuit	Used As
1MC	General Announcing System
2MC	Propulsion Plant Announcing
3MC	Aviator's System
4MC	Damage Control Announcing
5MC	Flight Deck Announcing
6MC	Intership (Bullhorn)
7MC	Submarine Control

Circuit	Used As
8MC	Troop Administration & Control
9MC	Underwater Troop Communications
18MC	Bridge
19MC	Aviation Control
21MC	Captain's Command Announcing
22MC	Electronic Control
23MC	Electrical Control
24MC	Flag Command Announcing
26MC	Machinery Control
27MC	Sonar/Radar Control
32MC	Weapons Control
39MC	Cargo Handling
40MC	Flag Administrative
42MC	CIC Coordinating
46MC	Aviation Ordnance/Missile Handling
53MC	Ship Administrative
54MC	Repair Officer's Control

The first woman Navy line officer
was commissioned in what year?   1942

*"A successful leader is a
coach and a cheerleader."*
From the book: **Successful Management Today**

*"It is human nature to want to be
recognized and rewarded for
special effort or achievement."*
From the book: **Successful Leadership Today**

CHAPTER 43

NAVY AIRCRAFT

All aircraft have military designations. A given aircraft bears the same alphanumeric identification symbol regardless of whether the aircraft is used by the Navy, Army, or Air Force.

Each basic designator consists of a letter and number combination. The letter specifies the basic mission of the aircraft.

A - Attack	O - Observation
B - Bomber	P `- Patrol
C - Cargo/Transport	R - Reconnaissance
E - Special Electronic	S - Antisubmarine
Installation	T - Trainer
F - Fighter	U - Utility
H - Helicopter	V - VTOL or STOL (vertical
K - Tanker	or short takeoff and landing
X - Research	capability)

The number following the letter indicates the design number of the type of aircraft. The designator P-3 means that the aircraft is a patrol aircraft and is the third design of that aircraft. If a particular design is modified, the design number is followed by another letter (A, B, E, etc.), the alphabetical order of which identifies the number of the modification. For example, P-3C. The "C" indicates the design has been modified three times.

When an aircraft is modified from its original mission, a mission modification letter precedes the basic mission symbol. The modification letters are as follows:

A - Attack	M - Missile Carrier
C - Cargo/Transport	Q - Drone
D - Director (for control	R - Reconnaissance
of drones)	S - Antisubmarine
E - Special Electronic	T - Trainer
Installation	U - Utility
H - Search and Rescue	V - Staff
K - Tanker	W - Weather
L - Cold Weather	

Using the above, if a P-3C was modified to be used as a drone, it would be identified as QP-3C.

NAVY ATTACK AIRCRAFT

Attack planes are used for low-level bombing, ground support, or nuclear strikes. They do not need the speed of fighters, but should be capable of heavy payloads, have good stability, and be able to carry enough fuel to remain on station for long periods of time.

A-7 CORSAIR II. A single-seat, lightweight carrier-based, single-engine aircraft. Used primarily for attack purposes. It can also be used as an inflight refueling tanker. The A-7 has folding wing tips for closer parking aboard aircraft carriers.

A-6 INTRUDER. An all-weather attack aircraft. It is fitted with complex and sophisticated electronic gear. The pilot and bombardier-navigator sit side by side.

AV-8A HARRIER. The Harrier is a fixed-wing vertical short takeoff or landing (V-STOL) strike aircraft. The Harrier can be operated from the decks of aircraft carriers and amphibious support ships.

NAVY FIGHTER AIRCRAFT

Fighters are high-performance aircraft generally employed to gain air superiority. They may be deployed defensively as interceptors, offensively as escorts for bombers, or on-ground support missions, or independently to counter enemy aircraft.

F-4 PHANTOM II. The Phantom is a twin-engine, Mach 2 aircraft. It is capable of both air intercept and ground support missions. Installed equipment permits all-weather operations.
F-14 TOMCAT. A high-speed, aircraft-carrier based, jet-powered aircraft. The main weapons systems are missiles.

F/A-18 HORNET. A supersonic, single seat, twin engine jet. There are fighter and attack versions of this aircraft. The Hornet is designed for agility, high reliability, high survivability, and reduced manpower maintenance requirements.

NAVY PATROL AIRCRAFT

Patrol craft are land-based, long-range multi-engine aircraft used primarily for ASW patrol.

P-3 ORION. The Orion is equipped with magnetic anomaly detection (MAD) gear, sonobuoys, radar, and other submarine detection systems. It is armed with torpedoes, bombs, rockets, and depth charges to "kill" submarines. The Orion can also serve as convoy escort, photographic mission duties, and aerial mining.

NAVY ANTISUBMARINE AIRCRAFT

Antisubmarine aircraft operate from aircraft carriers. They are used in conjunction with hunter-killer group helicopters and surface craft.

S-3 VIKING. The Viking is a high-wing, jet-powered, twin-engine carrier ASW aircraft. It carries surface and subsurface search equipment, and has direct attack capability with a variety of armament.

NAVY WARNING CLASS AIRCRAFT

Carrier-based airborne early warning (AEW) aircraft maintain station at some distance from a task force to provide early warning of approaching enemy aircraft and direct interceptors into attack position.

E-2 HAWKEYE. The Hawkeye has long-range antennas enclosed in a saucer-shaped, rotating disc atop the fuselage. It is equipped with the latest radar equipment and is manned by a crew of five.

TRANSPORT AIRCRAFT

Transport aircraft carry personnel and cargo.

C-9B SKYTRAIN. The primary mission of the Skytrain is fleet logistics support. Loading capacity is in excess of 30,000 pounds.

C-130 HERCULES. The Hercules is a multi-purpose transport aircraft. It is used for everything from search and rescue to cargo and troop transport.

C-2A GREYHOUND. This carrier on-board delivery (COD) is used to transport personnel and material from aircraft to shore locations, or from shore locations to aircraft carriers. It also serves to provide mail to and from carriers as well as the transport of medical evacuation personnel.

RECONNAISSANCE AIRCRAFT

EA-6B PROWLER. This aircraft specializes in tactical electronic warfare. This all-weather airplane provides active and passive defense to a task force. It is capable of jamming enemy defense electronics systems.

NAVY HELICOPTER AIRCRAFT

Helicopters are used in a variety of ways by the Navy: ASW; pilot rescue; transfer of supplies; mail; amphibious warfare; evacuation of wounded; counterinsurgency; minesweeping; and other duties.

CH-46 SEA KNIGHT (UH-46). The Sea Knight is a twin-engine transport vehicle that provides the fleet with a day/night underway replenishment capability. It is used primarily for supply missions at sea and for casualty evacuation. The Sea Knight can carry 25 troops or up to 4000 pounds of cargo. Rotor blades fold for shipboard use.

SH-3 SEA KING (SH-3H). The Sea King is a twin-turbine, all-weather helicopter designed for ASW use. It carries dipping sonar, torpedoes, and depth charges. Maximum speed 165 mph.

H-2 SEASPRITE (SH-2F). An ex-utility helicopter, the Seasprite serves aboard Navy destroyers in the LAMPS program. Maximum speed 160 mph.

SH-60B SEAHAWK. The Seahawk is placed aboard frigates and destroyers. It can detect, locate, and destroy submarines at long range. It has constant voice and data links with ship's CIC personnel. The Seahawk's primary mission is seeking and engaging submarines many miles from ships. It is also able to provide targeting information for over-the-horizon, surface-to-surface missiles. Maximum speed 125 mph.

RH-53D SEA STALLION (CH-53D). The Sea Stallion's mission is quick-reaction mine countermeasures, capable of rapid mobility and deployment of highly trained mine countermeasure detachments. Maximum speed 195 mph.

MH-53E SEA DRAGON Replacing the RH-53D Sea Stallion, this helicopter is used aboard the modern amphibious assault ships for mine countermeasures (MCM).

CH-53E SUPER STALLION. This large and powerful helicopter is designed for the lift and movement of heavy payloads. It has a lift capacity of over 30,000 pounds and a speed in excess of 175 miles per hour.

FLIGHT OPERATIONS

Flight operations (FLIGHT OPS) are almost a daily activity aboard an aircraft carrier at sea. When preparations are being made for FLIGHT OPS, the Air Department and Air Wing personnel go to "Flight Quarters" stations.

AIR BOSS	In overall charge of flight ops.
CATAPULT OFFICER (CAT OFFICER)	In direct charge of aircraft take-offs.
LANDING SIGNAL OFFICER (LSO)	In direct charge of aircraft landings

Flight deck and hangar personnel wear easily identifiable colors to avoid confusion. These colors are:

PLANE HANDLING	BLUE
FUELING	PURPLE
PLANE CAPTAINS	BROWN
MEDICAL PERSONNEL	WHITE
PLANE HANDLING OFFICER	YELLOW
ARRESTING GEAR, CATAPULT & MAINT.	GREEN
ORDNANCE, CRASH & SALVAGE	RED
ELEVATOR OPERATORS	WHITE & BLUE
ARRESTING GEAR/CATAPULT OFFICERS	GREEN & YELLOW
HELO CAPTAINS	RED & BROWN
PLANE INSPECTOR	GREEN & WHITE
TELEPHONE TALKERS & MESSENGERS	BLUE & WHITE

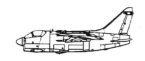

A-7 Corsair

A-6 Intruder

AV-8 Harrier

F-4 Phantom

F-14 Tomcat

F/A-18 Hornet

P-3 Orion

S-3 Viking

E-2 Hawkeye

C-9 Skytrain

C-130 Hercules

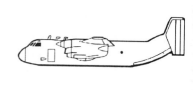

C-2A Greyhound

EA-6B Prowler

CH-46 Sea Knight

SH-3 Sea King

H-2 Seasprite

SH-60B Seahawk

RH-53D Sea Stallion

CHAPTER 44

NAVY WEAPONS SYSTEMS

MISSILE & ROCKET DESIGNATIONS. All missiles and rockets have three-letter designations. The first letter describes the launch environment. The second letter encompasses the mission. The third letter describes the type of mission.

FIRST LETTER	SECOND LETTER	THIRD LETTER
A - Air	D - Decoy	M - Guided Missile
B - Multiple	E - Special Electronic	R - Rocket
F - Individual	G - Surface Attack	
M - Mobile	I - Aerial Intercept	
P - Soft Pad	T - Training	
R - Ship	U - Underwater Attack	
U - Underwater	W - Weather	

FLEET BALLISTIC MISSILES

TRIDENT II (D-5). The Trident II (D-5) is the sixth generation of the U.S. Navy's Fleet Ballistic Missile (FBM) program. The Trident II is a 3-stage, solid propellant inertially guided FBM with a range of more than 4,000 nautical miles. The Trident/Ohio class submarines can each carry 24 Trident II missiles that can be launched under water or on the surface.

      Length: 44 feet
      Diameter: 83 inches
      Weight: 130,000 pounds
      Range: 4,000+ miles
      Warhead: Thermonuclear MIRV (Multiple
      Independently Targetable Re-entry Vehicle);
      Maneuverable (Re-entry Vehicle) Warhead

> *"No great man ever complains of want of opportunity."* RALPH WALDO EMERSON
> From the book: *Successful Leadership Today*

TRIDENT I (C-4). Trident I has a range almost double that of the Poseidon missile it replaces. It is being deployed in Ohio and Lafayette class fleet ballistic missile submarines.

Length: 34 feet
Diameter: 74 inches
Weight: 73,000 pounds
Range 4,000 nautical miles
Propulsion: Three-stage solid-fuel rocket, with   inertial
guidance
Warhead: Thermonuclear MIRV (Multiple
Independently Targeted Re-entry Vehicle) and
(Maneuverable Re-entry Vehicle) head

TOMAHAWK CRUISE MISSILE. The Tomahawk is a long range, subsonic cruise missile, conventionally armed for anti-surface warfare, and conventionally and nuclear armed for land attack versions. It is an all-weather attack missile. Tomahawk is a highly survivable weapon against predicted hostile defense systems. Radar detection is difficult because the missile has a very small cross-section and can fly at extremely low altitudes.

Length: 18 feet, 3 inches; 20 feet, 6 inches (with
booster)
Diameter: 20.4 inches
Wing Span: 8 feet, 9 inches
Weight: 2,650 pounds; 3,200 pounds with booster
Speed: 550 mph
Range: 1,350 nautical miles (land attack, nuclear
warhead) 600 nautical miles (land attack,
conventional warhead) 250 nautical miles (anti- ship
configuration)
Power Plant: Williams International FIO7-W-R-400
cruise turbo-fan engine; solid-fuel booster
Warhead: Conventional - 1,000 pounds bullput
Nuclear -W-80 conventional submunitions
dispenser with combined effect bomblets

HARPOON CRUISE MISSILE. The Harpoon's mission is to destroy hostile surface targets such as combatants, submarines, or other shipping. Harpoon is a medium range, rocket boosted, turbo sustained, anti-ship cruise missile capable of being launched from surface ships, submarines or from aircraft

Length: 15 feet (surface/submarine launched 12
feet, 7 inches (air launched)
Diameter: Missile Body, 1 foot, 2 inches
Wing Span: 3 feet (with booster fins and wings)

Power Plant: Turbojet and solid propellant booster
for surface/submarine launch
Warhead: 500 pounds, high explosive, blast
penetrator

STANDARD MISSILE. The Standard Missile (SM) is a two-model weapon which can be used against missiles, aircraft, and ships. It replaces the Terrier and Tartar missiles. The SM-2(MR)(Medium Range) is a medium range defense weapon. The SM-2(ER)(Extended Range) is an extended range area defense weapon.
CHARACTERISTICS: SM-1(MR), SM-2(MR)
Length: 14 feet, 7 inches
Diameter: 13.5 inches
Wingspan: 3 feet, 6 inches
Weight: 1,100 pounds (SM-1)
1,380 pounds (SM-2)
Power Plant: Dual thrust, solid fuel rocket
Warhead: Proximity fuse, high explosive

CHARACTERISTICS: SM-2(ER)
Length: 26 feet, 3 inches
Diameter: 13.5 inches
Wing Span: 5 feet, 2 inches
Weight: 2,980 pounds
Power Plant: Two-stage, solid-fuel rocket,
sustainer motor and booster motor
Warhead: Proximity fuse, high explosive

SPARROW MISSILE. The AIM/RIM-74 Sparrow Missile is a highly successful air-to-air and surface-to-air missile. It can be employed against attacking aircraft at all tactical speeds and altitudes in all weather.

The RIM-7M version, with folding wings and clipped tail fins, is compatible with the NATO Sea Sparrow launcher.
Length: 12 feet
Diameter: 8 inches
Wing Span: 3 feet, 4 inches
Weight: 510 pounds
Speed: 2,660+ mph
Range: 30+ nautical miles
Power Plant: Solid propellant rocket motor
Warhead: Blast Fragment, high explosive

PHOENIX MISSILE. The Phoenix missile is capable of long range tracking of multiple hostile air targets and can launch up to six missiles against six targets simultaneously. The missile has great range and intercept capability against high speed maneuvering targets at both high and low altitude.

> Length: 13 feet
> Diameter: 15 inches
> Wing Span: 3 feet
> Weight: 1,024 pounds
> Speed: 3,040+ mph
> Range: 100+ miles
> Power Plant: Solid propellant rocket motor
> Warhead: Proximity fuse, high explosive (weight 135 pounds)

HARM MISSILE. An air-to-surface missile designed to destroy or suppress enemy electronic emitters, especially those associated with radar sites used to detect anti-aircraft and surface-to-air missiles. It replaces the Shrike and Arm missiles.

> Length: 13 feet, 8 inches
> Diameter: 10 inches
> Wing Span: 3 feet, 8 inches
> Weight: 807 pounds
> Warhead Weight: 146 pounds
> Speed: 760+ mph
> Range: 50+ nautical miles
> Power Plant: Two-stage solid propellant rocket motor
> Warhead: Blast fragmentation

SIDEWINDER MISSILE. The Sidewinder air-to-air missile is a short-range, dogfight missile used by all Navy fighters and attack aircraft against hostile aircraft.

> Length: 9 feet, 5 inches
> Diameter: 5 inches
> Wing Span: 2 feet, 1 inch
> Weight: 195 pounds
> Speed: 1,900+ mph
> Range: 3.5+ nautical miles
> Power Plant: Single-stage, solid propellant reduced smoke motor
> Warhead: Annular blast fragmentation (25 pounds)

In what year did a jet aircraft operate off a Navy aircraft carrier? 1946

AMRAAM MISSILE. The AIM-120A, Advanced Medium Range Air-to-Air Missile (AMRAAM) is an all-weather, radar guided, beyond visual range missile designed to provide launch and leave capability and multiple target engagement capability. It is smaller, faster, lighter, and better able to attack at lower levels than the Sparrow Missile. The pilot will be able to aim and fire several missiles at multiple targets simultaneously.

Length: 12 feet
Diameter: 7 inches
Wing Span: 1 foot, 9 inches
Weight: 335 pounds
Speed: 760+ mph
Range: 35+ nautical miles
Power Plant: Directed rocket motor
Warhead: Blast high explosive

BOMBS.

Conventional aircraft bombs are designed for release over enemy targets to reduce and neutralize their war potential by destructive explosion, fire, or gases. The efficient destruction of various types of targets requires bombs that vary widely in size, construction content, and purpose.

Aircraft bombs are classified according to their payload.
1. Fire
2. Chemical
3. Smoke
4. Incendiary
5. Practice
6. Chemical
7. High Explosive (HE)

FIRE BOMBS. Fire bombs are of two types. Those designed for use against light, flammable targets are "scatter" bombs that contain a mixture of oil or gasoline and a thickening or gelling agent. This filler, called oil gel, is ignited and scattered by a small black powder charge when the bomb impacts. The gel is a thick material somewhat like rubber cement, and it adheres to the sides of structures, tents, and the like, setting them afire.

The ignition of more substantial targets, such as well-constructed buildings, is accomplished by dropping an "intensive" fire bomb filled with a mixture of aluminum powder and iron oxide (thermate or thermite), which burns at temperatures approximating the melting point of steel.

Fire bombs range in filled weight between 500 and 900 pounds. They carry between 75 and 112 gallons of filler.

CHEMICAL BOMBS. Chemical gas bombs (GBs) are designed for antipersonnel attack. Some bombs contain casualty agents that incapacitate or kill personnel; others contain harassing agents, such as tear or vomiting gases, which are of less potency but force the enemy to use masks and otherwise retard operations. Bomb weights run from 115 to 1,000 pounds. These bombs can be fuzzed to explode on impact or to provide an aerial blast.

SMOKE BOMBS. Smoke bombs are generally used for screening purposes to conceal shore areas and movements of ships and troops. The bomb shatters on impact, dispersing the smoke agent over an area of 30-50 square yards. An effective smoke screen may last up to 5 minutes.

INCENDIARY BOMBS. These bombs are designed for use against combustible land targets where numerous fires may cause serious damage, and over water to ignite oil slicks. When an incendiary equipped with a sodium igniter impacts in water, it bursts and scatters burning gobs of gel containing particles of sodium. The burning gel can produce temperatures up to 675 C for as long as 8 minutes.

PRACTICE BOMBS. The use of practice bombs makes it possible to train crews more economically and safely than can be done with live bombs. As the name indicates, a practice bomb simulates the ballistic properties of service-type bombs for target practice.

HIGH EXPLOSIVE (HE) BOMBS. High explosive bombs are sub-classified depending on their use:
1. General-Purpose (GP)   2. Low-drag General Purpose
3. Semi-Armor-Piercing (SAP) 4. Fragmentation (Frag)
5. Aircraft Depth (AD)

GENERAL-PURPOSE (GP) BOMBS. GP bombs are employed in the majority of bombing operations. Their cases are relatively light and the explosive filler ("payload") makes up about half of the bomb weight. These bombs range in size from 100 pounds to almost 2,000 pounds.

LOW-DRAG GENERAL-PURPOSE BOMBS. These bombs are designed to increase aerodynamic performance and bombing accuracy when used with high-speed aircraft. They are manufactured in four sizes weighing from 260 pounds to 2,000 pounds.

SEMI-ARMOR-PIERCING (SAP). The SAP bomb has a thicker case that gives greater penetration than a GP of comparable weight. These bombs weigh approximately 1,000 pounds.

FRAGMENTATION (Frag) BOMBS. The Frag bomb is fuzzed to explode before penetration. They cause destruction mainly by spraying the surrounding area with hundreds of case fragments. They are designed for the destruction or disablement of personnel and light targets. Frag bombs range in size from 4 to 260 pounds.

AIRCRAFT DEPTH (AD) BOMBS. Although the aircraft depth bomb is employed mainly against underwater targets (armed to explode at a preset depth), it has a secondary use as a demolition (impact) bomb. The standard AD bomb weighs approximately 350 pounds.

TORPEDOES

MK 50 TORPEDO. The mission of the MK 50 torpedo is to destroy hostile submarines. The MK 50 is an advanced lightweight torpedo for use against the faster, deeper-diving, and more sophisticated submarines. The MK 50 can be launched from all ASW aircraft, and from torpedo tubes aboard surface combatant ships. The MK 50 torpedo replaces the MK 46 torpedo.

> Length: 112 inches
> Diameter: 12.75 inches
> Weight: 750 pounds
> Speed: 40+ knots
> Power Plant: Stored Chemical Energy Propulsion System
> Guidance: Active/Passive Acoustic Homing

MK 48 and MK 48 ADVANCED CAPABILITY (ADCAP).

The mission of this family of torpedoes is to enable US submarines to sink hostile surface ships or submarines. The MK 48 is carried by all Navy attack and ballistic missile submarines. The improved version, the MK 48 ADCAP, is carried by some classes of submarines in addition to the newer SEAWOLF class. Both of these weapons are designed to combat fast, deep diving nuclear submarines and high performance surface ships. The MK 48 replaced both the MK 37 and MK 14 torpedoes in anti-submarine and anti-ship roles.

Length: 19 feet
Diameter: 21 inches
Weight: 3,434 pounds (MK 48),
3,695 pounds (MK 48 ADCAP)
Speed: 28+ knots
Power Plant: Piston engine, pump jet
Range: 5+ miles Depth: greater than 1200 feet
Warhead: 650 pounds high explosive

GUNS

PHALANX CLOSE-IN WEAPONS SYSTEM (CIWS).
The Phalanx CIWS was developed to provide the fleet with a close-range, hard defense against anti-ship cruise missiles, fixed-wing aircraft, and surface targets. It combines a single mount fire-control radar and a six-barrel Gatling gun firing depleted-uranium projectiles at a rate of 3,000 rounds per minute. Its projectiles are 2.5 times heavier than those made of steel.

Weight: 12,500 pounds
Gun: M61Al Vulcan (gatling-type)
Ammunition: 20mm with high density penetrating projectile
Magazine Capacity: 989 rounds
Firing Rate: 3,000 rounds per minute

*"By far the most valuable
possession is skill."* HIPPARCHUS
From the book: *Successful Leadership Today*

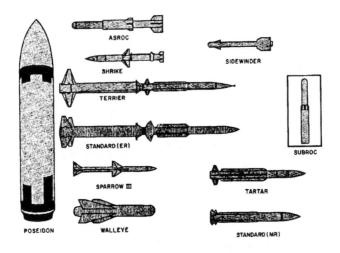

Navy Missiles and Rockets

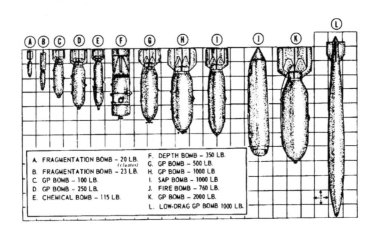

A. FRAGMENTATION BOMB – 20 LB. (cluster)
B. FRAGMENTATION BOMB – 23 LB.
C. GP BOMB – 100 LB.
D. GP BOMB – 250 LB.
E. CHEMICAL BOMB – 115 LB.
F. DEPTH BOMB – 350 LB.
G. GP BOMB – 500 LB.
H. GP BOMB – 1000 LB
I. SAP BOMB – 1000 LB
J. FIRE BOMB – 760 LB.
K. GP BOMB – 2000 LB.
L. LOW-DRAG GP BOMB 1000 LB.

Comparing Sizes of Some Conventional Bombs

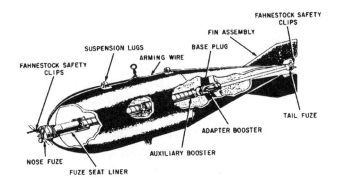

Conventional Bomb Components

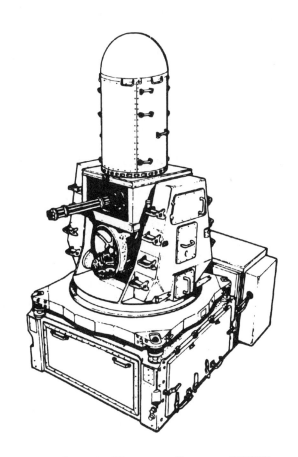

Close-In Weapons System (CIWS)

CHAPTER 45

REPAIR & MAINTENANCE: TERMS & DEFINITIONS

ALTERATION. Definition: Any change in the hull, machinery, equipment, or fittings that involves a change in design, materials, number, location, or relationship of an assembly's component parts whether the change is separate from, incidental to, or in conjunction with repairs.

Categories Of Alterations Are:
1. **APPROVED ALTERATION** Alteration approved for accomplishment, hut funding and year of accomplishment not identified.
2. **AUTHORIZED ALTERATION** Alteration approved for accomplishment with funding and year of accomplishment identified.
3. **ALTERATIONS EQUIVALENT TO A REPAIR (AER)**
An alteration which has one or more of the following attributes:
    a. The use of different materials which have been approved for like or similar use and are available from standard stock.
    b. The replacement of obsolete, worn-out or damaged parts, assemblies, or equipments, requiring renewal by those of later and more efficient design previously approved by the Systems Command concerned.
    c. The strengthening of parts which require repair or replacement in order to improve reliability of the parts and of the unit, provided no other change in design is involved.
    d. Minor modifications involving no significant changes in design or functioning of equipment but considered essential to prevent recurrence of unsatisfactory conditions.
    e. The replacement of parts, assemblies, or equipment with like items of later or more efficient design

when it can be demonstrated that the cost of installation and maintenance of the new parts, assemblies, or components is less than the cost of maintaining the installed parts, assemblies, or components.

   f.   Only the Systems Command exercising technical control over the article, or the authority to whom such technical control has been delegated by that command, shall designate an alteration as equivalent to a repair and approve it for accomplishment.

4. ELECTRONIC FIELD CHANGES. Any modification or alterations made to electrical equipment after delivery date to the government.

5. MILITARY ALTERATION. An alteration that changes or improves the military characteristics of a ship (CNO managed).

6. TECHNICAL ALTERATION. An alteration that affects safety, maintainability, reliability, or system performance (CNO managed).

7. ORDNANCE ALTERATION (ORDALT). Alteration to ordnance equipment under the technical cognizance of NAVSEA and composed of:

   a. ORDNANCE ALTERATION INSTRUCTION. Technical document containing instructions, drawings, test procedure, and directions to accomplish a material change, modification, repositioning, or alteration in the physical appearance of an installation of different parts in subassemblies, assemblies, or components in a weapon or system. Technical publication changes are supplied as part of that data package.

   b. ORDALT KIT. All the material and documentation required to perform an ORDALT, which may include materials and documentation necessary for testing, operating, and maintaining the equipment after alteration. ORDALT Kits include complete hardware, special tools if required, and a copy of ORDALT instruction. In some cases, a conjunctive SHIPALT may be required with an ORDALT.

8. **PROGRAMMED ALTERATION.** An alteration that is scheduled for accomplishment by CNO in SAMIS on a specific hull(s) in a specific fiscal year.

9. **SHIP ALTERATION (SHIPALT).** Any change in the hull, machinery, equipment, or fittings which involves change in design, materials, number, location, or relationship of the component parts of an assembly. SHIPALTs are classified by title, such as Title D alteration

SHIPALT TITLES

a. **TITLE D ALTERATION.** An alteration equivalent to a repair, approved by NAVSEA. Title D ship alterations are authorized by the TYCOM and funded under O&MN as operating expenses.

b. **TITLE F ALTERATION.** An alteration that can be accomplished by Forces Afloat and does not require special program material or centrally procured material for accomplishment. Title F alterations may only be authorized for accomplishment by TYCOMs, who must fund all costs except Design Services Allocation (DSA) and COSAL.

c. **TITLE K ALTERATION.** An alteration authorized for accomplishment through FMP and usually requiring special program material. It is accomplished by industrial activities and approved by CNO through the FMP process.

d. **TITLE K-P ALTERATION.** An alteration that changes the military or technical characteristics of a ship and involves installations of special program material, but is within Forces Afloat capability for installation. Special program and centrally procured materials required for accomplishment of these alterations are normally provided as a package by NAVSEA at no charge to TYCOM O&MN funds. Title K-P alterations may only be authorized for accomplishment by NAVSEA.

10. **UNPROGRAMMED ALTERATION.** An alteration not listed for accomplishment under one of the fiscal years in the FMP and listed in the "Unprogrammed" section to the FMP.

AVAILABILITY

Definition: Assignment of a ship to a repair activity for the purpose of accomplishing repairs or performing maintenance.

Specific types of availabilities assigned ships are:

1. **EXTENDED REFIT PERIOD (ERP).** A 60-day planned availability for SSBN nuclear submarines scheduled approximately 4 1/2 and 7 1/2 years after overhaul to accommodate accomplishment of major depot and intermediate level work items.

2. **FITTING OUT AVAILABILITY (FOA).** An availability at the shipyard designed as the fitting out activity to place onboard the material specified in the ship's allowance list.

3. **IMA AVAILABILITY (IMAV).** An availability at an Intermediate Maintenance Activity for the accomplishment of repair and alterations. These availabilities may be planned and scheduled or emergent. During these availabilities the ship may be rendered incapable of fully performing its assigned mission and tasks because of the nature of the repair work.

4. **REGULAR OVERHAUL (ROH).** An availability scheduled by CNO at a maintenance depot for general repairs and alterations, during which period the ship is rendered incapable of performing its assigned mission and tasks.

In what year did Congress end the punishment in the Navy known as "flogging?" 1850

---

5. **RESTRICTED AVAILABILITY (RAV).** An availability assigned for the accomplishment of specific items of work by an industrial activity with the ship present, during which time the ship is rendered incapable of fully performing its assigned missions and tasks. Restricted Availabilities are assigned by TYCOMs.

6. **SELECTED RESTRICTED AVAILABILITY (SRA).** An availability, normally at a depot level maintenance activity, scheduled by CNO which requires advance planning so that time and funds may be more effectively utilized.

7. **POST SHAKEDOWN AVAILABILITY (PSA).** An availability assigned to newly built, activated or converted ships upon completion of shakedown. The PSA will normally be of six calendar weeks duration and will be completed no later than the end of the eleventh month after completion of fitting out, at which time SCN funding and work authority terminates. Work performed shall be limited to correcting defects noted during shakedown and those remaining from the Acceptance Trials.

8. **TECHNICAL AVAILABILITY (TAV).** An availability for the accomplishment of specific items of work by a repair activity, normally with the ship not present, during which the ship's ability to fully perform its assigned mission and tasks is not affected.

9. **VOYAGE REPAIRS.** Emergency work necessary to enable a ship to continue on its mission and which can be accomplished without requiring a change in the ship's operating schedule or the general steaming notice in effect.

CLASSES OF SHIP SYSTEMS AND COMPONENT OVERHAULS

CLASS A. Work that requires such overhaul or repairs, modifications, field changes, ORDALTs or SHIPALTs as will sustain or improve the operating and performance characteristics of the system, subsystem, or component being repaired or altered to meet the "most recent" design and technical specifications for that item. It is intended that the end product be in "like new" condition in appearance as well as in operation and performance. All manufacturers' and technical manual performance standards and specifications, unless superseded by proper authority, will be met, as will all technical documentation. The repair activity will demonstrate that the end product successfully meets all performance criteria specified by the governing specifications.

Defining an overhaul as CLASS A means that all actions required to meet the definitions are authorized. The definition is applicable to all components, subsystems, and systems whether machinery, electrical, hull, electronics, or weapons.

CLASS B. Work that requires such overhaul or repairs as will restore the operating and performance characteristics of a system, subsystem, or component to its "original" design and technical specifications. If it is required to restore the operating and performance characteristics of an item to other than its original design and technical specifications, it must be so specified and the performance criteria defined. SHIPALTs, ORDALTs, field changes, and modifications, even if applicable, are not to be accomplished unless specified by the customer. Maintenance adjustment and calibration routines specified by the applicable instruction manual, unless superseded by authority, are required. The repair activity will demonstrate that the end product successfully meets all performance criteria specified by the governing specifications.

CLASS C. Repair work on a system, subsystem, or component specified by the work request or that work required to correct the particular deficiencies or malfunctions specified by the customer. The repair activity must demonstrate that the work requested has been accomplished or that the conditions or malfunctions described have been corrected, but the repairing activity has no responsibility for the repair or proper operation of the associated components of the equipment or for the operation of the system as a whole.

CLASS D. Work associated with the "Open, Inspect, and Report" type of work request in which the customer cannot be specific about what is or may be wrong with the item. This class of work is intended to be diagnostic and thus may require various tests, followed by inspection, to assist in a complete diagnosis. The repair activity will report findings, recommendations, and cost estimates to the customer for authorization prior to any repair work. When requested by the customer, minor repairs and adjustments may be accomplished without prior authorization to the extent specified.

CLASS E. Work required to incorporate all alterations and modifications specified for a designated system, subsystem, or component. The repair activity will demonstrate the successful checkout of the work accomplished to assure compliance with the performance standards established for the modification only to the extent of the work performed. When required by the customer, the repair activity will conduct system tests to prove system operability through affected interfaces. Repairs, if any, are minor.

MACHINERY ALTERATION (MACHALT) PROGRAM

A kit concept which enables HM&E changes to be accomplished in an expeditious manner, eliminating these changes from formal SHIPALT process. A MACHALT is defined as a planned change, modification, or alteration to any HM&E equipment in service (shipboard or shore activities) when it has been determined by the MACHALT Configuration Control Board (CCB) that the alteration or modification meets all of the following conditions:

    a. Can be accomplished without changing an interface external to the equipment or system.

    b. Is a modification made within the equipment boundary or is a direct replacement of the original equipment design.

c. Can be accomplished without the ship being in an industrial activity.

d. Will be accomplished individually and not conjunctively with a SHIPALT or other MACHALT.

MAINTENANCE LEVELS

The three levels of ship maintenance are:

1. **ORGANIZATIONAL MAINTENANCE.** That maintenance which is the responsibility of and performed by the using organization on its assigned equipment. Its phases normally consist of inspecting, servicing, lubricating, adjusting, and the replacing of parts, minor assemblies, and subassemblies.

2. **INTERMEDIATE MAINTENANCE.** That maintenance which is the responsibility of and performed by designated maintenance activities for direct support of using organizations. Its phases normally consist of calibration, repair, or replacement of damaged or unserviceable parts, components, or assemblies; the emergency manufacture of nonavailable parts; and the provision of technical assistance to using organizations.

3. **DEPOT MAINTENANCE.** That maintenance performed on material requiring major overhaul or a complete rebuild of parts, assemblies, subassemblies, and end items, including the manufacture of parts, modifications, testing, and reclamation as required.

Depot maintenance serves to support lower categories of maintenance by providing technical assistance and performing that maintenance beyond their responsibility. Depot maintenance provides stocks of serviceable equipment by using more extensive facilities for repair than are available in lower level maintenance activities.

"Leadership is action not position."
DONALD McGANNON
From the book: *Successful Leadership Today*

OVERHAULS

A major ship availability established for general maintenance and alterations at a naval shipyard or other shore-based depot-level repair activity.

During this period, the ship generally undergoes the installation of alterations and modifications to update its capabilities and large-scale maintenance that cannot be undertaken at other times.

The categories of overhauls are:

1. **BASELINE OVERHAUL (BOH).** An overhaul that is designed to restore a ship's systems, subsystems, and equipment to a baseline condition before the ship is placed on an engineered operating cycle.

The intent of the BOH is to provide an extensive overhaul that, together with a well engineered and executed maintenance program, will enable the ship to carry out its mission throughout the extended operating cycle.

2. **REGULAR OVERHAUL (ROH).** An availability for the accomplishment of general repairs and alterations at a naval shipyard, commercial shipyard, or other shore-based repair activity, normally scheduled in advance and in accordance with an established cycle.

3. **COMPLEX OVERHAUL (COH).** An overhaul that, due to cost, duration, or manpower constraints or the complexity or interrelationship of the various ship subsystems affected by the overhaul work packages, requires coordination and extensive management of both the planning and industrial phases of the overhaul in order to provide a high level of confidence that the overhaul can be satisfactorily completed.

> In 1857 Congress established a rank above Captain for the first time. What was this rank originally called?   FLAG OFFICER

4. INTEGRATED LOGISTIC OVERHAUL (ILO). The work involved in improving the material readiness of a ship by bringing storeroom repair part inventories up to the level prescribed in updated allowance and load lists or to the endurance level prescribed by appropriate fleet authority. Attainment of this broad objective requires the successful conduct of many separate but related actions.

---

*"Good thoughts about an individual
do no good unless expressed."*
From the book: **Successful Leadership Today**

In what year did Congress establish the
ranks of Rear Admiral, Commodore,
Lieutenant Commander, and Ensign?   1862

---

*"Frequent verbal support from a superior
is a great motivator."*
From the book: **Successful Leadership Today**

Congress authorized the Medal of Honor in 1861.
Officers were not eligible for this award until
what year?   1915

PERA (PLANNING AND ENGINEERING FOR REPAIRS AND ALTERATIONS)

A program for improving the advance planning, integration, and control procedures associated with overhaul. The primary objective of the PERA Program is to provide intensive management for the accomplishment of effective, efficient, orderly, and timely ship overhauls.

There are currently five PERA offices:
1. PERA - Submarine, located at Portsmouth NAVSHIPYD.
2. PERA - Aircraft carriers and other aviation-type ships, located at Puget Sound NAVSHIPYD.
3. PERA (CRUDES) - Cruisers/Destroyers, located at Philadelphia NAVSHIPYD.
4. PERA (CSS) - Combatant Support Ships, located at NAVSEA San Francisco.
5. PERA (ASC) - Amphibious Ships and Craft, located at Norfolk NAVSHIPYD

The PERA offices, as extensions of the NAVSEA Ship Logistics Divisions, integrate the requirements of the various systems and TYCOMs and manage the planning and engineering efforts for overhauls of assigned ship types and vital interrelated programs pertaining thereto.

On the basis of ship modernization planning documents, they assist the Ship Logistics Divisions and TYCOMs in the development of class modernization and maintenance packages for assigned ships.

The PERAs develop a complete and integrated ship overhaul planning work package that is usable by an overhauling activity with minimum translation and minimum additional planning.

PRE-OVERHAUL TEST AND INSPECTION (POT&I)

Tests and inspections performed to determine overhaul and RAV work requirements. It is necessary for some equipment to undergo a test in order for technicians to determine its repair requirements.

TYPE COMMANDER ALTERATIONS (TYCOMALT)

Type commanders are authorized to approve temporary changes to compartments of ships other than nuclear powered ships or ship nuclear support facilities through use of Type Commander Alterations (TYCOMALT) subject to the following requirements and criteria (Reference OPNAVINST 4720.93).

    1. Military characteristics of the ships must not be affected (for purposes of this instruction, increasing the number of berths is not considered to be a change in military characteristics).

    2. Only those temporary changes necessary to meet the requirements of higher authority shall be proposed for accomplishment.

    3. All proposed TYCOMALTs must be submitted formally to Naval Sea Systems Command for review and technical approval. The Naval Sea Systems Command review shall consider safety damage control coordination and effectiveness, ship stability, traffic flow, materials and installation methods.

    4. Watertight integrity or the ability to establish damage control material condition must not be affected.

    5. Operation or maintenance of installed equipments must not be interfered with.

    6. Fluid, electrical, heating, cooling ventilation, plumbing or electrical systems must not be involved.

    7. Changes must not require additional COSAL support.

    8. Compartments or areas covered by non-deviation drawings must not be involved.

    9. Installed equipment must not be modified.

    10. Materials must meet approved MILSPEC standards.

    11. Installation must be accomplished in accordance with approved methods and procedures.

"A leader inspires and motivates people toward a common purpose."
From the book: ***Successful Leadership Today***

CHAPTER 46

CODE OF CONDUCT

Any military person who is captured by enemy or unfriendly forces must be guided by the Code of Conduct.

ARTICLE 1

I am an American, fighting in the forces which guard my country and our way of life. I am prepared to give my life in their defense.

ARTICLE 2

I will never surrender of my own free will. If in command, I will never surrender the members of my command while they still have the means to resist.

ARTICLE 3

If I am captured I will continue to resist, by all means available. I will make every effort to escape and aid others to escape. I will accept neither parole nor special favors from the enemy.

ARTICLE 4

If I become a prisoner of war, I will keep faith with my fellow prisoners. I will give no information or take part in any action that might be harmful to my comrades. If I am senior, I will take command. If not, I will obey the lawful orders of those appointed over me and will back them up in every way.

ARTICLE 5

When questioned, should I become a prisoner of war, I am required to give name, rank, service number, and date of birth. I will evade answering further questions to the utmost of my ability. I will make no oral or written statements disloyal to my country and its allies or harmful to their cause.

ARTICLE 6
I will never forget that I am an American, fighting for freedom, responsible for my actions, and dedicated to the principles which made my country free. I will trust in my God and in the United States of America.

> "No matter what may be the ability of the officer, if he loses the confidence of his troops, disaster must sooner or later ensue."
> GEN ROBERT E. LEE
> From the book: **Successful Leadership Today**

> "The wise are instructed by reason;
> the ordinary minds by experience;
> the stupid by necessity;
> and brutes by instinct." CICERO
> From the book: **Successful Leadership Today**

> In what year did the first black person enter the U.S. Naval Academy?   1872

307

CHAPTER 47

GENERAL ORDERS OF SENTRIES

1. To take charge of this post and all government property in view.

2. To walk my post in a military manner, keeping always on the alert, and observing everything that takes place within sight or hearing.

3. To report all violations of orders I am instructed to enforce.

4. To repeat all calls from posts more distant from the guard house than my own.

5. To quit my post only when properly relieved.

6. To receive, obey, and pass on to the sentry who relieves me all orders from the commanding officer, command duty officer, officer of the deck, and officers and petty officers of the watch only.

7. To talk to no one except in line of duty.

8. To give the alarm in case of fire or disorder.

9. To call the officer of the deck in any case not covered by instructions.

10. To salute all officers, and all colors and standards not cased.

11. To be especially watchful at night, and, during the time for challenging, to challenge all persons on or near my post and to allow no one to pass without proper authority.

CHAPTER 48

COURTS-MARTIAL

The Uniform Code of Military Justice (Article 16) identifies three types of courts-martial.

1. SUMMARY COURT-MARTIAL (SCM)
-Consists of one commissioned officer.
-SENTENCE AWARD. Any sentence that may be given at captain's mast, and the additional punishments of confinement for 1 month, and hard labor without confinement for 45 days.
-A person awarded a summary court-martial has the right to refuse such trial. A special or general court-martial will then be held, as appropriate.

2. SPECIAL COURT-MARTIAL (SPCM)
-Consists of not less than 3 members. The accused can request that enlisted personnel serve on the court. In that event, enlisted personnel make up at least one-third of the court membership.
-SENTENCE AWARD. Any sentence that may be given at a summary court martial, and additional punishments such as a bad conduct discharge, confinement for up to 6 months, loss of two-thirds pay per month for 6 months, and hard labor without confinement for up to 3 months.

3. GENERAL COURT-MARTIAL (GCM)
-Consists of a military judge and not less than 5 members. As in a special court-martial, the accused may request that enlisted personnel serve on the court.
-SENTENCE AWARD. A general court-martial can award any punishment not forbidden by the UCMJ, including death when authorized for the offense.

> What is the name of the oldest United States Navy vessel?
> CONSTELLATION (launched in 1797)

CHAPTER 49

TYPES OF DISCHARGES

There are five types of discharges from naval service.

HONORABLE DISCHARGE. To receive an honorable discharge, a person's service to the Navy must have been from good to excellent. A final overall average mark must not be lower than 2.7, and an average conduct mark must be not less than 3.0. A person that normally would be eligible for a general discharge may receive an honorable discharge if that person is being separated because of a disability incurred in the line of duty, or if that person received any awards for gallantry in action, heroism, or other meritorious service.

GENERAL (UNDER HONORABLE CONDITIONS) DISCHARGE. A general discharge is a separation from the service, under honorable conditions, of a person whose military record is not sufficiently meritorious to deserve an honorable discharge. There is only one honorable discharge. A general discharge indicates satisfactory service but not to the established standard of the Navy.

OTHER THAN HONORABLE (OTH) DISCHARGE. A discharge under other than honorable conditions may be issued for misconduct or security reasons.

BAD CONDUCT DISCHARGE (BCD). A bad conduct discharge is a separation from the service under conditions other than honorable. A bad conduct discharge may be given only by approved sentence of a general or a special court-martial.

DISHONORABLE DISCHARGE (DD). A dishonorable discharge is a separation from the service under dishonorable conditions. A dishonorable discharge may be given only by a general court-martial and is appropriate for serious offenses calling for dishonorable separation as part of the punishment.

"Before everything else, getting ready is the secret of success." HENRY FORD
From the book: *Successful Leadership Today*

"Recognize and reward creativity and resourcefulness."
From the book: *Successful Leadership Today*

When was the rank of Chief Warrant Officer established in the U.S. Navy?   1899

The term "seven seas" refers to what seven bodies of water?
1- North Atlantic   2- South Atlantic
3- North Pacific   4- South Pacific
5- Indian Ocean   6- Arctic Ocean
7- Antarctic Ocean

CHAPTER 50

UNIFORM CODE OF MILITARY JUSTICE

The punitive articles of the UCMJ are those numbered 77 through 134. As a quick reference, these article titles are listed below:

ARTICLE 77 - PRINCIPALS (who can be charged)
ARTICLE 78 - ACCESSORY AFTER THE FACT
ARTICLE 79 - CONVICTION OF LESSER INCLUDED OFFENSE
ARTICLE 80 - ATTEMPTS
ARTICLE 81 - CONSPIRACY
ARTICLE 82 - SOLICITATION
ARTICLE 83 - FRAUDULENT ENLISTMENT, APPOINTMENT, OR SEPARATION
ARTICLE 84 - UNLAWFUL ENLISTMENT, APPOINTMENT, OR SEPARATION
ARTICLE 85 - DESERTION
ARTICLE 86 - ABSENCE WITHOUT LEAVE
ARTICLE 87 - MISSING MOVEMENT
ARTICLE 88 - CONTEMPT TOWARD OFFICIALS
ARTICLE 89 - DISRESPECT TOWARD SUPERIOR COMMISSIONED OFFICER
ARTICLE 90 - ASSAULTING OR WILLFULLY DISOBEYING SUPERIOR COMMISSIONED OFFICER
ARTICLE 91 - INSUBORDINATE CONDUCT TOWARD OFFICER, OR PETTY OFFICER WARRANT OFFICER, NONCOMMISSIONED
ARTICLE 92 - FAILURE TO OBEY ORDER OR REGULATION
ARTICLE 93 - CRUELTY AND MALTREATMENT
ARTICLE 94 - MUTINY OR SEDITION
ARTICLE 95 - RESISTANCE, BREACH OF ARREST, AND ESCAPE
ARTICLE 96 - RELEASING PRISONER WITHOUT PROPER AUTHORITY
ARTICLE 97 - UNLAWFUL DETENTION
ARTICLE 98 - NONCOMPLIANCE WITH PROCEDURAL RULES
ARTICLE 99 - MISBEHAVIOR BEFORE THE ENEMY
ARTICLE 100 - SUBORDINATE COMPELLING SURRENDER
ARTICLE 101 - IMPROPER USE OF COUNTER SIGN
ARTICLE 102 - FORCING A SAFEGUARD

ARTICLE 103 - CAPTURED OR ABANDONED PROPERTY
ARTICLE 104 - AIDING THE ENEMY
ARTICLE 105 - MISCONDUCT AS PRISONER
ARTICLE 106 - SPIES
ARTICLE 107 - FALSE OFFICIAL STATEMENTS
ARTICLE 108 - MILITARY PROPERTY OF THE UNITED
                    STATES -- LOSS, DAMAGE, DESTRUCTION,
                    OR WRONGFUL DISPOSITION
ARTICLE 109 - PROPERTY OTHER THAN MILITARY
                    PROPERTY OF UNITED STATES--WASTE,
                    SPOILAGE, OR DESTRUCTION
ARTICLE 110 - IMPROPER HAZARDING OF VESSEL
ARTICLE 111 - DRUNKEN OR RECKLESS DRIVING
ARTICLE 112 - DRUNK ON DUTY
ARTICLE 113 - MISBEHAVIOR OF SENTINEL
ARTICLE 114 - DUELING
ARTICLE 115 - MALINGERING
ARTICLE 116 - RIOT OR BREACH OF PEACE
ARTICLE 117 - PROVOKING SPEECHES OR GESTURES
ARTICLE 118 - MURDER
ARTICLE 119 - MANSLAUGHTER
ARTICLE 120 - RAPE AND CARNAL KNOWLEDGE
ARTICLE 121 - LARCENY AND WRONGFUL APPROPRIATION
ARTICLE 122 - ROBBERY
ARTICLE 123 - FORGERY
ARTICLE 123a- MAKING, DRAWING, OR UTTERING CHECK,
                    DRAFT, OR ORDER WITHOUT SUFFICIENT
                    FUNDS
ARTICLE 124 - MAIMING
ARTICLE 125 - SODOMY
ARTICLE 126 - ARSON
ARTICLE 127 - EXTORTION
ARTICLE 128 - ASSAULT
ARTICLE 129 - BURGLARY
ARTICLE 130 - HOUSEBREAKING
ARTICLE 131 - PERJURY
ARTICLE 132 - FRAUDS AGAINST THE UNITED STATES
ARTICLE 133 - CONDUCT UNBECOMING AN OFFICER AND
                    A GENTLEMAN
ARTICLE 134 - GENERAL ARTICLE (This article makes punishable acts or omissions not specifically mentioned in other articles the UCMJ.)

313

Punishment	PUNISHMENT IMPOSED BY			
	Flag or general officer in command	CO if LCDR or above	CO if below LCDR	OIC—any grade
OFFICER				
Admonition or reprimand	Yes	Yes	Yes	No
Restriction	60 days	30 days	15 days —JAG Man. 0101-	No
Arrest in quarters	30 days	No	No	No
Forfeiture of pay	1/2 of 1 mo. pay per mo. for 2 mo.	No	No	No
Detention of pay	1/2 of 1 mo. pay per mo. for 3 mo.	No	No	No

	Any officer commanding, LCDR and above	Commanding officers below LCDR; OICs, any grade
ENLISTED		
Admonition or reprimand	Yes	Yes
Confinement on B&W or diminished rations	3 consecutive days (only on E-3 and below, aboard ship) —JAG Man. 0101-	3 consecutive days (only on E-3 and below, aboard ship) —JAG Man. 0101-
Correctional custody	30 consecutive days (only on E-3 and below) —JAG Man. 0101-	7 consecutive days (only on E-3 and below) —JAG Man. 0101-
Forfeiture of pay	1/2 of 1 mo. pay per mo. for 2 mo.	7 days' pay
Reduction in grade	To next inferior grade —JAG Man. 0101-	To next inferior grade
Extra duty	45 days	14 days
Restriction	60 days	14 days
Detention of pay	1/2 of 1 mo. pay per mo. for 3 mo.	14 days' pay

Maximum Punishments Authorized by Article 15, UCMJ

CHAPTER 51

SECURITY

All information or material that is considered vital to the safety of the United States is given a security classification. Each security classification indicates the amount of protection the information and material requires to safeguard it against unauthorized disclosure. The three security classifications are TOP SECRET, SECRET, and CONFIDENTIAL.

TOP SECRET. This classification applies to defense information or material requiring the highest degree of protection. The unauthorized disclosure of top secret information could result in exceptionally grave damage to the United States and its allies.

SECRET. This classification is given to information or material which is less vital to our security than top secret. Serious damage to the United States and its allies could result in the unauthorized disclosure of secret information.

CONFIDENTIAL. Confidential is the security classification given to information or material that is disclosed to unauthorized persons could cause identifiable damage to the nation's security.

FOR OFFICIAL USE ONLY (FOUO). FOUO is not a security classification. It means that only those persons whose official duty requires access to this information should view the information. This includes such items as the Plan of the Day, logs, records, personnel records, etc.

SECURITY AREAS

Spaces that contain classified material are known as security areas. These areas have varying degrees of restriction of access and control of movement, depending on the nature of the work, information, or materials concerned. There are three levels of security areas:

LEVEL 3: (Formerly called EXCLUSION AREA) This type area contains classified information of such nature that merely being in the area constitutes access to the information. Level 3 areas require the strictest control of access. All entrances and exits are guarded or secured, and a system of positive identification of personnel is required.

LEVEL 2: (Formerly called LIMITED AREA). This area is one in which uncontrolled movement of personnel would permit access to classified information. Access to the information may be prevented, however, by escort and other internal controls. Entrances and exits are guarded or controlled by attendants who check personal identification.

LEVEL 1: (Formerly called CONTROLLED AREA). This type area serves as a buffer zone to provide administrative control, safety, and protection for other areas. Uncontrolled movement may or may not permit access to a security interest or asset.

So that their relative sensitivity may not be outwardly determined, these areas are not marked as such. Each of these areas is clearly marked "Restricted Area."

OPERATIONAL SECURITY. Operational security (OPSEC) are measures taken to prevent an enemy, or possible enemy, from obtaining operational information. There are four parts of OPSEC designed to prevent the enemy from collecting bits and pieces of information.

COMMUNICATIONS SECURITY. Includes communications by teletype, radio, mail, other communications methods

OPERATIONAL INFORMATION. Includes equipment (movement),maps, photographs, and plans, ship and air squadron movements.

ELECTRONIC SECURITY. Includes radar, sonar, Identification, Friend or Foe (IFF), and any non-communications methods.

PHYSICAL SECURITY. The guarding of classified areas and spaces against unlawful entry & sabotage.

SECURITY CONTAINERS

Combinations to security containers must be changed when:
1. First installed.
2. An individual with combination no longer has or requires access.
3. When combination has been compromised.
4. When container is found open and unattended.
5. When none of the above apply, all combinations must be changed once a year.

PERSONAL SECURITY INVESTIGATIONS

DEFINITION. An official inquiry into an individual's activities and background to develop information regarding loyalty, trustworthiness, and reliability. All DOD investigations are performed by the Defense Investigative Service (DIS).

TYPES OF INVESTIGATIONS

1. NATIONAL AGENCY CHECK (NAC).
a. Initial investigation of records and files of FBI, DIS, and Naval Criminal Investigative Service (NCIS). This is preceded by the initiation of an entrance NAC (ENTNAC).
b. Check with the Civil Service Commission, Immigration and Naturalization Service, etc.
c. Check with other armed services.
d. Grants a clearance up to and including SECRET.

2. BACKGROUND INVESTIGATION (BI).
A thorough check of all records including:
a. NAC
b. Birth records
c. Education
d. Employment/references/neighbors (conducted by a field investigator)
e. Criminal records
f. Foreign connections
g. Citizenship
h. Credit
i. Personal interview
j. Grants a clearance up to and including TOP SECRET.

3. SPECIAL BACKGROUND INVESTIGATION (SBI).

a. Similar to a BI, but is much more detailed making it the most exhaustive of all security investigations conducted by the DIS.

b. Grants clearances to special classification categories.

INFORMATION A Periodic Reinvestigation (PR) is conducted every five years for intelligence and other top security billets.

All investigations include a field investigation except a NAC.

DEFINITION. Definition of security clearance: An administrative determination that an individual is eligible for access to classified information. A clearance DOES NOT automatically guarantee access authorization.

TYPE CLEARANCES

1. **INTERIM.** Granted to individuals pending the completion of a formal investigation and prior to being granted a final clearance. MAXIMUM DURATION OF SIX MONTHS.

2. **FINAL.** Granted to an individual upon completion of the formal investigation.

CLEARANCE LEVEL	INTERIM	FINAL
CONFIDENTIAL	SCREEN OF LOCAL RECORDS	COMPLETED NAC
SECRET	SCREEN OF DEFENSE CENTRAL INDEX OF INVESTIGATIONS (DCII) FILES	COMPLETED NAC
TOP SECRET	COMPLETED NAC	COMPLETED BI

ACCESS TO CLASSIFIED INFORMATION

All of the below prerequisites are required to be fulfilled to be granted access to classified material. Access cannot be granted unless all three of the criteria are maintained.

1. Appropriate Clearance
2. "Need to Know"
3. Commanding Officer's Approval

THIS PAGE RESERVED FOR YOUR NOTES

CHAPTER 52

INSTRUCTIONS & PUBLICATIONS

ACCEPTANCE OF GIFTS	SECNAVINST 4001.2
ALCOHOL & DRUG ABUSE PREVENTION AND CONTROL	OPNAVINST 5350.4
ADVANCE PAY	MILPERSMAN 2650100
AWARDS	SECNAVINST 1650.1
	MILPERSMAN 3410200
ADVISORY BOARDS (COMMISSARY, EXCHANGE & BEQ)	OPNAVINST 1700.2
BIOGRAPHIES (OFFICER)	MILPERSMAN 5020140
BOARD FOR CORRECTION Of NAVAL RECORDS	MILPERSMAN 5040200
BROADENED OPPORTUNITY FOR OFFICER SELECTION AND TRAINING (BOOST)	OPNAVNOTE 1500
CASUALTY ASSISTANCE CALLS PROGRAM (CACP)	NMPCINST 1770.1
CASUALTY ASSISTANCE CALLS AND FUNERAL HONORS SUPPORT PROGRAM COORDINATION	OPNAVINST 1770.1
COMMAND ADVANCEMENT PROGRAM (CAP)	BUPERSINST 1430.17
CASH AWARDS FOR MILITARY PERSONNEL FOR SUGGESTIONS, INVENTIONS, SCIENTIFIC ACHIEVEMENTS & DISCLOSURES	OPNAVINST 1650.8
CAREER COUNSELOR PROGRAM	TRANSMAN 9.09
CAREER PLANNING (OFFICER)	OPNAV 13-P-1
CIVILIAN HEALTH & MEDICAL PROGRAM OF THE UNIFORMED SERVICES (CHAMPUS)	SECNAVINST 6320.8
CHANGE IN RATE OR RATING	OPNAVINST 1133.3
	BUPERSINST 1430.16
CONGRESSIONAL CORRESPONDENCE	MILPERSMAN 5410120
CRUISE BOOKS	OPNAVINST 5070.1
CWO MANUAL	NAVPERS 18455
COMMAND RETENTION TEAM	NAVPERS 15878
CORRESPONDENCE MANUAL (DEPARTMENT OF THE NAVY)	SECNAVINST 5216.5

COMMAND INDOCTRINATION PROGRAM	OPNAVINST 5351.1
DIRECTIVES ISSUANCE SYSTEM (DEPARTMENT OF THE NAVY)	SECNAVINST 5215.1
DRILL AND CEREMONIES MANUAL	SECNAVINST 5060.22
DEGREE COMPLETION PROGRAM	OPNAVINST 1500.45
DEFENSE ACTIVITY FOR NON-TRADITIONAL EDUCATION SUPPORT (DANTES)	OPNAVNOTE 5450
DEPENDENTS INDEMNITY COMPENSATION	NAVPERS 15878
DISCRIMINATION COMPLAINTS	OPNAVINST 5354.1
DRUG ABUSE PROGRAM	SECNAVINST 5355.1
ENLISTED PERFORMANCE EVALUATION SYSTEM	NMPCINST 1616.1
ENLISTED CLASSIFICATION	MILPERSMAN 1440100 MILPERSMAN 1440220
ENLISTED COMMISSIONING PROGRAM	OPNAVNOTE 1530
ENLISTED EDUCATION ADVANCEMENT PROGRAM	OPNAVNOTE 1510
EQUAL OPPORTUNITY MANUAL	OPNAVINST 5354.1
ENLISTED TRANSFER MANUAL	NAVPERS 15909
FOOD SERVICE MANAGEMENT-OFFICERS' QUARTERS AND MESSES & CHIEF PETTY OFFICERS' MESSES AFLOAT	NAVSUP PUB 486 VOL II AFLOAT
FLAGS, PENNANTS, AND CUSTOMS	NTP 13
FAMILY ADVOCACY PROGRAM	OPNAVINST 1752.2
FAMILY SERVICE CENTER PROGRAM	OPNAVINST 1754.1
FITNESS REPORTS (OFFICER)	NMPCINST 1611.1
FAMILY OMBUDSMAN MANUAL	NAVPERS 15571
FAMILY OMBUDSMAN PROGRAM	OPNAVINST 1750.1
FAMILY HOUSING	OPNAVINST 11101.13
GENERAL MILITARY TRAINING (GMT)	OPNAVNST 1500.22
GIFTS	SECNAVINST 4001.2
GUARANTEED ASSIGNMENT RETENTION DETAILING PROGRAM (GUARD III)	TRANSMAN 8.01
HISTORY CARD (OFFICER)	MILPERSMAN 1820140
HUMAN GOALS TRAINING PLAN	OPNAVINST 1543.48
HUMANITARIAN DISCHARGE	MILPERSMAN 3850240
HUMANITARIAN DUTY	TRANSMAN 18

HUMAN RELATIONS COUNCIL	OPNAVINST 5420.3
INSTRUCTOR DUTY	TRANSMAN 10
JOINT STAFF BILLETS	MILPERSMAN 1860300
	TRANSMAN 9.19
LETTER OF SEPARATION	MILPERSMAN 3810240
LETTER OF COMMENDATION	MILPERSMAN 3410200
LIMITED DUTY OFFICER MANUAL	NAVPERS 18564
LIMITED DUTY OFFICER PROGRAM	SECNAVINST 1120.3
NO COST TRANSFERS	TRANSMAN 16
	NAVPERS 15980
OPERATION OF NAVY MESSES	BUPERSINST 1710.13
ASHORE & PACKAGE STORES	
OFFICER CLASSIFICATION	NAVPERS 15839
OFFICER DATA CARDS	MILPERSMAN 1820140
	MILPERSMAN 5020220
OFFICER CANDIDATE SCHOOL	NAVPERS 15878
(OCS) PROGRAM	BUPERSINST 1120.35
PHYSICAL READINESS PROGRAM	OPNAVINST 6110.1
PUBLIC AFFAIRS POLICY AND	SECNAVINST 5720.44
REGULATIONS	
PROGRAM FOR AFLOAT COLLEGE	OPNAVINST 1500.45
EDUCATION (PACE)	
PHOTOGRAPHS (OFFICERS)	MILPERSMAN 5020140
POLITICAL ACTIVITY	MILPERSMAN 6210240
PETTY OFFICER QUALITY	MILPERSMAN 3410180
CONTROL BOARD	
QUALIFICATIONS QUESTIONNAIRE	MILPERSMAN 5020180
(OFFICER)	
RETENTION TEAM MANUAL	NAVPERS 15878
RECREATION PROGRAMS AFLOAT	NMPCINST 1710.31
RECRUITING DUTY	TRANSMAN 11
RETIREMENT CEREMONY	MILPERSMAN 3810240
RETIREMENT	MILPERSMAN 3860380
	MILPERSMAN 3860400
STANDARD ORGANIZATION AND	OPNAVINST 3120.32
REGULATIONS OF THE U.S. NAVY	
SOCIAL USAGE AND PROTOCOL	OPNAVINST 1710.7
HANDBOOK	
SPONSOR PROGRAM	SECNAVINST 1740.3
STANDARDS OF CONDUCT AND	SECNAVINST 5370.2
GOVERNMENT ETHICS	
SAILOR OF THE MONTH,	OPNAVINST 1700.10
QUARTER, & YEAR PROGRAM	
SCHOLARSHIP PROGRAM	SECNAVINST 1500.4
SEPARATION	MILPERSMAN 3810460

SUBSTANCE ABUSE	MILPERSMAN 3850280
SCHOOL QUOTAS	MILPERSMAN 3810170
SECURITY PROGRAM	OPNAVINST 5350.4
	TRANSMAN 7
	DODINST 5200.1
	OPNAVINST 5510.1
SPONSOR PROGRAM	OPNAVINST 1750.1
UNRESTRICTED LINE OFFICER	NAVPERS 15197
CAREER PLANNING GUIDE BOOK	
UNIFORM REGULATIONS	NAVPERS 15665
WIVES ORGANIZATIONS	MILPERSMAN 3450200

Why were early sailors sometimes called "tars?"
EARLY SAILORS WOULD PUT TAR ON THEIR
CLOTHING TO MAKE IT WATERPROOF

Success if 1% inspiration
and 99% perspiration.

"Courage is grace under pressure."
ERNEST HEMMINGWAY
From the book: *Successful Leadership Today*

---

*"No one is offended by
writing that is easy to understand."*
From the book: *Successful Leadership Today*

CHAPTER 48

NAVY COMMUNICATIONS
COLOR CODES FOR
ALPHABET/NUMERAL FLAGS

ALFA -	WHITE/ BLUE	**MIKE -**	BLUE/ WHITE	**YANKEE -**	YELLOW/ RED
BRAVO-	RED	**NOVEMBER -**	BLUE/ WHITE	**ZULU -**	BLACK/ YELLOW/ BLUE/ RED
CHARLIE -	BLUE/ WHITE/ RED/ WHITE/ BLUE	**OSCAR -**	RED/ YELLOW		
		PAPA -	BLUE/ WHITE	**ONE -**	RED/ YELLOW/ RED
DELTA -	YELLOW/ BLUE/ YELLOW	**QUEBEC -**	YELLOW	**TWO -**	YELLOW/ RED/ YELLOW
ECHO -	BLUE/ RED	**ROMEO -**	RED/ YELLOW	**THREE -**	BLUE/ RED/ BLUE
FOXTROT-	WHITE/ RED				
GOLF -	YELLOW/ BLUE/ YELLOW/ BLUE/ YELLOW/ BLUE	**SIERRA -**	WHITE/ BLUE	**FOUR -**	RED/ WHITE
		TANGO -	RED/ WHITE/ BLUE	**FIVE -**	YELLOW/ BLUE
				SIX -	WHITE/ BLUE
HOTEL -	WHITE/ RED	**UNIFORM -**	RED/ WHITE	**SEVEN -**	RED/ WHITE/ RED
INDIA -	YELLOW/ BLACK	**VICTOR -**	WHITE/ RED	**EIGHT -**	YELLOW/ BLUE/ YELLOW
JULIETT -	BLUE/ WHITE/ BLUE	**WHISKEY -**	BLUE/ WHITE/ RED	**NINE -**	BLUE/ WHITE/ BLUE
KILO -	YELLOW/ BLUE				
LIMA -	YELLOW/ BLACK	**XRAY -**	WHITE/ BLUE	**ZERO**	WHITE/ BLUE

ALPHABET & NUMERAL FLAGS

FLAG and NAME	Spoken	Written	FLAG and NAME	Spoken	Written	FLAG and NAME	Spoken	Written
A	ALFA	A	M	MIKE	M	Y	YANKEE	Y
B	BRAVO	B	N	NOVEMBER	N	Z	ZULU	Z
C	CHARLIE	C	O	OSCAR	O	1	ONE	1
D	DELTA	D	P	PAPA	P	2	TWO	2
E	ECHO	E	Q	QUEBEC	Q	3	THREE	3
F	FOXTROT	F	R	ROMEO	R	4	FOUR	4
G	GOLF	G	S	SIERRA	S	5	FIVE	5
H	HOTEL	H	T	TANGO	T	6	SIX	6
I	INDIA	I	U	UNIFORM	U	7	SEVEN	7
J	JULIETT	J	V	VICTOR	V	8	EIGHT	8
K	KILO	K	W	WHISKEY	W	9	NINE	9
L	LIMA	L	X	XRAY	X	0	ZERO	0

COLOR CODES FOR
PENNANTS/SPECIAL FLAGS

PENNANT ONE	WHITE/RED	**CODE or ANSWER**	RED/ WHITE/ RED/ WHITE/ RED	**NEGATIVE**	BLUE/ YELLOW
PENNANT TWO	BLUE/WHITE			**PREPARATIVE**	YELLOW/ GREEN/ YELLOW
PENNANT THREE	RED/WHITE/ BLUE	**SCREEN**	BLACK		
		CORPEN	RED/ WHITE	**PORT**	RED/ WHITE/ RED/ WHITE/ RED/ WHITE/ RED
PENNANT FOUR	RED/WHITE	**DESIG- NATION**	WHITE/ BLUE/ WHITE		
PENNANT FIVE	YELLOW/ BLUE	**DIVISION**	RED/ WHITE/ BLUE/ YELLOW	**SPEED**	RED
PENNANT SIX	BLACK/ WHITE			**SQUADRON**	BLUE/ YELLOW/ RED/ WHITE
PENNANT SEVEN	YELLOW/ RED	**EMERGENCY**	RED/ WHITE	**STARBOARD**	GREEN/ WHITE/ GREEN
PENNANT EIGHT	WHITE/ RED	**FLOTILLA**	WHITE/ BLUE	**STATION**	WHITE/ RED
PENNANT NINE	WHITE/ BLACK/ YELLOW/ RED	**FORMATION**	RED/ WHITE/ BLUE	**SUBDIVISION**	BLUE
		INTER- ROGATIVE	WHITE/ RED	**TURN**	WHITE/BLUE/ WHITE/BLUE/ WHITE/BLUE
PENNANT ZERO	YELLOW/ RED/ YELLOW				

1ST SUBSTITUTE BLUE/YELLOW	**3RD SUBSTITUTE** WHITE/BLACK
2ND SUBSTITUTE BLUE/WHITE	**4TH SUBSTITUTE** RED/YELLOW

NUMERAL PENNANTS, SPECIAL FLAGS & PENNANTS

PENNANT and NAME	Spoken	Written	PENNANT or FLAG	Spoken	Written	PENNANT or FLAG	Spoken	Written
1	PENNANT ONE	p1	CODE or ANSWER	CODE or ANSWER	CODE or ANS —	NEGATIVE	NEGAT	NEGAT
2	PENNANT TWO	p2	SCREEN	SCREEN	SCREEN	PREPARATIVE	PREP	PREP
3	PENNANT THREE	p3	CORPEN	CORPEN	CORPEN	PORT	PORT	PORT
4	PENNANT FOUR	p4	DESIG-NATION	DESIG	DESIG	SPEED	SPEED	SPEED
5	PENNANT FIVE	p5	DIVISION	DIV	DIV	SQUADRON	SQUAD	SQUAD
6	PENNANT SIX	p6	EMERGENCY	EMERGENCY	EMERG	STARBOARD	STARBOARD	STBD
7	PENNANT SEVEN	p7	FLOTILLA	FLOT	FLOT	STATION	STATION	STATION
8	PENNANT EIGHT	p8	FORMATION	FORMATION	FORM	SUBDIVISION	SUBDIV	SUBDIV
9	PENNANT NINE	p9	INTER-ROGATIVE	INTER-ROGATIVE	INT	TURN	TURN	TURN
0	PENNANT ZERO	p0						
TACK LINE	TACK							

SUBSTITUTES

	Spoken	Written		Spoken	Written
1st. SUBSTITUTE	FIRST SUB	1st.	3rd. SUBSTITUTE	THIRD SUB	3rd.
2nd. SUBSTITUTE	SECOND SUB	2nd.	4th. SUBSTITUTE	FOURTH SUB	4th.

PHONETIC ALPHABET & MORSE CODE

Letter	Phonetic Alphabet	Pronunciation Guide	International Morse Code
A	ALFA	AL FA	. —
B	BRAVO	BRAH VOH	— . . .
C	CHARLIE	CHAR LEE	— . — .
D	DELTA	DELL TAH	— . .
E	ECHO	ECK OH	.
F	FOXTROT	FOKS TROT	. . — .
G	GOLF	GOLF	— — .
H	HOTEL	HOH TELL	. . . .
I	INDIA	IN DEE AH	. .
J	JULIETT	JEW LEE ETT	. — — —
K	KILO	KEY LOH	— . —
L	LIMA	LEE MAH	. — . .
M	MIKE	MIKE	— —
N	NOVEMBER	NO VEM BER	— .
O	OSCAR	OSS CAH	— — —
P	PAPA	PAH PAH	. — — .
Q	QUEBEC	KAY BECK	— — . —
R	ROMEO	ROW ME OH	. — .
S	SIERRA	SEE AIR RAH	. . .
T	TANGO	TANG GO	—
U	UNIFORM	YOU NEE FORM	. . —
V	VICTOR	VIK TAH	. . . —
W	WHISKEY	WISS KEY	. — —
X	XRAY	ECKS RAY	— . . —
Y	YANKEE	YANG KEY	— . — —
Z	ZULU	ZOO LOO	— — . .

Number	Pronunciation Guide	International Morse Code
1	WUN	. — — — —
2	TOO	. . — — —
3	THUH-REE	. . . — —
4	FO-WER	. . . . —
5	FI-YIV	. . . . .
6	SIX	— . . . .
7	SEVEN	— — . . .
8	ATE	— — — . .
9	NINER	— — — — .
0	ZERO	— — — — —

SEMAPHORE ALPHABET

CHAPTER 54

NAVY VOCABULARY

ABAFT	-Farther aft, as, "Abaft the beam."
ABEAM	-On a relative bearing 90º (abeam to starboard), or 270º (abeam to port).
ABOARD	-On a ship or naval activity
ABREAST	-Same as abeam. Side by side.
ACCOMMODATION LADDER	-A ladder suspended over and inclining down the side of a ship to facilitate boarding the ship from boats.
ACE	-Pilot with five or more downed enemy aircraft.
ACOUSTIC TORPEDO	-Torpedo guided by sound
ADRIFT	-Loose from moorings and out of control. Applied to anything which is lost, out of and, or left lying about (as adrift clothing items placed in the lucky bag.).
AFLOAT	-Resting on water
AFT	-Toward the stern.
AFTER	-That which is farthest or most aft (as "after fireroom").
AFTERMOST	-More aft, nearest stern.
AFTERNOON WATCH	-The 1200-1600 watch.
AGROUND	-Resting fast to the bottom.
AHOY	-A hail or demand for attention (as "boat ahoy").
AIR BEDDING	-Bring bedding topside to air out, expose to fresh air.
AIR BOSS	-Slang: Air officer aboard an aircraft carrier or large ship with an air department.
AIR WING	-Squadrons aboard an aircraft carrier.
AIRDALE	-Slang: Naval aviation personnel
ALEE	-In the direction toward which wind is blowing. Downwind.
ALIVE	-Lively, energetic. ("Look alive.")
ALL FAST	-Lashed down or tied as necessary.
ALL HANDS	-Collective term for everyone at the command.

ALOFT	-Any area above the highest deck of a ship.
ALONGSIDE	-Next to or near a ship or pier.
AMIDSHIPS	-At, in, toward the middle.
ANCHORAGE	-An area designated to be used by ships for anchoring.
ANCHOR BALL	-Black ball hoisted to indicate ship at anchorage.
ANCHOR BUOY	-Small float attached to anchor. Used to locate anchor in case it breaks loose from a ship.
ANCHOR CABLE	-The wire, chain, or cable attached between the anchor and the ship.
ANCHOR LIGHTS	-Lights required to be lit when a vessel is anchored.
ANCHOR WATCH	-People made available to the OOD outside normal work hours for duties such as heaving in or paying out the anchor cable.
ARMAMENT	-The weapons of a ship.
ARMOR	-Extra heavy metal for protection against missiles, torpedoes, etc.
ARMORED DECK	-A deck below the main deck that provides added protection to vital spaces of a ship.
ARMORY	-Shipboard compartment where small arms are stowed.
ARRESTING CABLES	-Cables aboard an aircraft carrier flight deck used to safely "catch" the tailhook of a landing aircraft.
ASHORE	-On shore or beach.
ASSAULT CRAFT	-Vessels used in amphibious landings.
ASTERN	-Directly behind the ship.
ATHWART	-Across, at right angles to.
AUTO CAT	-Aircraft used to relay messages to/from ships.
AVAST	-Nautical word for stop ("avast heaving").
AWEIGH	-Nautical word meaning anchor is off the bottom.
AYE AYE	-Reply to a command or order meaning, "I understand and will obey."
BACKORDER	-A requisition that cannot be filled until additional stock is received.

BACKSTAY	-Piece of standing rigging leading aft.
BACKWASH	-Aft-running water caused by ship's propeller.
BALLAST	-Weight loaded into a ship to increase stability.
BALLISTIC MISSILE	-Has a two-stage flight path. In the first stage, a preset guidance system guides the missile on its flight path to the target. In the last stage, the missile is in a free trajectory. In contrast, a guided missile has a system that constantly updates and corrects the missile's heading until impact with the target.
BAR	-A long, narrow shoal across a harbor entrance.
BARGE	-(1) Type of small craft used to haul supplies or garbage; or, (2) Type of motorboat assigned for the personal use of a flag officer.
BARNACLES	-Small shellfish that attach themselves to bottoms of vessels and other submerged structures.
BATTEN DOWN	-To close any watertight fixture.
BATTERY	-Navy gun mounts are referred to as batteries. They may be called "main battery," "surface battery," or "machine gun battery."
BATTLE DRESS	-Protective clothing procedures in effect at general quarters.
BATTLE GROUP	-Group of different types of ships together in one organization/operation. Usually consists of an aircraft carrier & various surface ships. May include logistic ships.
BEAM	-(1) The extreme breadth of a vessel; or, (2) A transverse frame supporting a deck.
BEAR A HAND	-Provide assistance or expedite ("bear a hand with the field day").
BECKET	-Fitting on a block to which the dead end of a fall is attached.
BECKET BEND	-Simple knot used to tie two lines together.

BELAY	-(1) To secure a line to a fixed point; or, (2) Order to disregard a previous order, or to stop an action ("belay that last order").
BELOW	-Downward, or underneath present location.
BERTH	-(1) Bunk or rack; or (2) Duty assignment; or, (3) Mooring space assigned to a vessel.
BIGHT	-The middle part of a line, or a loop in a line.
BILGE	-Bottom of the hull near the keel.
BILGE KEEL	-A keel attached to the outside of a ship's hull, near the turn of the bilge, to reduce rolling.
BILGE PUMP	-Pump used to extract water from bilge.
BILLET	-Place or duty to which one is assigned.
BINNACLE	-Stand containing a magnetic compass.
BINNACLE LIST	-List of persons excused from duty because of illness.
BIRD FARM	-Slang: Aircraft carrier.
BITT	-Cylindrical upright fixture to which mooring or towing lines are secured aboard ship.
BITTER END	-The free or loose end of a line.
BLUEJACKET	-Enlisted person below E-7.
BOARD	-The action of going aboard a ship.
BOAT	-(1) Small craft capable of being carried aboard a ship; or, (2) A submarine.
BOAT BOOM	-A spar rigged out from the side of an anchored or moored ship to which boats are tied when not in use.
BOAT FALLS	-Tackle used to hoist and lower a boat in davits.
BOATHOOK	-A staff having a hook at one end, usually made of wood.
BOATSWAIN'S CHAIR	-A seat attached to a line for hoisting a person aloft.
BOATSWAIN'S LOCKER	-A compartment, usually forward on a ship, where lines and other equipment used by deck personnel are stowed.
BOGEY-	-Unidentified aircraft.
BOMB	-A "free-falling" weapon. It may or may not be guided by a guidance system.

BOOM	-A spar used for hoisting items aboard ship.
BOOMER	-Slang: Ballistic submarine.
BOOT TOPPING	-Black paint applied to a ship's sides along the waterline.
BOW	-The forward end of a vessel.
BRASSARD	-Arm band worn by shore patrol, OODs, etc.
BREAK OUT	-To bring out (as "break out supplies").
BREAST LINE	-Mooring line that leads from a ship to the pier at right angles to the ship.
BRIDGE	-The area in the superstructure of a ship from which the ship is operated.
BRIG	-Navy prison or place of confinement.
BRIGHTWORK	-Brass & other metals that require polishing.
BROW	-Another name for gangplank. Used to go from a ship to a pier, or from one ship to another ship.
BROWN BAGGER	-Person who brings lunch to work.
BULKHEAD	-A vertical partition in a ship.
BULL ENSIGN	-Senior ensign at a command.
BULWARK	-Solid barrier along the edges of weather decks.
BUNK	-Bed.
BUNTING	-Signal flags.
BUOY	-An anchored float used as an aid to navigation, or to mark the location of an object.
CABIN	-The living compartment of a ship's commanding officer ("the captain's cabin").
CAME	-Large timber or rectangular structure used as a fender between a ship and the pier.
CANNIBALIZE	-Remove good parts from one equipment to put into another equipment.
CAPSIZE	-To turn over, upside down.
CARGO HOLDS	-Large spaces with hatch openings on the main deck. Used to carry cargo for other ships.
CARRY ON	-Command given to resume or continue normal activity.

CAST OFF	-To throw off, as mooring lines
CAT	-Short for catapult
CATAPULT	-Device used to launch aircraft off an aircraft carrier.
CATWALK	-Walkway that avoids obstructions aboard a ship.
CHAIN LOCKER	-Space where the anchor chain is stowed.
CHART	-A nautical map.
CHARTHOUSE	-Contains navigational instruments. Usually located just aft of pilothouse.
CHOCK	-Deck fitting through which mooring lines are led.
CHOP	-To change operational commanders. Outchop from one commander. Inchop to another commander.
CHOW	-Food.
CLAMP DOWN	-To mop with a damp swab, or light water with a dry swab.
CLEAT	-A metal casting with two projecting arms to which a line is passed.
CLOSE UP	-To hoist all the way up. Two-block.
COAMING	-Bulwark around a hatch opening.
COFFERDAM	-Void between shipboard compartments.
COLORS	-(1) The national ensign; or, (2) The act of raising or lowering the ensign in the morning and in the evening.
COMBATANT SHIP	-A ship whose primary mission is combat.
COMBAT INFORMATION CENTER(CIC)	-This is the nerve center of a ship This is where combat information is collected, evaluated, and acted upon.
COMMISSION	-(1) Ship entering active naval service. (2) Person attaining commissioned officer status.
COMMISSION PENNANT	-A long, narrow, starred and striped pennant flown only aboard a commissioned ship.
COMPANIONWAY	-A deck opening giving access to a ladder to go from one deck to another deck.
COMPARTMENT	-An interior space, or room, aboard a ship.
CONN	-Station from which a ship is controlled.

CONSUMABLE SUPPLIES	-Administrative & housekeeping items, routine maintenance tools, & general purpose hardware.
CONTROLLED EQUIPAGE	-Selected items of equipage which required increase management control due to high cost, vulnerability to pilferage, or essential to the ship's mission.
COPPERS	-Large cooking pots in a galley.
CORRECTIONAL CUSTODY	-The physical restraint (confinement) of a person during duty or nonduty hours, or both.
COURSE	-A ship's desired direction of travel.
COVER	-Slang for headgear, hat.
COXSWAIN	-Enlisted person in charge of a boat.
CREW	-Enlisted persons aboard a ship.
CRUISE	-The deployment of a ship or squadron, usually overseas, that lasts several months.
DAMAGE CONTROL CENTRAL(DCC)	-Maintains damage control information for the entire ship. Ensures proper material conditions are set and maintained. Coordinates any and all damage control repairs, and makes reports to the bridge.
DARKEN SHIP	-To turn off all external lights and close all openings through which lights could be seen from outside the ship.
DAVEY JONES LOCKER	-The bottom of the ocean.
DEAD AHEAD	-Directly ahead, bearing 000 degrees.
DEAD ASTERN	-Directly behind, bearing 180 degrees.
DEAD HORSE	-Drawing advance pay. When paying it back it is referred to as paying off a "dead horse."
DECK	-Horizontal planking or plating which divides a ship into horizontal layers.
DECK LOG	-Official record maintained aboard a commissioned ship.
DEEP SIX	-To throw something over the side of a ship.
DEPLOYMENT	-To deploy away from home port. See cruise.

DEPTH CHARGE	-An antisubmarine weapons system. Can be fired or dropped by ships or aircraft. Set to explode at certain depths or in close proximity to a submarine.
DIP	-The act of lowering a flag part way down and then raising it again, as in a salute or honoring of another ship.
DISPENSARY	-Small medical facility with less services than a hospital.
DOG	-Metal fitting used to close portholes or hatches.
DOG DOWN	-To set the dogs on a door or hatch.
DOG WATCH	-The dividing of the 1600-2000 watch. The first dog watch is 1600-1800. The second dog watch is 1800-2000.
DOUBLE UP	-Act of doubling the number of mooring lines used.
DRAFT	-The vertical distance from the keel to the waterline.
DRIFT	-The speed at which a vessel is pushed off course by wind and current.
DRY RUN	-A practice exercise before actual event/activity.
DUNNAGE	-Material (such as lumber or burlap) used in stowing material to provide protection to both the material & the ship.
EASE OFF	-To slacken, make slack.
EBB	-Referring to a falling tide.
EQUIPAGE	-Items of a durable nature not consumed in use and are essential to the ship's mission.
EVAPORATOR	-Equipment used to make fresh water from seawater.
EXPENDITURE	-Any act which results in a decrease in Navy assets (material or funds).
EXTRA DUTY	-The assignment of any duty to be performed after a person's regular work hours, not to exceed two hours daily, and not performed on holidays. Petty officers may not be assigned extra duties that would demean their grade or position.

EYES	-The most forward part of the forecastle.
FALL IN	-Command given to get into ranks at attention.
FALL OUT	-Dispersal command given at conclusion of formal activities.
FANTAIL	-The after end of the main deck.
FATHOM	-A unit of depth measure equal to six feet.
FEED WATER	-Fresh distilled water for ship's boilers made from salt water by ship's evaporators.
FENDER	-A cushioning device hung over the side of a ship to prevent contact between a ship and a pier, or another ship.
FIELD DAY	-A time or day devoted to a complete clean-up of a space or ship.
FIREMAIN	-Piping system to which fire hydrants are connected aboard ship.
FISCAL YEAR	-A 12-month period selected for accounting purposes. The government fiscal year begins 1 October and ends 30 September of the following year.
FLAG BAG	-Storage container for ship's flags.
FLAG OFFICER	-An admiral. Authorized to fly personal flag.
FLAGSTAFF	-Vertical staff at the stern to which the ensign is hoisted when moored or at anchorage.
FLANK SPEED	-Make maximum possible speed.
FLIGHT DECK	-Top deck of an aircraft carrier. Used for aircraft take-offs & landings.
FLYING BRIDGE	-The uppermost part of a ship.
FOGY	-A longevity pay increase.
FORE AND AFT	-The entire length of a vessel.
FORECASTLE	-Forward section of the main deck (pronounced "fok-sul").
FOREMAST	-The first mast aft of the bow.
FORENOON WATCH	-The 0800-1200 watch (also called the morning watch).
FORESTAY	-A stay leading forward.
FOUL ANCHOR	-An anchor entangled with its line/chain or other obstruction.
FOUL UP	-Make mistake. Getting into trouble.

FRAME	-The athwartship strength member of a ship's hull.
FREEBOARD	-Distance from water line to weather deck.
FROCK	-To wear rank of next higher pay grade without receiving higher pay. This might be done prior to actual promotion to next grade.
GAFF	-A light spar set at an angle from the upper part of a mast. The ensign is usually flown from the gaff underway.
GALLEY	-Space where food is prepared aboard ship.
GENERAL MESSAGE	-A message originated at a high Navy level & distributed to the entire Navy, or large segments of the Navy.
GENERAL QUARTERS	-Battle stations aboard ship.
GEORGE	-The junior ensign at a command.
GIG	-Boat assigned for the commanding officer's personal use.
GOLDBRICK	-One who loafs, goofs off.
GRANNY KNOT	-An incorrectly tied square knot.
GROMMET	-Reinforced hole in canvas.
GROUND TACKLE	-The collective term for the articles of equipment used in connection with anchoring and mooring.
GUIDED MISSILE	-Has a guidance system that constantly updates and corrects the missile's heading until impact with a target.
HALF MAST	-Flying the flag half way up mast/pole. Done in honor of someone recently deceased.
HALYARD	-A light line used to hoist a flag or pennant.
HANGAR DECK	-Large deck below flight deck where airplanes are stored and serviced.
HARD OVER	-Condition of a rudder which has been turned to the maximum possible rudder angle.
HASH MARK	-Service stripe indicating four years of Naval Service.
HATCH	-A square or rectangular access in a deck.

339

HAUL DOWN	-Action of lowering signal flags.
HAWSEPIPE	-Opening through which the anchor cable runs from the deck out through the side.
HAWSER	-Any heavy wire or line used for towing or mooring.
HEAD	-Latrine, washroom.
HEADING	-The direction toward which the ship is pointed.
HEAVE	-To throw.
HEAVE IN	-Take in line or cable.
HEAVE TO	-The act of a ship in stopping or reducing headway just enough to maintain steerageway.
HELM	-Mechanical device used to turn the rudder. Usually a wheel aboard a ship.
HITCH	-Slang for reenlistment term.
HOLIDAY	-Space on a painted surface which was not painted.
HOLIDAY ROUTINE	-A day off from normal ship's routine.
HULL	-The shell, or plating, of a ship.
INBOARD	-Toward the centerline.
INLET	-A narrow strip of sea extending into land.
INSHORE	-Close to the shore.
IRISH PENNANT	-A loose end of line left dangling. Loose thread on clothes.
ISLAND	-Superstructure on starboard side of flight deck of an aircraft carrier.
JACK	-Starred blue flag flown at the jackstay of a commissioned ship not underway.
JACKSTAFF	-Vertical spar at the stem to which the jack is hoisted.
JACOB'S LADDER	-A portable rope or wire ladder.
JETTISON	-Throw over the side.
JUMP SHIP	-The act of deserting a ship.
JURY RIG	-Any makeshift device or apparatus.
KEEL	-The lowermost longitudinal strength member from which the frames and plating rise.
KNIFE EDGE	-Rim of hatch or door frame.
KNOCK OFF	-Quit work(ing).

KNOT	-(1) Measure of speed (See nautical mile). (2) "Ties" in lines of ropes.
LADDER	-A shipboard flight of steps.
LANDING CRAFT	-Vessel especially designed for landing troops and equipment directly on the beach (such as an LCU).
LANDLUBBER	-Nautical term for someone who has not been to sea.
LASH	-To secure an object by turns of line, wire, or chain.
LEE	-An area sheltered from the wind. Downwind.
LEEWARD	-Direction toward which the wind is blowing.
LIBERTY	-Permission to be absent from a ship or station for less than a period of leave.
LIFELINES	-Wire ropes supported by stanchions.
LIGHT OFF	-To start up equipment.
LINE	-A term applied to any rope which is not wire rope.
LINE OFFICER	-An officer eligible to assume command at sea duties. Staff officers (Medical, Supply, etc,) cannot assume command at sea.
LIST	-Refers to athwartship balance (port or starboard) of a ship.
LOG ROOM	-Engineer's record space/room aboard ship.
LOOK ALIVE	-Admonishment meaning "be alert," or "move faster."
LUCKY BAG	-Locker used to stow gear found adrift. Usually controlled by Master-at-Arms.
MAE WEST	-Nautical term for specific type of life jacket.
MAGAZINE	-Compartment used for the stowage of ammunition.
MANNING THE RAIL	-Event where ship's crew lines up on the rails of a ship to honor an event or a person.
MARLINESPIKE	-Tapered tool used to help splice rope and wire.
MATE	-Another sailor.
MAY DAY	-International voice distress call.

MEATBALL	-Slang for battle efficiency pennant.
MESSAGE CENTER	-The secure place aboard ship where messages are sent/received to and from other ships/shore stations.
MESS DECK	-Space where ship's crew eats (General Mess).
MIDSHIPMAN	-An officer-in-training student at the U. S. Naval Academy or a member of an NROTC unit at a college/university.
MIDWATCH	-The 0000-0400 watch.
MINE	-An underwater explosive weapon, usually put in a fixed position. A mine can explode when a ship touches it or comes close to it, depending on the type of mine.
MISSILE	-A self-propelled weapon containing an explosion section, a propulsion section, and a guidance section. A missile can change its direction, or heading, after it has been fired.
MONKEY FIST	-Weighted knot on a heaving line.
MOOR	-To dock or secure ship to a pier.
MOORING LINE	-Line used to secure ship to a pier.
MORSE CODE	-Signals consisting of dots and dashes.
MUSTER	-A roll call.
NAUTICAL MILE	-The equivalent of 6,076 feet.
NEST	-Two of more ships tied up alongside each other.
ORDNANCE	-A term that includes everything that makes up a ship's or aircraft's firepower. This includes guns, missiles, rockets, ammunition, gun mounts and turrets.
OUTBOARD	-Away from the centerline. More outward.
OUTSTANDING REQUISITION	-A requisition for which not all requested material has been received.
OVERHEAD	-The underside of a deck.
OVER THE HILL	-Slang: To desert.
PASSAGEWAY	-A corridor aboard a ship.
PAY OUT	-To feed out, as a line.
PIER	-Structure extending from land out into the water. Used for mooring ships.

PILOTHOUSE	-Enclosure on the bridge housing the main steering controls.
PITCH	-Vertical rise and fall of a ship's bow caused by ocean currents.
PLANKOWNER	-A person stationed on a ship when it is placed in commission.
PLAN OF THE DAY	-A listing of the daily activities and events of a command.
POLLYWOG	-A sailor who has never crossed the Equator.
PORK CHOP	-Slang: Supply officers
PORT	-The left side.
PRIVATE MESS	-A mess (such as the wardroom mess) in which the cost involved is not met by appropriated funds.
PROCUREMENT	-The act of obtaining materials or services.
PROPELLER GUARDS	-Steel braces above the propellers to prevent them from hitting a dock, pier, or other objects.
PYROTECHNICS	-Ammunition containing chemicals that produce smoke or light.
QUARTERDECK	-Deck area designated by the commanding officer as the place to carry out official functions.
QUARTERS	-(1) Stations for shipboard evolutions; or (2) Living spaces.
QUAY	-Solid structure along a bank used for loading and off-loading ships.
RACK	-Slang: Bunk
RAT GUARDS	-Metal cones placed on mooring lines to prevent rats from gaining access aboard ship by climbing up on the mooring lines.
RATIONS	-Meal. Food.
REEF	-An underwater ledge rising abruptly from the ocean's floor.
RESTRICTION	-The requirement to remain within certain specified limits (ship, station, etc.).
ROCKET	-A self-propelled weapon with an explosive and a propulsion section. Once a rocket has been fired, it is

	unable to change its direction or movement pattern.
ROPEYARN SUNDAY	-Term applied to an otherwise workday which has been granted as a holiday for the purpose of taking care of personal business.
SACK	-Slang: Bunk. Rack.
SCRAMBLED EGGS	-Slang for gold ornament on commander & above officer hat bills.
SCREW	-Ship's propeller.
SCUTTLE	-The act of deliberately sinking a vessel.
SCUTTLEBUTT	-(1) Water or drinking fountain; or, (2) Navy rumor.
SEA CABIN	-Captain's sleeping quarters. Usually located near the bridge.
SEA LAWYER	-A sailor who supposedly knows all the rules and laws, and freely passes out this information.
SECONDARY CONN	-Contains equipment needed for ship's control in the event of control loss in primary control.
SECURE	-(1) To make fast; or, (2) To stop doing something.
SEMAPHORE	-Form of visual communications.
SET THE WATCH	-Establish normal watch conditions.
SHAKE A LEG	-Admonishment to move faster.
SHELLBACK	-A sailor who has crossed the Equator and survived King Neptune's court punishment.
SHIFT COLORS	-To change the arrangement of colors when getting underway, mooring, or anchoring.
SHIPMATE	-A sailor friend.
SHIP'S COMPANY	-Every one assigned to a particular navy command/ship.
SHIP'S CONTROL CONSOLE	-Consists of the engine and propeller order sections. Controls the speed and direction of the ship.
SHOAL	-Place of shallow water.
SHORE LEAVE	-Officer's liberty.
SICKBAY	-Shipboard hospital.
SIDE BOY	-Sailor(s) who form(s) ranks at quarterdeck or gangway in part of official functions.

SIGNAL BRIDGE	-Open area on the superstructure equipped with signal searchlights, flags, yardarm blinker controls, and other equipment used by Signalmen aboard ship.
SINGLE UP	-Act of un-doubling, or bringing the number of securing lines from ship to pier from two to one.
SKIVVY(IES)	-Nautical term for underwear.
SKYLARK	-To play around.
SLIP	-A narrow space between two piers.
SMALL STORES	-A shop that sells clothing items to sailors.
SNIPE	-Slang: Engineering person.
SPANNER	-A wrench used for tightening couplings on a firehose.
SQUARE AWAY	-To put in proper order, make right.
STAFF CORPS OFFICER	-Officers not eligible to assume command at sea duties. Includes: supply, medical, dental corps.
STANCHION	-Vertical post used for supporting decks, lifelines, etc.
STANDBY	-To wait.
STARBOARD	-The right side.
STATEROOM	-A living compartment for officers aboard ship.
STEM	-The forward most part of a ship.
STERN	-The point at the aft end of the ship where port and starboard meet.
SUPERSTRUCTURE	-Ship's structure above the main deck.
SURVEY	-The procedure used to expend material from stock records and accounts when it is deteriorated, damaged, lost, missing, or otherwise unavailable for its intended use.
SWAB	-Navy "mop."
TATTOO	-Call to announce taps (turn in) in 5 minutes.
TIN CAN	-Slang: Destroyer (ship).
TOPSIDE	-General term meaning above decks, or the weather decks.
TORPEDO	-Self-propelled underwater missile device. It can be used against surface or underwater vessels.

TRIM	-The relationship between the fore and aft draft.
TURN IN	-Go to bed.
TURN TO	-Commence work.
UNDERWAY	-Term meaning a ship has cast off all lines to pier (or hoisted anchor) and is at sea under own power.
VOID	-An empty space or tank aboard ship.
WAKE	-Trail left by moving vessel in the water.
WARDROOM	-Space aboard ship where officers eat.
WATERLINE	-The point where the hull meets the surface of the water.
WATERTIGHT INTEGRITY	-The degree or quality of watertightness.
WEATHER DECK	-Ship's decks exposed to the weather.
WEAPON SYSTEM	-Consists of a weapon and the associated equipment required to operate and control the weapon.
WHARF	-Somewhat like a quay but built in the fashion of a pier.
WHEELHOUSE	-Pilot house.
WHITE HAT	-Slang: Enlisted person E-1 to E-6.
WORKING PARTY	-Group of people (usually junior in rank) assigned to carry out a specific short-term task.

CHAPTER 55

NAVY ACRONYMS

AA	Anti-Aircraft
AAA	Anti-Aircraft Artillery
AAB	Aircraft Accident Board
AAFES	Army & Air Force Exchange System
AAI	Aircraft Accident Investigation
AAM	Air-to-Air Missile
AAP	Affirmative Action Plan
AAR	Aircraft Accident Report
AAW	Anti-Air Warfare
AAWC	Anti-Air Warfare Center
ABM	Anti-Ballistic Missile
A/C	Aircraft
AC	Aircraft Commander
ACB	Amphibious Construction Battalion
ACBD	Active Commission Base Date
ACDU	Active Duty
ACDUTRA	Active Duty for Training
ACE	American Council on Education
ACFT	Aircraft
ACIP	Aviation Career Incentive Pay
ACNO	Assistant Chief of Naval Operations
ACOS	Assistant Chief of Staff
ACR	Allowance Change Request
ACP	Allied Communications Publication
ACTY	Activity
AD	Destroyer Tender (Ship)
ADBD	Active Duty Base Date
ADCOM	Administrative Command
ADP	Automatic Data Processing
ADTAKE	Advise When Action Taken
ADV	Advance/Advancement
AE	Ammunition Ship
AEL	Allowance Equipage List
AEP	Advanced Education Program
AER	Alteration Equivalent to a Repair
AEW	Airborne Early Warning
AFFF	Aqueous Film Forming Foam
AFQT	Armed Forces Qualification Test
AFRS	Armed Forces Radio Service

347

AFRTS	American Forces Radio and Television Service
AFS	Combat Stores Ship
A/G	Air-Ground
AGM	Air-to-Ground Missile
AH	Hospital Ship
AIB	Aircraft Instrument Bulletin
AIG	Address Indicating Group
AIROPS	Air Operations
AIS	Automated Information System
ALCOM	All Commands
ALNAV	All Navy Activities. General Message
ALT	Alteration
AMB	Aircraft Mishap Board
AMEB	American Embassy
AMPHIB	Amphibious
AMRAAM	Advanced Medium Range Air-to-Air Missile
AO	Oiler (Ships)
AOC	Aviation Officer Candidate
AOCP	Aviation Officer Continuation Pay
AOE	Fast Combat Support Ship
AOR	Replenishment Oiler
A/P	Airplane
APL	Allowance Parts List
APO	Army Post Office
AR	Repair Ship
ARC	American Red Cross
	Alcohol Rehabilitation Center
ARFCOS	Armed Forces Courier Service
ARFCOSTA	Armed Forces Courier Station
ARM	Anti-Radiation Missile
ARS	Salvage & Rescue Ship
	Alcohol Rehabilitation Services
A/S	Air Speed
AS	Submarine Tender (Ship)
ASAP	As Soon As Possible
ASBD	Active Service Base Date
ASCOMM	Antisubmarine Warfare Communications
ASMD	Anti-Ship Missile Defense
ASO	Aviation Safety/Supply Office
ASR	Submarine Rescue Ship
ASROC	Anti-Submarine Rocket
ASVAB	Armed Services Vocational Aptitude Battery
ASW	Anti-Submarine Warfare
ASWOC	Antisubmarine Warfare Operational Center
ATCO	Air Traffic Control Office(r)

ATD	Airborne Technical Data (system operator)
ATF	Fleet Ocean Tug
ATP	Allied Tactical Publication
AUTODIN	Automatic Digital Network
AWCLS	All-Weather Carrier Landing System
AWOL	Absent Without Leave
AXP	Allied Exercise Publication
BAQ	Basic Allowance for Quarters
BAS	Basic Allowance for Subsistence
BASEOPS	Base Operations
BCD	Bad Conduct Discharge
BDS	Battle Dressing Station
BG	Battle Group
BI	Background Investigation
BMOW	Boatswain's Mate of the Watch
BOH	Baseline Overhaul
BOOST	Broadened Opportunity for Officer Selection & Training
BOQ	Bachelor Officers Quarters
BP	Base Pay
CAAC	Counseling and Assistance Center
CACO	Casualty Assistance Calls Officer
CACP	Casualty Assistance Calls Program
CAG	Carrier Air Group
CAGE	Commercial And Government Entity
CANTRAC	Catalog of Navy Training Courses
CAP	Civic Action Program
	Combat Air Patrol
CARDIV	Carrier Division
CARQUAL	Carrier Qualification
CASCOR	Casualty Correction Report
CASREP	Casualty Report
CAT	Civil Action Team (Seabees)
CATCC	Carrier Air Traffic Control Center
CAW	Carrier Air Wing
CBO	Congressional Budget Office
CBMU	Construction Battalion Maintenance Unit Seabees)
CBU	Construction Battalion Unit (Seabees)
CCB	Configuration Control Board
CDO	Command Duty Officer
CDP	College Degree Program
CEC	Civil Engineer Corps

CG	Guided Missile Cruiser
	Coast Guard
CGN	Nuclear Powered Guided Missile Cruiser
CHAMPUS	Civilian Health & Medical Program of the Uniformed Services
CHC	Chaplain Corps
CIC	Combat Information Center
CID	Criminal Investigative Division
CINC	Commander-in-Chief
CIWS	Close-in Weapon System
CMA	Clothing Maintenance Allowance
C/MC	Command Master Chief
CMAA	Chief Master-at-Arms
CMIO	Communications Material Issuing Office
CMS	Communications Security Material System
CNO	Chief of Naval Operations
CO	Commanding Officer
COB	Chief of the Boat
COD	Carrier Onboard Delivery
CODAA	Collateral Duty Alcoholism Advisor
COH	Complex Overhaul
COLA	Cost of Living Allowance
COMMSTA	Communications Station
COMRATS	Commuted Rations
COMSEC	Communications Security
CONUS	Continental United States
COSAL	Coordinated Shipboard Allowance List
CPO	Chief Petty Officer
CPX	Command Post Exercise
C/SC	Command Senior Chief
CSMP	Current Ship's Maintenance Project
CTE	Commander, Task Element
CTF	Commander, Task Force
CTG	Commander, Task Group
CTT	Command Training Team
CTU	Commander, Task Unit
CV	Multipurpose Aircraft Carrier
CVBG	Carrier Battle Group
CVN	Nuclear Multipurpose Aircraft Carrier
CW	Continuous Wave (Morse code)
CWO	Chief Warrant Officer
	Communications Watch Officer
DACOWITS	Defense Advisory Committee on Women in the Service

DANTES	Defense Activity for Nontraditional Education Support
DAPA	Drug and Alcohol Program Advisor
DC	Damage Control
DCA	Damage Control Assistant
	Defense Communications Agency
DCAOC	Defense Communications Agency Operations Center
DCC	Damage Control Central
DCNO	Deputy, Chief of Naval Operations
DCS	Defense Communications System
DD	Destroyer (Ship)
	Dishonorable Discharge
DDCCPO	Department Damage Control Chief Petty Officer
DDCPO	Division Damage Control Chief Petty Officer
DDG	Guided Missile Destroyer (Ship)
DEERS	Defense Enrollment Eligibility Reporting System
DELREP	Delay in Reporting
DET	Detachment
DIA	Defense Intelligence Agency
DIC	Dependency and Indemnity Compensation
DICOMP	Dependents Indemnity Compensation
DIFDEN	Duty in A Flying Status Not Involving Flying
DIFOT	Duty in Flying Status Involving Operational or Training Flights
DIS	Defense Investigative Service
DLA	Defense Logistic Agency
	Dislocation Allowance
DO	Duty Officer
DOB	Date of Birth
DOD	Department of Defense
DODDS	Department of Defense Dependent School(s)
DON	Department of the Navy
DR	Dead Reckoning
DRT	Dead Reckoning Tracer
DSC	Defense Supply Center
DSRV	Deep-Submergence Rescue Vehicle
DTG	Date-Time-Group
DUFLY	Duty Involving Flying Status
DUNIS	Duty Under Instruction
EAM	Emergency Action Message
EAOS	End Active Obligated Service
EAWS	Enlisted Aviation Warfare Specialist
ECM	Electronic Countermeasures

ECP	Emergency Command Post
	Enlisted Commissioning Program
EDO	Engineering Duty Officer
EDVR	Enlisted Distribution Verification Report
EEAP	Enlisted Education Advancement Program
EEFI	Essential Elements of Friendly Information
EGL	Equipage Guide List
EIC	Equipment Identification Code
EMI	Extra Military Instruction
EMO	Electronics Material Officer
ENL	Enlisted
ENTNAC	Entrance National Agency Check (security clearance)
EO	Equal Opportunity
EOD	Explosive Ordnance Disposal
EOH	End of Overhaul
ERP	Extended Refit Program
ESO	Educational Services Officer
ESRA	Extended Selected Restricted Availability
ESWS	Enlisted Surface Warfare Specialist
ETA	Estimated Time of Arrival
ETD	Estimated Time of Departure
ETP	Education and Training Program
EVAL	Evaluation
FAA	Federal Aviation Administration
FAAWC	Force Anti-Air Warfare Coordinator
FAC	Facility
FASO	Field Aviation Supply Office
FAU	Flag Administrative Unit
FAW	Fleet Air Wing
FBM	Fleet Ballistic Missile
FDHD	Flight Deck Hazardous Duty
FF	Frigate
FFG	Guided Missile Frigate
FIT	Fleet Indoctrination Team
FITREP	Fitness Report (officers & CPOs)
FITRON	Fighter Squadron
FLTSATCOM	Fleet Satellite Communications
FOA	Fitting Out Availability
FOUO	For Official Use Only
F M/C	Force Master Chief
FMP	Fleet Maintenance Program
FMSO	Fleet Material Support Office
FNAEB	Field Naval Aviation Evaluation Board

FPO	Fleet Post Office
FRAG	Fragmentation (bomb or hand grenade)
FRAMP	Fleet Readiness Aviation Maintenance Personnel
FSA	Family Separation Allowance
FSC	Family Services Center
	Federal Supply Classification
GAO	Government Accounting Office
GCA	Ground-Controlled Approach
GCI	Ground-Controlled Interception
GCM	General Court-Martial
GFE	Government Furnished Equipment
GMT	General Military Training
GPO	Government Printing Office
GUARD III	Guaranteed Assignment Retention Detailing (program)
HEAT	High-Explosive Anti-Tank (rocket warhead)
HHG	Household Goods
HRO	Housing Referral Office
HSG	Housing
HUK	Hunter-Killer
HUMS	Humanitarian Reassignment
HZ	Hertz (Cycles)
IAW	In Accordance With
ICBM	Intercontinental Ballistic Missile
ID	Identification
IFF	Identification, Friend or Foe
IG	Inspector General
ILO	Integrated Logistics Overhaul
ILS	Integrated Logistics Support
IMA	Intermediate Maintenance Activity
INSURV	Inspection and Survey Board
IRBM	Intermediate Range Ballistic Missile
IRR	Individual Ready Reserve
JA	Judge Advocate
JAG	Judge Advocate General
JAGC	Judge Advocate General Corps
JANAP	Joint Army-Navy-Air Force Publication
JANCOM	Joint Army-Navy Communications
JARCC	Joint Air Reconnaissance Coordination Center
JCN	Job Control Number

JML	Job Material List
JNROTC	Junior Naval Reserve Officers Training Corps
JO	Junior Officer
	Job Order
JOOD	Junior Officer of the Day/Deck
JOOW	Junior Officer of the Watch
JOPREP	Joint Operational Reporting
JRCC	Joint Rescue Coordination Center
JSN	Job Sequence Number
JTF	Joint Task Force
JTG	Joint Task Group
JTR	Joint Travel Regulations
JUMPS	Joint Uniform Military Pay System
KIA	Killed In Action
KISS	Keep It Simple Stupid (The "KISS" principle)
LAMPS	Light Airborne Multipurpose System (helos on ships)
LANT	Atlantic
LAO	Legal Assistance Office(r)
LARP	Launch and Recovery Platform
LCC	Amphibious Command Ship
LCPO	Leading Chief Petty Officer
LDO	Limited Duty Officer
LEP	Law Education Program
	List of Effective Pages
LES	Leave and Earnings Statement
LHA	Amphibious Assault Ship
LHD	Amphibious Warfare Ship
LKA	Amphibious Cargo Ship
LMET	Leadership and Management Education and Training
LOD	Line of Departure
LOE	Light Off Examination
LOEP	List Of Effective Pages
LOGREP	Logistics Replenishment
LORAN	Long-Range Navigation
LOS	Line of Sight
LOX	Liquid Oxygen
LPD	Amphibious Transport Dock (Ship)
LPH	Amphibious Assault Ship
LPO	Leading Petty Officer
LSD	Dock Landing Ship
LSO	Landing Signal Officer

LST	Tank Landing Ship
LV	Leave
LVRATS	Leave Rations
MAA	Master-At-Arms
MAAG	Military Assistance Advisory Group
MAB	Marine Amphibious Brigade
MACHALT	Machine Alteration
MAD	Magnetic Anomaly Detection
MARBKS	Marine Barracks
MARDET	Marine Detachment
(MMM)3M	Maintenance and Material Management (System)
MAU	Marine Amphibious Unit
MAW	Marine Air Wing
MCAS	Marine Corps Air Station
MCM	Mine Countermeasures
	Manual for Courts-Martial
MCPO	Master Chief Petty Officer
MCPON	Master Chief Petty Officer of the Navy
MDCS	Maintenance Data Collection Subsystem
	Maintenance Data System
MEPS	Military Enlistment Processing Station
MGT	Management
MIA	Missing in Action
MIDN	Midshipman
MIJI	Meconing, Intrusion, Jamming and Interference
MILCON	Military Construction
MILSPEC	Military Specification
MILSTRIP	Military Standard Requisitioning and Issue Procedure
MILPERSMAN	Military Personnel Manual
MIP	Maintenance Index Page
MIRV	Multiple Independently Targetable Reentry Vehicle
MIS	Management Information System
MISC	Miscellaneous
MK	Mark
MMR	Main Machinery Room
MOD	Modification
MOQ	Married Officers' Quarters
MOTU	Mobile Technical Unit
MRC	Movement Reporting Center
	Maintenance Requirement Card
MRE	Meals Ready-to-Eat

MRO	Movement Reporting Office
MSC	Military Sealift Command
	Medical Service Corps
MSG	Message
MSO	Minesweeper (Ship)
NAAF	Naval Auxiliary Air Field
NAAS	Naval Auxiliary Air Station
NAB	Naval Amphibious Base
NAC	National Agency Check
NADC	Naval Air Development Center
NAF	Naval Air Facility
NAG	Naval Advisory Group
NALC	Naval Ammunition Logistic Code
NAPS	Naval Academy Preparatory School
NAR	No Action Required
NAS	Naval Air Station
NASAP	Navy Alcohol Safety Action Program
NATO	North Atlantic Treaty Organization
NATOPS	Naval Air Training & Operating Procedures Standardization Program
NAVACT	Naval Activity
NAVCAD	Naval Academy
NAVFAC	Naval Facility
NAVFOR	Naval Forces
NAVSTA	Naval Station
NCB	Naval Construction Brigade (Seabees)
NCFSU	Naval Construction Forces Support Unit (Seabees)
NCIS	Naval Criminal Investigative Service
NCR	Naval Construction Regiment (Seabees)
NCTAMS	Naval Computer & Telecommunications Area Master Station
NCTS	Naval Computer & Telecommunications Station
NEC	Navy Enlisted Classification
NEX	Navy Exchange
NFCU	Navy Federal Credit Union
NFO	Naval Flight Officer
NIS	Not In Stock
NJP	Nonjudicial Punishment
NLT	No/Not Later Than
NMCB	Naval Mobile Construction Battalion (Seabees)
NMPC	Naval Military Personnel Command
NOBC	Naval Officers Billet Code
NOL	Naval Ordnance Laboratory

NOTAL	Not To All
NOTAM	Notice to Airmen
NOTU	Naval Ordnance Test Unit
NPPSO	Navy Publication and Printing Services Office
NPS	Naval Postgraduate School
NR	Naval Reserve
NRCC	Nonresident Career Course
NRL	Naval Research Laboratory
NROTC	Naval Reserve Officer Training Corps
NRS	Navy Relief Society
NSC	Naval Supply Center
NSFO	Navy Standard Fuel Oil
NSGA	Naval Security Group Activity
NSN	National Stock Number
NSU	Naval Support Unit (Seabees)
NSWC	Naval Surface Weapons Center
NTC	Naval Training Center
NTCC	Naval Telecommunication Center
NTDS	Naval Technical Data System
NTP	Naval Telecommunication Publication
	Navy Training Plan
NTS	Naval Training Station
NUPOC	Nuclear Propulsion Officer Candidate Program
NWCA	Navy Wives Club of America
NWIP	Naval Warfare Information Publication
NWP	Naval Warfare Publication
NWPL	Naval Warfare Publication Library
NWT	Non-Watertight Door
OBA	Oxygen Breathing Apparatus
OCC	Officer Correspondence Course
OCHAMPUS	Office of the Civilian Health & Medical Program
	of the Uniformed Services
OCS	Officer Candidate School
OHA	Overseas Housing Allowance
OJAG	Office of the Judge Advocate General
OJT	On-the-Job Training
OLA	Office of Legislative Affairs
OOD	Officer of the Day/Deck
OPNAV	Office of the Chief of Naval Operations
OPORD	Operations Order
OPREP	Operational Report
OPS	Operations
OPSIG	Operating Signal
OPTAR	Operating Target (budget)

ORD	Ordnance
ORDALT	Ordnance Alteration
ORE	Operational Readiness Evaluation
ORI	Operational Readiness Inspection
OSR	Officer Summary Record
OTC	Officer in Tactical Command
OTH	Other Than Honorable (discharge)
OUTCONUS	Outside Continental United States
OUTUS	Outside Continental United States
OVHD	Overhead
OVHL	Overhaul
OWL	Officers' Wives League
PAC	Pacific
PACE	Program for Afloat College Education
PAR	Personnel Advancement Requirement
PASEP	Passed Separately
PCB	Printed Circuit Board
PCO	Prospective Commanding Officer
PCS	Permanent Change of Station
PDL	Pass Down Log
PEB	Propulsion Examining Board
PEBD	Pay Entry Base Date
PEP	Personnel Exchange Program
PERA	Planning & Engineering for Repairs & Alterations
PG	Post Graduate
PHIB	Amphibious
PHIBCB	Amphibious Construction Battalion (Seabees)
PI	Personnel Inspection
PKP	Purple K Powder
PLAD	Plain Language Address Directory
PMEL	Precision Measuring Equipment Laboratory
PMS	Planned Maintenance System
	Preventive Maintenance System
PNA	Passed, Not Advanced
POC	Point of Contact
POD	Plan of the Day
POOW	Petty Officer of the Watch
POT&I	Pre-Overhaul Test & Inspection
POV	Privately Owned Vehicle
POW	Prisoner of War
PPO	Police Petty Officer
PQS	Personnel Qualification Standard
PRAV	Planned Restricted Availability

PRD	Projected Rotation Date
PRECOM	Precommissioning
PREP	Preparatory (signal flag)
PRP	Personnel Reliability Program (security)
PSA	Personnel Support Activity
	Post-Shakedown Availability
PSD	Personnel Support Detachment
PT	Physical Training
PUB	Publication
PWC	Public Works Center
PXO	Prospective Executive Officer
QA	Quality Assurance
QMOW	Quartermaster of the Watch
QUALS	Qualifications
R&D	Research and Development
RADHAZ	Radiation Hazard
RATT	Radio Teletype
RAV	Restricted Availability
RDD	Required Delivery Date
RDT&E	Research, Development, Test, and Evaluation
RDY	Ready
RFS	Ready For Sea
RHIP	Rank Has Its Privileges
RIF	Reduction In Force
RIO	Radar Intercept Officer
RL	Restricted Line (officer designation)
ROICC	Resident Officer-in-Charge of Construction
RNCF	Reserve Naval Construction Force (Seabees)
ROH	Regular Overhaul
ROTC	Reserve Officers Training Corps
R/T	Radiotelephone
RTC	Recruit Training Command
RTM	Rate Training Manual
S/A	Ship Alteration
SACO	Substance Abuse Control Officer
SAG	Surface Action Group
SAMID	Ship Anti-Missile Integrated Defense
SAP	Semi-Armor-Piercing
SAR	Sea-Air Rescue
SBI	Special Background Investigation
SBP	Survivor Benefit Plan
SCM	Summary Court-Martial

SCORE	Selective Conversion and Reenlistment
SCPO	Senior Chief Petty Officer
SEA	Senior Enlisted Advisor
SEAL	Sea-Air-Land (special forces unit)
SECDEF	Secretary of Defense
SECNAV	Secretary of the Navy
SER	Selected Early Retirement
SELRES	Selected Reserves
SF	Ship's Force
SFOMS	Ship's Force Overhaul Management System
SGLI	Servicemen's Group Life Insurance
SHIPALT	Ship Alteration
SINS	Ship's Inertial Navigation System
SIOP	Single Integrated Operational Plan (security)
SIOP-ESI	Single Integrated Operational Plan - Extremely Sensitive Information
SIQ	Sick in Quarters
SLEP	Service Life Extension Program
SNDL	Standard Navy Distribution List
SOAP	Supply Operations Assistance Program
SOC	Servicemen's Opportunity College
SOP	Standard Operating Procedure
	Senior Officer Present
SOPA	Senior Officer Present Afloat/Ashore
SOQ	Senior Officers' Quarters
SOS	Save Our Ship (morse code distress call)
SP	Shore Patrol
SPCC	Ship Parts Control Center
SPCM	Special Court-Martial
SPECAT	Special Category (security)
SPECOM	Special Communications
SRA	Selected Restricted Availability
SRB	Selective Reenlistment Bonus
SS	Submarine
SSBN	Fleet Ballistic Missile Submarine
SSD	Survival Support Device
SSN	Nuclear Attack Submarine
STAR	Selective Training and Reenlistment
SUBROC	Submarine Rocket
SUPSHIP	Supervisor of Shipbuilding, Conversion, and Repair
SWO	Surface Warfare Officer
	Senior Watch Officer
TA	Tuition Assistance

TAV	Technical Availability
T&E	Test and Evaluation
T&T	Travel and Transportation
TACAMO	Take Action and Move Out
TACAN	Tactical Air Navigation
TACO	Tactical Coordinator
TAD	Temporary Additional Duty
TAO	Tactical Action Officer
TAP	Tuition Assistance Program
TAR	Training and Administration of Reserves
TAV	Technical Availability
TE	Task Element
TEMMAD	Temporary Additional Duty
TF	Task Force
TG	Task Group
TIR	Time in Rate
TIS	Time in Service
TRE	Training Readiness Evaluation
TU	Task Unit
TYCOM	Type Commander
TYCOMALT	Type Commander Alteration
UA	Unauthorized Absence
UCMJ	Uniform Code of Military Justice
UCT	Underwater Construction Team (Seabees)
UDT	Underwater Demolition Team
UI	Under Instruction
	Unit of Issue
UIC	Unit Identification Code
UNREP	Underway Replenishment
UNSECNAV	Under Secretary of the Navy
URL	Unrestricted Line (officer designation)
USHBP	Uniformed Services Health Benefits Program
USN	United States Navy
USNA	United States Naval Academy
USNR	United States Naval Reserve
USNS	United States Naval Ship
USO	United Services Organization
USS	United States Ship
VA	Veterans Administration
VCNO	Vice Chief of Naval Operations
VEAP	Veteran's Education Assistance Program
VERTREP	Vertical Replenishment

VGLI	Veteran's Group Life Insurance
VHA	Variable Housing Allowance
WESTPAC	Western Pacific
WO	Warrant Officer
WQ&S	Watch, Quarter & Station (Bill)
WT	Watertight (doors and hatches)
WX	Weather
XO	Executive Officer
ZI	Zone Inspection

INDEX